THE DEATH (

THE DEATH OF THE LEFT

Why We Must Begin
from the Beginning Again

Simon Winlow and Steve Hall

First published in Great Britain in 2023 by

Policy Press, an imprint of
Bristol University Press
University of Bristol
1-9 Old Park Hill
Bristol
BS2 8BB
UK
t: +44 (0)117 374 6645
e: bup-info@bristol.ac.uk

Details of international sales and distribution partners are available at
policy.bristoluniversitypress.co.uk

British Library Cataloguing in Publication Data
A catalogue record for this book is available from the British Library

ISBN 978-1-4473-5415-4 paperback
ISBN 978-1-4473-5416-1 ePub
ISBN 978-1-4473-5418-5 ePdf

Cover design: Nicky Boroweic
Front cover image: Adobe/eNjoy Istyle

Bristol University Press and Policy Press use
environmentally responsible print partners.

Printed and bound in Great Britain by TJ Books, Padstow

Contents

Acknowledgements

We would like to take this opportunity to thank colleagues and students who have both inspired and supported us throughout our careers. The names of those who have helped us are too numerous to list here, but of particular significance are James Treadwell, Dan Briggs, Anthony Lloyd, Justin Kotzé, Tereza Kuldova, Tom Raymen, Tammy Ayres, Rowland Atkinson, Olly Smith, Luke Telford, Tony Ellis, Keith Hayward, Pat Carlen, David Wilson, Dick Hobbs, Robert Reiner, Philip Whitehead, Sarah Soppitt, Mark Horsley, Nick Gibbs, David Temple, Saabirah Osman, Liam Brolan, Dan Rusu, Kate Tudor, Adam Lynes, Craig Kelly, Deirdre O'Neill, Alex Hochuli, George Hoare, Lisa Mckenzie, Philip Cunliffe, Lee Jones and Thomas Fazi. We hasten to add that these academics do not necessarily agree with the thesis advanced here, but have nonetheless engaged us in respectful, intelligent and productive debate about intellectual matters. We would also like to thank Victoria Pittman and the rest of the Policy Press team for giving us the opportunity to write and publish this book, and for doing such a great job bringing it to fruition.

We would also like to briefly thank our friends, most of whom sensibly avoided involvement in the university sector. We would particularly like to thank Neil, Sam and Evan McGhin, Julian and Donna Cliff, David Knox, Mike and Liz Randall, and Rod and Cat Sinclair.

And now to the real stuff. Simon Winlow would like to thank his beautiful, faultless wife Emma for bathing his entire life in sunlight. He would also like to thank his perfect boy, Gabriel, and his wonderful parents, Alan and Liz.

Steve Hall would like to thank his one true love Christine, his son Christopher, daughter Alex, Emily, Michael, and granddaughters Erin and Sophie for surrounding him with the joy of family.

Acknowledgements

We would also like to make it abundantly clearly that our thesis here is totally divorced from ultra-realism, the theoretical framework we have developed in the fields of sociology and criminology.

Acknowledgments

We would like to thank ... ...

and ...

Introduction

We have taken no pleasure in writing this book. For years we debated whether it was worth writing at all. The political dimension of our adult lives has been filled with frustration, sadness and occasional anger as we watched the British left endure serial defeats and celebrate its own fragmentation. However, until quite recently we were pulled back from dark desolation by the hope that someday soon the left's comedy of errors would come to an end as a new generation of political and intellectual leaders emerged to drive it forward with vision and purpose.

It was not to be. Since 1979, the British left seems to have grown comfortable with electoral failure. The Labour governments of Blair and Brown achieved success only by conforming to the core demands of neoliberalism's global economic project. In the United States, Obama's presidency carried considerable symbolic importance, but he achieved absolutely nothing in terms of overcoming the economic orthodoxies that pushed so many Americans into poverty and insecurity. This pattern was replicated across all developed and developing nations. In or out of government, ostensibly left-wing parties busied themselves advocating neoliberal economic policies that harmed the very people they were supposed to defend. The left won elections only when it accepted the rules of the global market. Even formerly Maoist China joined the club.

The left has clearly undergone fundamental change. It no longer offers a genuine alternative to the existing order of things, whether reformist or revolutionary. Now, as we move further into the twenty-first century, the left seems to have discarded its traditional identity as a mass movement intent on achieving political power. It displays little interest in protecting – let alone improving – the prosperity and security of multi-ethnic working populations. Centre-left political projects of the past – such as

1

Roosevelt's New Deal in the 1930s or the British Labour Party's programme of economic restructuring after 1945 – achieved electoral success on the back of a compelling range of policy initiatives made comprehensible to their electorates. Electorates continue to yearn for the genuine kind of economic change that would provide a platform of material security. However, today's left has little to offer.

The left abandoned its traditional commitments and transformed itself into a cultural hub serving mildly apologetic neoliberals and a range of bespoke activist movements that oppose what they see as historical structures of social injustice. This cultural or identitarian left has accepted neoliberalism's individualised mode of social competition and rejected democratic socialism's appeal to solidarity and common interests. The radical elements of this loose identitarian network believe that a politicised alliance of minority activists can achieve solidarity in the project of bringing down white male elites. However, this alliance is built upon the shakiest of foundations. It is an instrumental alliance devoid of genuine unity, unlikely to draw the mass support required to win elections and almost certain to leave the multi-ethnic majority unprotected as we stumble blindly towards an uncertain future.

While the mildly apologetic neoliberals at the forefront of the left's major parties stick rigidly to an electoral strategy that involves little more than a commitment to budgetary discipline and an attempt to be slightly less loathsome than their opponents, the activist left continues to provide its opponents with limitless opportunities to satirise its political naivety. Satire is an effective ideological weapon in any political contest, and the right has prospered from the left's refusal to face reality. However, our goal is not to mock the banality of the left's mainstream political parties or poke fun at the activist left. For us, the death of a realistic, serious, ambitious and electable left is tragic in its consequences and deserves to be treated with a degree of solemnity.

That does not mean that we will restrict ourselves to describing the anatomy of our current tragedy. Much has been written about the insecurity, austerity, unemployment, underemployment and social fragmentation that blight many regions of the West. Where neoliberalism has been a playground for the successful it has been an abyss for those who have failed to succeed. Rather than pick through neoliberalism's destructive effects and tentatively identify partial administrative solutions, we will focus on the epicentre of the tragedy – the left's voluntary disintegration, to the extent that it now faces imminent erasure as a political force.

The left's descent into terminal illness is inextricably tied to the much grander historical narrative of its nineteenth-century origins and the convulsions it experienced throughout the twentieth century. The left of which we speak was not modelled on the French Revolution – the alliance of lawyers, bankers and businessmen who replaced the Ancien Régime with the *laissez-faire* political economy that presaged today's neoliberalism – but on periodic attempts to politicise and institutionalise the groundswell of discontent expressed by the working class. To offer explanatory power this narrative must be structured by crucial events that bring into clear relief the left's failure to rise to historic challenges and opportunities. It must also identify the perennial problems the left has faced in the essential political task of building alliances and attracting committed support. As we will see, the left has always been held back by a range of external and internal forces that have worked tirelessly to attenuate genuine resistance to the market economy's overreach into all aspects of human life.

The dominant force constantly active in diluting and diverting the left was a loose and sometimes tense alliance of movements that ranged across a spectrum from economic liberalism to cultural libertinism. Traditional conservatism and modern socialism were both transformed as this broad liberal alliance burrowed into their foundations. The transformations of modern socialism and conservatism were complex processes but, to put it very crudely for the moment, the socialist left ditched socialism and the conservative right ditched conservatism, clearing the way for a transformed liberal alliance – with the neoliberals on the right and the cultural liberals on the left – to stumble onwards unopposed.

It is, of course, now broadly accepted that as neoliberalism became an unchallengeable orthodoxy, the political field became barren, alienating, and incapable of driving history forward with purpose. The effects of this fundamental shift have been enormous,[1] and in some cases too daunting for governments, mass media and academic experts to confront squarely. As we shall see, the multifaceted and long-running failure of the left – the most important features of which are the fragmentation of its ideological discourse, the degeneration of its cultural values and the capitulation of its political parties – has played a significant role in fomenting and reproducing our present troubles.

We must now be brave enough to acknowledge an uncomfortable truth – Western civil society has been heading downhill for decades. Given the sterile nature of our politics, there is currently little for us to be optimistic about. To varying degrees, Western nations are riven by simmering internal hostilities. A sense of shared interests, together with an acknowledgement of our common fate and interdependence, are increasingly hard to find. Things of great value are gradually disappearing, and little that might nourish our collective life is being created.

As time passed, we watched the left drift further and further away from its fundamental task of fighting for the prosperity and security of ordinary people. The very people most in need of a fully committed and tactically astute left were thoughtlessly abandoned by those who presented themselves as their representatives. Throughout our careers, from our vantage point in the deindustrialised North of England, we have investigated this depressing reality in detail. We gathered data as formerly prosperous and stable communities disintegrated, as drug markets and violence became normalised and antisocial individualism decimated fragile projects of cultural and political solidarity.

The traditional industries and labour markets that allowed ordinary people to improve their lives and look to the future with optimism are now long gone. The effects of this fundamental change are with us still. Echoes from a lost world continue to reverberate through the lives of those who remember that another future was once possible. We watched with sadness and growing detachment as politics descended into bland administration and the left's traditional commitment to equality, fairness and the common good withered and died.

4

But hope can be a powerful emotional drive. It was this hope that brought us together as researchers and writers at the beginning of the millennium. We clung to it tightly, advocating in our academic work the return of a politics capable of addressing the problems that scarred the old industrial regions left behind by neoliberalism's financialised economy. We scanned the horizon for signs of a break from current orthodoxies. Now, finally, these orthodoxies are indeed disintegrating, but not under circumstances of the left's choosing, and certainly not because the left had persuaded a majority that it could offer a feasible and attractive alternative.

As the years rolled by and the increasingly liberalised left continued its journey into abstraction, our hopes faltered as new emotions came to the fore. We greeted gains made by the political right with resignation and watched dispassionately as the left's key institutions seemed to ditch the fight for solidarity and economic justice as they adopted the principles of the new liberal radicalism. We watched as virtually every authentic working-class voice on the left was silenced and each traditional value and cultural form was scrutinised with a view to throwing it into history's dustbin.

Amid all these convulsions it was impossible to look back on 40 years of political failure without asking why a once-electable left had become so strategically inept and divorced from reality. What is this 'left' we see before us today? How and why did it take its present form? Why did the current focus on cultural justice displace the old focus on economic justice? Who controls the shape and tone of leftist politics, and might it be possible for the left to reconnect with ordinary people and once again represent their interests? Or should we simply accept that those days are gone?

Being brutally honest with oneself can be mightily disruptive, but it can also produce a positive outcome. Should we now embrace the possibility that the left has reached a stage of such fragmentation and incoherence that it no longer exists as a credible political force? If so, what does the political future hold? Should the now fully incorporated institutions of the left be abandoned and the way cleared for the creation of something new, something built upon a commitment to address the real problems that haunt the present and the future, something that acknowledges and respects our collective past, yet still strives to carve out a path to a better future? These questions have preoccupied us since we entered the new millennium. Eventually we concluded that they must be answered.

The fruits of our investigation of the political left in the Anglophone world provide the substance of this book. We have postponed writing it for years, largely because it became obvious to us that many on the left today refuse to accept any searching criticism, no matter how constructive or well-intentioned it may be. Some still labour under the misapprehension that the left continues to represent the interests of the people, and that a rising tide of progressive cultural sentiment will soon sweep it to power. It also seems to us perfectly obvious that many of those in positions of power on the left are convinced that it is on the path to future electoral success, and maybe even beyond that to an era of genuine social transformation.

Regrettably, today's activist left seems incapable of attracting electoral support, or promoting a public understanding of concentrated structural power in political economy. It appears far more concerned with stoking hostile intersectional culture wars. Clearly, the core function of the cultural left's media commentariat is not to help the left win, but to help the left retain its public presence despite its ongoing defeat. As we shall see, those invited onto TV shows to articulate a 'left-wing point of view' are certainly not neoliberalism's true antagonists. Rather, they serve the neoliberal system well by ignoring or obscuring fundamental issues and restricting their critique to cultural matters, which does not even mildly inconvenience the political and economic processes that ensure the system's continuity.

Few on today's left can see any reason to identify past errors of judgement or the junctures at which it turned in the wrong direction. After years of intellectual mismanagement and reductive political tribalism, they prefer instead to wage a ceaseless symbolic war that condemns the political right as 'unfit to govern' in the vague hope that their moralistic denunciations will lead them to a historic and long overdue victory. We can see no signs indicating that such negative politics will lead the left to the sort of positive electoral victory it needs to effect social change.

The internal politics of the activist left have not evolved dialectically by engaging in self-critique or wrestling with contradictions and alternative points of view. Rather, they have evolved only on their own terms. The left's activist elite imagines itself, its values and its ideas to be flawless and progressive. All who disagree are categorised as uneducated bigots. If electorates or traditional fellow-travellers are not persuaded or refuse to proclaim their agreement with enough enthusiasm, they reveal only their prejudices and inability to get with the programme.

The list of distasteful slurs aimed at the cultural left's critics is truly something to behold. Many once committed leftists, dismayed by the left's refusal to prioritise the construction of a new economic platform capable of preventing millions of ordinary people sliding to the brink of financial ruin, or appalled that divisive identity politics has captured the movement's commanding heights, have either dropped out or learnt to suffer their dissatisfaction in silence. More concerning is the denunciation of millions of ordinary men and women who have refused to support the left's decaying mainstream political parties, the majority of which continue to propose economic policies crafted by the neoliberal right. All who fail to support the current crop of leftist political leaders and social media influencers are, it would seem, idiots, racists, xenophobes, boomers, gammon, and so on. The list of insults is quite extensive, but the general message is the same. They are, as Hillary Clinton put it, 'a basket of deplorables'. Only horrifying prejudices and intellectual deficiencies, the activist left opine, could have led these men and women to abstain or vote for the parties of the political right. Of course, such relentless vilification reduces the chance that these ordinary people will ever again vote for the parties of the left.

Clearly, now is not a good time to be a leftist critic of the left. Our prolonged sojourn in academia was replete with dire warnings that, if we know what's good for us, we should withhold our critical history of the modern and postmodern left. However, after lengthy and often fraught discussions, we decided to go for it and let the chips fall where they may.

Certainly, there are many less contentious books we could have written. However, we are committed to this one.

Throughout our lives we have invested heavily in the principles and ideals of the left, only to watch it fail, fail again, and then gradually mutate into a clannish, exclusive, intellectually bereft and politically suicidal melee of disparate cultural groups, some of which now appear to be as belligerently disconnected from each other as they are from the population at large. Perhaps, deep down, we still believe that a belated acknowledgement of the left's calamitous errors will pave the way to renewal. Perhaps things can be turned around. However, to cling on to this possibility would be to let the heart rule the head.

We have always wanted the left to be better, not simply in the moral but also the functional sense. We wanted it to be a force committed not only to righting wrongs but also to building a better society for all to enjoy. For us it is now vital that we take on the task of building something new where the left once stood. Having some understanding of how and why the left died might, we hope, serve a new generation of brave individuals as they seek to build new institutions committed to advancing the common good.

What follows here is, we hope, a brief and accessible account of the forces that have carried the left to its present position of permanent unelectability. We hope that what we have found will contribute to our shared understanding of why the left regularly failed and eventually died. Our intention is not to dispirit the reader. Rather, we hope that out of adversity clearly understood renewed strength might emerge. The purpose is to learn from past mistakes and sketch out how political organisations that actually serve the people can be built. We warmly welcome you to the book and we hope that in it you can find something to deepen and clarify your understanding of contemporary politics and the rather precarious state we are in today.

1

The mortgage on the left's
future foreclosed

The 2008 global financial crisis was an event of huge significance. We continue to live in its aftermath. It should have heralded the end of an epoch. The dogma, corruption, disinformation, errors and misunderstandings that structured neoliberalism's financialised market system were revealed in grim detail. However, the best the mainstream left could do in response was to offer a moralising critique of corporate bankers' untrammelled greed and the connivance and laxity of the sector's regulators. Key figures on the left nodded along with the neoliberal right's claim that the system had broken down, or that it had been in some way corrupted. None were willing to acknowledge that these malfunctions and corrupt practices were simply surface effects of deep flaws in the system's core.

The truth of the matter is that a crisis had been building since the serial financial shocks of the 1980s, and – given that pretty much every politician believed that the positive outcomes of 'the markets' far outweigh the negative – in many respects it was inevitable. What we needed was a new system of democratically regulated money creation and investment. We needed democratic state institutions that controlled the animal spirits of the market and forced financiers to play within strictly policed rules. We needed a fully inclusive economy replete with secure, well-paid and socially useful jobs. And, of course, we needed politicians who were not totally committed to the rigid doctrines of the financial sector. The left's popular message should have been this: *the way we organise our economy is deeply flawed; we need to rebuild on firm foundations; the economy we build should be guided by the best available understanding of how our monetary system works and driven forward by an unyielding commitment to the common good.*

Some on the margins of the left did make such arguments, but it was their willingness to make them that saw them marginalised in the first place. Bowing and quaking before the unforgiving goddess TINA ('there is no alternative'), the left had abandoned the economic engine room and handed it to financial technocrats decades before the 2008 crisis.

It really should have been unsurprising that, as the global economy crashed, the left had very little of substance to say about it. That the laxity of business and trading regulations would lead to this bleak destination had been inevitable. The left should have courted the best heterodox economists, made the modern post-1971 economic system comprehensible to the public, talked clearly about its inherent problems and potential benefits, and proposed an attractive, feasible alternative that would greatly improve the lives of the vast majority. Instead, yet another historic opportunity was missed, and cynicism became even more deeply embedded in the West's popular culture.[1]

As we shall see, the neoliberal market system was reanimated by the state and stumbled on in a zombified form, lowering wages, imposing austerity measures, sowing disharmony, indebting individuals and whole nations, enriching elites and commodifying everything it encountered. After spending barely imaginable sums of money bailing out banks and corporations, those in government then ran for cover, denying that the state had the capacity to create employment, extinguish poverty, and repair the crumbling economic foundations that underpinned a rapidly splintering civil society. Clearly, there was a virtually inexhaustible supply of money available to bail out the banking sector and hand out contracts to the corporate sector, but for some reason the state had to be frugal when it came to assisting ordinary people to overcome their very real problems.

The austerity that followed the 2008 crisis turned millions away from the left. As ostensibly leftist parties across the West resigned themselves to administering austerity, many voters concluded that the left cared nothing about the suffering of everyday people. Although some continued to vote for these parties simply because they continued to represent the best of a very bad bunch, true commitment virtually disappeared, and politics took on a decidedly negative hue. Rather than positively endorse a political party and its policy agenda, a growing number of people felt they had no choice but to vote for the party they found least appalling. Other voters, who had supported the broad left only to witness leftist parties enact policies that further enriched oligarchs and made getting and keeping a decent job that much harder, withdrew their votes. Others still – disgusted by mainstream politics' absurd pantomime and the entrenched ineptitude of the political elite – dropped out of politics and ignored electoral democracy's symbolically rich but increasingly hollow rituals.[2]

As social researchers during the early years of the twenty-first century, we heard time and again versions of the same joke: 'Don't vote; it only encourages them.' Some people were angry, many more simply frustrated and resigned to negativity. They could see nothing on the field of politics to truly believe in. They could not identify a single politician who did not appear to be in some way 'out for themselves'. Others, of course, refused to give in to cynicism and clung on to hope, but the traditional alignments and institutional values that once characterised our modern political system were simply evaporating.

It is perfectly clear that austerity eroded the traditional relationship between the left and the multi-ethnic working class. As we shall see later, other issues loomed large in this process, but austerity hardened attitudes and forced many previously committed left-of-centre voters to re-evaluate their position. Huge numbers had become poorer despite leftist political parties' regular terms in office. Millions of working people looked at influential figures in the left's political parties and its high-profile media commentariat only to conclude that they had absolutely nothing in common with them. It was inevitable that many traditional leftist voters would begin to open themselves up to alternative voices.

How could it really be argued that the left was 'for the people', when, with its policy decisions, it made the majority poorer and less secure? Rather than fight against the injustices of neoliberalism, and for a functioning economic system in which all were valued and included, the mainstream left implemented austerity in the hope that private sector investors could be lured from their foxholes by the prospect of high returns, low taxes and cuts to state spending. In the aftermath of the crash, the mainstream left's priorities were absolutely clear.

Given the deep harms created by the crisis and the austerity that followed, we should not understate the magnitude of the mainstream left's failure. As we write these words, once again we find ourselves at a historical juncture bursting with potential. The COVID-19 pandemic has revealed the state's ability to invest and hire labour without causing runaway inflation, and fundamental changes to the world's energy and transport infrastructure are already in motion. Unfortunately, there is no sign that the left has the wherewithal to seize the opportunities at hand and finally recuperate the failures of the past. Our pessimism on this point is rooted not in nostalgia or grubby parochialism but on a careful and objective reading of the history of the left in the West. Its failures, past and present, need to be dragged out from underneath the carpet and explained.

Greed is good

In the years building up to the crash, everyone could see that neoliberalism's financialised global economy had been cut adrift from the real-world economies in which ordinary men and women earn a living. It was glaringly obvious that the colossal gains made by the titans of Wall Street and the City of London had not and never would trickle down to enrich the lives of the hoi polloi. Yet, when the crash came, it was ultimately ordinary men and women who paid the price. In the years leading up to the crash, housing and consumer debt had risen to clearly unsustainable levels, yet the mortgage finance boom continued. Risks were not reflected and priced in financial markets. Doomsayers were silenced by a cacophony of voices proclaiming that in Western economies the boom would continue and this time it would be different.[3] It was not.

The human costs of the crisis and its aftermath were particularly severe. In the United States, for example, millions of jobs were lost, wages declined rapidly, and trillions of dollars were wiped from the nation's household wealth.[4] It's easy to brush past this figure without fully digesting its scale. A billion is a thousand million. A trillion is a thousand billion. Household wealth is, we accept, not always the best measure of a nation's economic well-being, but this is still a figure to boggle the mind. Inevitably, hundreds of thousands of American families fell into poverty, and millions lost their homes.[5] Similar effects were seen across the developed world. In 2008 alone, household wealth in the UK declined by around £815 billion. This massive reduction equates to a loss of around £31,000 for each household in the UK.[6]

The causes of the crisis are quite complex and beyond the remit of this book but, at a fundamental level, its roots can be found in neoliberalism's drive to remove restrictive business and investment regulations so that finance capital could pursue profit unhindered. And throughout the 1990s and the early years of the twenty-first century, that is precisely what capital did. As a broad range of new financial instruments was created for investors keen to secure ever greater returns, financial markets grew with incredible speed. Money ruled and unrestrained leveraging – borrowing at a lower rate to lend, often irresponsibly at high risk, for a higher rate of return – was normalised. The financial elite either repressed all knowledge of the social consequences of irresponsible moneylending or dipped into neoliberalism's variegated ideological support systems to pass off their anti-social self-interest as the creativity and innovation required for general prosperity.

The phrase 'greed is good', taken from Oliver Stone's 1987 movie *Wall Street*, is often used to give some sense of the ethos behind neoliberalism's acquisitive culture. While the phrase inevitably omits many important issues, it actually captures quite well the core economic beliefs of mainstream politicians of both left and right in the years that led to the crisis. The boundless drive of financial elites to acquire more would grow national economies, create jobs and, they imagined, secure the tax revenues needed to fund public spending. Mainstream politicians agreed that the genius of the investment class was powering forward whole societies, and to impede their activities would jeopardise the livelihoods of ordinary taxpayers. Politicians in the Conservative Party in Britain, the Republican Party in the United States, and right-of-centre political parties in the larger European countries were happy to preach this often and loud. Politicians from the left of centre tended to be less vociferous in their praise of the global financial elite, but they were resigned to the claim that limiting its acquisitiveness would be counterproductive.

Abstract investment markets had grown steadily in the wake of the Big Bang that announced Thatcher's deregulation of the financial sector in 1986. As the twentieth century gave way to the twenty-first, once dominant productive and distributive markets virtually disappeared as money moved into speculative financial markets. Financial instruments of various kinds – for example futures, which are agreements to trade at a specific price and time, and futures options, which form an accompanying market in the buying and selling of futures – came to dominate Wall Street and the City of London during the 1990s. Many of these markets produced large profits for those who knew how to play the game. Safer investments in the economy of real products and services that produced smaller profits appeared dull and unimaginative by comparison.

On the New York Stock Exchange, high-frequency trading, in which the actual ownership of equities or commodities is held for only a fraction of a second before being returned to the market, grew in terms of overall volume by 164 per cent between 2005 and 2009. The market quickly became 'a technological arms race'[7] that left many traditional investors trailing behind complex trading algorithms devised by tech-savvy university graduates who had bypassed traditional occupational fields and flooded into the finance sector in search of personal enrichment. Some of these new markets, for example in asset-backed securities – the most infamous of which is the collateralised debt obligation[8] – appear to have been poorly understood by regulators who were, in any case, resolutely committed to non-intervention.

Credit rating agencies played along. Risky investments packaged and sold as low-risk opportunities flooded into the market. Tranches of debt were packaged up, graded AAA by one of the three world-leading ratings agencies – Moody's, Standard & Poor's or Fitch – and sold on the market as rock-solid investment opportunities to pension funds and other investors too trusting, hurried or ill-informed to identify what lay behind the AAA rating. Often, these debt packages contained risky mortgages hidden among safer debts; and, often, obviously risky debt packages containing toxic elements were nonetheless graded as if they were safe. Of course, as the economy started to head south, much that was considered safe during boom times suddenly became decidedly less so.

Many banks, giddy at the opportunities suddenly available in the financial sector, had lent staggering amounts to borrowers of various kinds, and the amount of debt these banks carried often dwarfed the value of assets they held in reserve. The American housing market had been growing rapidly for years and, on the surface, taking out a mortgage to buy a house seemed like the sensible thing to do. Banks profited as aspiring homeowners rushed into the market. However, 2005 saw growing numbers of mortgage defaults and this trend continued in 2006. At this stage, panic had yet to set in. Many market operators remained sure that high yields were still to be found in the housing market and the subsidiary markets in mortgages and mortgage insurance.

But away from the glitz of Wall Street lay a reality about which few investors were cognisant. The mortgage market contained within it many predatory lenders – especially mortgage brokers and financial consultants interested in grabbing commission payments – who had sold mortgages with excessively high interest rates. These high rates were often hidden behind initially low rates used to hook borrowers keen to get onto the housing ladder. After a year or so, the far higher interest rate kicked in and the borrowers were left wondering how to make ends meet. The boosterism of estate agents and others attached to the housing market exacerbated matters. In a rising market that appeared set to rise for years to come, the important thing was to buy a house quickly and profit from rising asset prices. A large mortgage may seem daunting now, many buyers were told, but as the value of your house continues to rise, in years to come it will prove to be the wisest investment you have ever made.

Of course, when mortgages moved over onto the higher interest rate many homeowners struggled with repayments. For others, circumstances changed, and this was especially true when employers started to cut jobs as the first seismic rumblings of financial collapse could be heard in the distance. Many who had bought property as an investment were understandably terrified at the prospect of holding mortgage debt that far outweighed the value of their property. House prices tumbled faster as more properties flooded onto the market. Many who found themselves in desperate financial straits after the economy started to decline were forced to hand the keys to their dream home to the bank, who then half-heartedly pushed such properties into an already saturated market in which there were progressively fewer buyers. What became known as the American sub-prime mortgage crisis spilled over into a broader crisis of the American financial system, and this in turn prompted a global financial crisis that would have repercussions for many years to come.

The collapse of Bear Stearns, the New York investment bank, is usually considered the first key indicator that this was not simply another one of the frequent downturns experienced in Western finance systems since the 1980s. For years, Bear Stearns had been a major player in the American mortgage securities industry, profiting handsomely as the housing market continued to grow. The collapse of that market left the bank hideously overexposed. The Federal Reserve provided some initial liquidity to allow it to limp on, but it was not enough. Bear Stearns was later sold to JPMorgan Chase at a knockdown price. Some years later, JPMorgan Chase agreed to pay a record $13 billion settlement to regulators over a string of investigations into its risky mortgage deals between 2005 and 2008. As the dust began to settle, it became clear that few banks remained unscathed, and those which had disregarded high street operations and jumped into the market in abstract investment mechanisms suffered most.

In Britain, Northern Rock found itself flailing around desperately in search of a secure foothold that might prevent it from sinking deeper into the mire. The bank had invested heavily in the housing market and found itself totally unprepared as the market deflated and mortgage defaults increased. Anxiety spread as the bank's problems became common knowledge. Many savers concluded that it would be best to withdraw their money, and an old-fashioned bank run began. Given the scale of the debt carried by many banks relative to their rather limited reserves, the British economy could ill afford for such fears to spread and infect the entire financial system. Spokespeople for the Labour government made it clear that the savings of regular customers were guaranteed under the Financial Services Compensation Scheme and that the state would stand shoulder to shoulder with ordinary savers and investors threatened by events in the banking sector. However, when a buyer for Northern Rock could not be found, the state was forced to step in and nationalise the bank in the hope of stabilising the sector and assuaging the anxieties of an increasingly rattled public. Bradford & Bingley, another former mutual building society with a longstanding presence on British high streets, was also split up and sold off, and some parts of it nationalised.

Despite the state's efforts, new problems began to emerge with dazzling rapidity. In the United States, the Treasury Department stepped in to take control of Fannie Mae and Freddie Mac, the two state-sponsored cornerstones of the US housing market. While the size of these takeovers stands out, the list of banks and other financial institutions that found themselves in desperate need of the state's help is quite expansive. The US government, in its Troubled Asset Relief Program – which was initially allocated some $700 billion to buy toxic assets in the hope of keeping financial institutions trading, and generally stabilising the US economy – offered crucial assistance to such notable institutions as General Motors, Goldman Sachs, AIG, JPMorgan Chase, Morgan Stanley, Chrysler and Wells Fargo. There were, of course, many others.

The US federal government was for the most part willing to help ailing financial institutions that found themselves in trouble, but Lehman Brothers represented a step too far. During the boom years preceding the crash it had reaped a bountiful harvest from its high-risk investments. Satisfied that its financiers had the acumen needed to continually pick winners, Lehman leveraged in enormous sums to fund its investments. At the time of the bank's eventual collapse its leverage ratio was an amazing 31 : 1 and it held assets with a notional value of $600 billion.[9] Lehman's bankruptcy remains the biggest on record.

For many, Lehman Brothers became the archetype of corporate banking excess. The bank's chief executive, Dick Fuld, nicknamed 'the gorilla of Wall Street', had earned a personal income in excess of $500 million in the eight years preceding the collapse, and somehow managed to walk away from the whole debacle unscathed.

Fuld was certainly not the only figure to inspire hatred. In Britain, Fred Goodwin, Chief Executive Officer of the Royal Bank of Scotland (RBS) and nicknamed 'Fred the Shred', attracted a great deal of opprobrium. The extravagantly remunerated Goodwin had grown RBS from a small regional bank into a sprawling global entity by abandoning the relatively sedate banking culture of the modern age to dive headlong into the twenty-first century's market in abstract investment mechanisms. It seems that Goodwin was driven by a desire to grow the bank as much as possible, and to do that he was willing to take wild gambles on investments he did not appear to fully understand.[10] Gordon Brown's Labour government agreed to bail out RBS, to the tune of around £45 billion. Goodwin was stripped of his knighthood, but he suffered no penalty beyond that. He quickly left the public stage to take up early retirement, cushioned by the millions in bonuses he had earned during the boom years and the millions more he had stored away in his pension pot.

A contagion of toxic debt quickly spread throughout the financial system. Stock prices on Wall Street and in the City of London collapsed. Morgan Stanley and Goldman Sachs withdrew from investment banking and repositioned themselves as commercial banks. As Keynes had shown all those years ago, the business cycle and levels of employment in the private sector are driven by 'animal spirits', waves of sub-rational optimism and pessimism about future demand and investment returns. For years both banks and private sector companies had been excessively optimistic about what lay ahead, which had emboldened them to increase their debt-to-equity ratio and adopt illiquid positions. When news of the crash first broke, optimism turned to pessimism. Many banks and businesses suddenly sought to adopt liquid positions.

As Hyman Minsky[11] once suggested, stability appears to breed instability. In making this claim, Minsky was directing our attention to the attitudes and investing strategies that become normalised in times of economic stability. Confidence and a degree of optimism about future returns on investments can, it seems, lead to carelessness, or indeed outright recklessness. Animal spirits rise and risks are taken on investment opportunities that should be subjected to greater critical interrogation. When prices seem set to rise further, great emphasis is placed upon investing quickly, and, if need be, borrowing the funds to invest. Securing the maximum return on one's investment is the focus of attention; far less attention is given to the actual viability of the assets one buys or whether or not the asset is appropriately priced. Of course, as the financial crisis grew progressively worse, many found it incredibly difficult to offload rapidly depreciating assets as they tried to secure the liquidity that would give them room to manoeuvre. As time passed, it became increasingly clear that many debts would not be repaid. Many formidable institutions crashed to the ground.

Ultimately, the music in neoliberalism's financialised economy had stopped, and the main players were scrambling desperately to find somewhere they could safely sit down. Capital investment, the lifeblood of the financialised economy, had dried up, and the entire system came shuddering to a standstill. Every potential investment opportunity suddenly seemed polluted by risk. Many of those who still possessed investment capital retreated to their preferred tax havens to wait out the storm. The allegedly responsive and adaptable global free market had completely seized up. It had no internal mechanisms that could allow it to adjust and overcome the problems it faced. Predictably enough, all eyes turned to the much-maligned state for answers.

Throughout the industrial era the Western nation-state had played a central role in the growth of technology and industry.[12] Yet since the 1970s neoliberal ideologues have denounced it as hopelessly slow, uninventive, and incapable of responding to the needs and desires of thoroughly consumerised individuals who, we were told, had left behind archaic notions of nationhood and saw themselves as cosmopolitan citizens of the world. The political elites of the neoliberal age all seemed to have been fully inculcated with the flawed logic spouted by the global free-trade lobby, which for decades had worked tirelessly behind the scenes to ensure that the basic tenets of neoliberalism were regarded as common sense, pragmatic, and the best means of growing national economies whilst avoiding geopolitical tension and runaway inflation.[13]

Since the 1970s, neoliberalism has ascended to the level of indisputable orthodoxy in many Western nations. Since the 1980s, almost all mainstream economists, finance ministers and economics commentators have assumed that it is up to the private sector to create jobs. Economic growth, a plethora of attractive investment opportunities, low taxes and high profits made business owners optimistic about the future. To take advantage of the opportunities that lay ahead, businesses would invest in fixed assets and expand their workforce. This would in turn boost productivity, consumer spending and the overall health of the economy.

However, it was Keynes' insights that had shaped the economies of most Western nations from the close of the Second World War until neoliberalism's takeover of Western political economy in the early 1980s. Put very simply, Keynes claimed that the state can and should engage in deficit spending during times of economic contraction in the private sector to maintain full employment, prevent destructive economic crashes and ensure continued incremental economic growth. The state, Keynes maintained, had the ability to create productive employment, and it was in the interests of all that it did so. As growth in the private sector flattened out and pessimism set in, the state could create jobs with an obvious public purpose, and this would ensure continued demand and a rapid return to moderate and managed growth. These jobs could also be used to upgrade infrastructure with a view to driving innovation while boosting productivity and the nation's Gross Domestic Product. As the economy heated up, the state could reduce spending to prevent sharp inflation and the creation of dangerous bubbles.

Keynes' goal was to create steady, incremental growth and move beyond the boom-and-bust cycle that plagues the unregulated market. After the horrors of war, in which so many had sacrificed so much, Britain and many other Western nations refused to accept a return to the instability and injustices of the pre-war years. Even the old one-nation aristocrats of the Tory

Party hoped to build a land fit for heroes.[14] Housing, stable and fairly paid work, political representation and high-quality education and healthcare rapidly became rights demanded by citizens across the West, and at the time few mainstream politicians were willing to stand in their way.

The Marshall Plan[15] greatly assisted a number of European nations as they sought to rebuild after the war. While Keynes, who represented Britain in negotiations, did not get everything he hoped for from George Marshall, who headed up the American team, eventually the United States agreed to provide an initial $17 billion to assist the battered European nations to rebuild. More money was forthcoming. Of course, the Marshall Plan and the various initiatives that followed were not wholly the product of boundless generosity. The United States had by this time turned its attention to the threat of the Soviet Union, and it did not want other European nations to fall victim to the evils of communism. American liberalism must triumph, and its huge wealth was to be a crucial weapon in the fight. And, as Keynes was eager to stress, the United States had a strong economic case for funding European recovery. The Marshall Plan was an investment rather than a gift. The United States had by this time clearly surpassed Britain to take up the title of 'the workshop of the world', and, with their loans and investments, the Americans were effectively nurturing current and future export markets. Once they had received Marshall Plan funds, Britain, France and West Germany, who were the principal beneficiaries, would turn to American industry to buy what they needed to rebuild, and they would continue to buy American as their economies grew. In a roundabout way, the Marshall Plan was an investment in American industry, and consequently in American jobs. Keynes was also not blind to the global political picture. The Marshall Plan drew the largest and most strategically important European economies closer to the United States in an era that was set to be defined by a tense Cold War.

Keynes exerted considerable influence on the West's post-war economic order. He was certainly not, as some of his contemporaries suggested, a radical leftist. Indeed, he formed part of the Bloomsbury set and was well connected with literary, financial and political elites throughout Europe and North America. He seems to have been, by nature and by upbringing, a liberal conservative, greatly influenced by the work of Edmund Burke, and the philosopher G.E. Moore, who was one of the architects of analytic philosophy.

Keynes was a confirmed elitist rather than a man of the people, but he was brave enough to defy convention and commit himself to truthfully representing financial and monetary systems. His boundary-redefining book, *The General Theory of Employment, Interest and Money*,[16] is rather dry and occasionally self-indulgent. It contains little of the style and verve to be found elsewhere in both his scholarly and popular books and articles. However, despite its aesthetic flaws, Keynes' already titanic status as an economist, philosopher and political commentator compelled many British economists to persevere with it. In the fullness of time, and with the support of significant academic economists in British and American universities,[17] Keynes' deeply unfashionable assessment of the global financial system and the role of the nation-state in economic management established itself as an orthodoxy, despite the continued attempts of many representatives of capital to denigrate his work and the reputations of economists who committed to his model.[18]

Despite initial scepticism, Roosevelt drew confidence from Keynes' work and launched his New Deal in 1933 as a response to the terrible social impact of the Wall Street Crash and the Great Depression. In the years that followed, deficit spending would combine with his other principle of capital controls to become something of a panacea as nations sought to manage their economies more equitably. Keynes knew the power of the public purse, and he saw little logic in relying entirely upon the inherently unstable market to provide the jobs and economic growth nations needed to advance in a reasonably stable and civilised manner. Keynes also saw little sense in restricting the economic remit of the state to monetary policy.

In time, most mainstream economists and politicians came to agree that by itself the private sector would not sustain full employment. Boom and bust were not avoided entirely, often because politicians refused to implement Keynes' suggested measures with due diligence and foresight, but also because

Keynes' original theoretical work was over time diluted by those aligned to private sector interests. However, for the most part the economies of Britain, the United States, West Germany and France grew steadily. Welfare states were created, and, after a fashion, full employment was maintained. Crucial infrastructure projects were completed, and productivity steadily rose.

The balance between welfare and industrial investment was different across nations but, overall, Keynesian economic management had a positive impact on the lives of ordinary men and women. The consumer economy diversified, and memories of desperate poverty faded from view. Functional communities, sustained by steady and occasionally satisfying employment that paid enough to raise a family, looked to the future with optimism. The long shadow of the Second World War encouraged many to feel a sense of investment in the collective project of nationhood. They were citizens who had contributed to this prevailing mood of well-being and relative affluence. The bad times were behind them. Their work was valued, and their contribution acknowledged. Men and women became gradually more secure, and a modicum of assuredness could be discerned in their cultural lives.

Much of this fell away as Western nations voyaged out further onto neoliberalism's dark sea. The recession and stagflation of the 1970s – which, as we shall see later, could have been avoided – eroded faith in Keynesianism. Neoliberalism rose in credibility and was carried into office by a new generation of politicians committed to liberalising national economies. The state was stripped of many of the tools that had served it so well during the post-war era. The very idea that the state should create employment – or spend and invest in ways likely to create employment – became unthinkable, and tantamount to heresy. Politicians mandated to wield the huge power of the nation-state began to disavow the concentrated power they possessed. They also did what they could to convince the public that the nation's economic well-being depended solely upon the ability of investors and financiers to identify profitable investment opportunities.

Tax cuts, variable interest rates, financial deregulation and allowing unemployment to rise to its so-called 'naturally occurring rate' were, from the 1980s onwards, the only tools neoliberal finance ministers seemed willing to deploy. Should unemployment rise too fast and its deleterious social effects become obvious, the basic political drive was limited to encouraging the private sector to create employment. The only solutions neoliberals would consider were to offer tax incentives, adjust interest rates, clear away regulatory impediments, and generally do everything possible to allow investors to realise significant and sustained profits. As part of that process, workers needed to adjust their expectations and accept lower wages, reduced job security and worse conditions.

In the post-war era, the pendulum had moved in favour of workers and citizens, but now it was moving at breakneck speed in the opposite direction. Throughout the middle third of the twentieth century, the investment class had judged it expedient to accept higher taxes, higher wages and better conditions because the threat of a significant political move to the left was certainly not beyond the bounds of imagination. Profits had fallen, but markets were expanding and diversifying, and political stability needed to be maintained. The investment class put up with the demands of bold trade unionists, the restrictions of the Keynesian economic model and the regulations imposed by the democratic state. However, they were merely biding their time.

The economic crises of the 1970s signalled that the time had come to push back. Investors demanded higher returns, and a new generation of political leaders believed that they were entitled to make such demands. The people would have to change. They would have to put up with lower wages, economic insecurity and worsening conditions. Cheap consumer goods imported from abroad would be their only compensation. They were told that this was the only possible way to stabilise the global economy and guarantee a better future. They would simply have to get used to instability and be prepared to abandon the towns, cities, regions and nations of their birth to head off to wherever employment became available.

The state had willingly made itself the handmaiden of global investment capital. Politicians accepted that potential profits must be high to attract private investment. The tried-and-tested way to keep profits high is to suppress production costs. Throughout the neoliberal era, wages declined significantly in real terms, especially in labour markets that did not require a university education. Other costs were cut too, but workers suffered most. Jobs became gradually more unstable and short term, while wage growth stagnated or declined even as productivity and profits climbed higher.[19] Workforces were nothing more than – in the vulgar accounting logic proper to neoliberalism – a unit cost. Hardly ever were the men and women who toiled in the downgraded labour markets of the new market economy considered a valuable resource. Low-wage service workers were more expendable than they ever had been. Quickly it became accepted that they would constantly transit from one onerous, underpaid and unstable job to the next in the vague hope that something better would materialise further along the road.[20]

As the neoliberal age wore on and welfare states were cut back, the state's drive to dispense with assets, managerial responsibilities and economic entanglements was often accompanied by the hope that charities and private citizens could be relied upon to address the social consequences of poverty, unemployment and underemployment.[21] Representatives from the main political parties – which by this stage treated the shibboleths of neoliberalism as if they were the word of God – steadfastly refused to step forward to advocate for the public investment and real jobs ailing nations so sorely needed.

Throughout the neoliberal era, most mainstream politicians agreed that the state should be kept small while the market was encouraged to run wild. This meant that, in the crucial dimension of the economy, the political spectrum no longer existed. Blair, Brown, Clinton, Schröder, Mitterrand and many others adopted Thatcher and Reagan's faith in markets, and the new globalised corporate business and financial class was the principal beneficiary. All seemed to agree that the state should have at most a 'light-touch' regulatory role in economic planning,[22] guaranteed not to stifle the redoubtable ingenuity of the nation's swashbuckling financiers.

The incoming Labour government's decision to grant the Bank of England independence in 1997 – and in so doing cede significant powers to an unelected banking elite tasked with managing inflation by controlling interest rates – signalled the final triumph of neoliberal economics amongst mainstream leftist politicians. Throughout, neoliberal economists continually tried to convince themselves and those in government that nations need to maintain an 'optimal rate of unemployment' to prevent inflation.[23] It's worth letting that phrase percolate in the brain for a moment: an 'optimal rate of unemployment'. Even if low unemployment guaranteed rapidly rising inflation, which it does not, clearly these people believe that keeping inflation in check is far more important than attempting to ease the insecurity and suffering of ordinary people.

From the late 1980s onwards, many notable social scientists suggested that a war was taking place between the state and the market. However, if this really was a war, only one side seemed to be fighting. Faced squarely, it looked nothing like war. It was more like a clear-up operation against what little remained of the defeated democratic political resistance to neoliberalism. If a war had indeed taken place, the state's representatives had done all they could to secure its eventual defeat.

Once the key political battles were over, a new normal established itself. For us, as denizens of northern England, the key battle was the 1984–85 miners' strike. The symbolic significance of this conflict was huge. Thatcher's Conservative government – which, once the traditional one-nation Tories had been purged, was staffed entirely by free-market neoliberals – set out to disarm and discredit the British trade union movement. It was willing to use any means necessary to achieve that end.[24] But that was not all. The defeat of the miners signalled the death of a valuable way of life, rooted in clear and comprehensible symbolism, a way of life that had allowed generations of British working-class men and women a degree of freedom and cultural vitality that they had not experienced before in the modern age. Despite what many contemporary cosmopolitan leftists suggest, the death of industrialism in Britain did not free ordinary people to widen their horizons and begin a process of personal transformation, growth and progress. To this day, many post-industrial areas across Britain continue to exhibit a sense of despondency, grievance and loss.

Throughout the neoliberal era, politicians in government were very often vocal advocates of the market and stern critics of the state. They carried their anti-statist banner high and proud, promising to free the electorate from the state's pathological tendency towards coercive control. And to many mainstream commentators, markets were capable of wonders. Markets were vital, powerful, innovative, adaptable and free, and a haven for all who want to push technology forward and dash towards a brighter future. States were old and sclerotic, composed of dusty bureaucracies and dreary institutions, things of the past rather than the future.

Even when it was inconceivable for those in government to fully dispense with a key feature of state activity – for example, in Britain, where the National Health Service (NHS) is still considered one of the nation's crowning achievements and a key feature of the nation's identity – the goal became to draw the market into existing bureaucratic systems. The NHS, for example, had many of its services 'contracted out' (a process that involves giving out contracts to private businesses to carry out functions once provided directly by state employees). This allowed Blair to claim he had spent a growing proportion of the nation's wealth on the NHS despite the fact that the overall quality of healthcare provision and other services did not improve.

Blair and many other mainstream politicians believed that businesses were naturally geared towards cutting waste, improving efficiency and satisfying customers. However, the contracting-out of state services, such as health, usually meant a stark decline in quality and overall satisfaction. It didn't work for the citizens who used these services, many of whom could clearly see the overall decline of the NHS and the pressure its overstretched staff were under, and it didn't work for the majority of those who worked in the NHS, because contracting out almost always meant those once employed by the state were hired back by private sector contractors on worse pay and conditions and with a greater workload. It did work, however, for the business owners and investors to whom the state gave contracts.[25]

Politics became dominated by neoliberal dogma and its reductive assumptions. By the 1990s, few mainstream politicians

27

were willing to back the state or even make the argument that the state should at least act to prevent the spread of the market into every aspect of human life. As the social democratic age faded into history, only a few remaining old socialists, usually on the backbenches of the Labour Party, believed the state should once again assume a central role in the nation's economy. Labour's front benches, by this time, were occupied by graduates parachuted into safe seats, who brought with them little experience of the real world and no experience at all of the drudgeries of working in the downgraded service sector. They were media-savvy, ambitious, often startlingly self-confident, and totally dedicated to doing whatever needed to be done to win office. And of course, they were, first and foremost, liberals rather than socialists.

This new parachute regiment of liberal-leftist career politicians showed little interest in the left's fundamental values or the lives of the increasingly frustrated voters upon whom they had traditionally relied. It was easy to make the excuse that the working class no longer existed, whereas in reality it had merely made the transition from relatively secure industrial work to insecure service work, and it was thus no longer visible in large moving crowds outside shipyard gates. The new careerist politicians rarely looked beyond the election-time sales pitch. Every five years or so, these leftist party apparatchiks would knock on doors, make some promises, then disappear again. No fidelity, no values, no sense of mutual support or common fate, and no meaningful representation. It was no longer a historical, cultural or political relationship in the true sense. It wasn't even a meagre contractual relationship. As the left embraced neoliberalism, the relationship that existed between leftist political parties and their core support in the working class was, if anything, extractive. Leftist political parties still grabbed votes, but nothing at all moved in the opposite direction.

This situation could not endure. As dedicated pragmatists, the left's new generation of careerist politicians should have understood that they could not continue indefinitely taking their core voters for granted. Sooner or later, despite historical allegiances, disgruntled voters would withhold their votes or give them to a rival. However, the new generation of career politicians continued to forge ahead, sure that stripping back business regulations and state spending would spur private investment, which would in turn create the jobs that would bring dying post-industrial regions back to life.

Such an audacious economic transformation would have been impossible without firm and widespread ideological support. By the turn of the millennium all Western politicians and influential cultural figures accepted and, in the main, actively promoted the idea that global neoliberalism is the only possible route to a brighter, wealthier future. The past was ideologically transformed into something impoverished, repressive, parochial, drab and inward-looking, and those associated with it were believed to be similarly inclined. The future in neoliberalism's global village was open, dynamic, and alive with opportunity, diversity, innovation and progressive cultural change. If you were willing to disengage from reality and accept the world as it was presented by the culture industries, the end of history appeared to have so much going for it. Advocating a return to the politics of the state, and suggesting the nation withdraw from the vigorous cut and thrust of global free trade in order to protect jobs, increase wages and bolster national supply chains, elicited only guffaws of laughter from those who had seized control of mainstream political parties and mass media institutions.

However, the great irony is that in the wake of the biggest financial crisis in living memory, it was to the state that everyone turned in the hope that it would steady the ship and chart a course to recovery. Only the state had the power to intervene at a fundamental level to prevent further catastrophe. Only the state could truly do what needed to be done, yet it was almost impossible to find a single politician willing to say anything positive about it.

Britain's Chancellor of the Exchequer at the time of the crisis, Alistair Darling, in his memoir *Back from the Brink*, discusses with admirable candour the feeling of being engulfed by the crisis as one institution after another decided to come clean about the gaping hole in their finances. Darling acknowledges just how close he came to shutting off the cash machines and effectively closing down the economy in the hope of halting the contagion.[26] Ben Bernanke, too, at that time chair of the

Federal Reserve in the United States, has not attempted to minimise the scale and complexity of the crisis.[27] For him, the global financial crisis of 2008 was a once-in-a-lifetime event of even greater magnitude than the Great Depression of the 1930s. For years the staunchest of free-market advocates, he admitted the crisis had revealed to him the financialised global economy's underlying structural faults. Only the state could respond, and all the banking technocrats and politicians knew it.

The 2008 financial crisis was not simply a crisis of the banking sector. It quickly metamorphosed into what became known as the European sovereign debt crisis. Portugal, Ireland, Greece, Cyprus and Spain, a collection of countries unflatteringly nicknamed the 'PIGS', found themselves unable to repay or refinance their debts and unable to assist their own banks as they stumbled towards collapse from the latter half of 2008 onwards. These nations faced a fundamental problem. Because they had given up their sovereign currencies for the euro, they could not, in the usual manner, devalue their currency to manage debts. The 2008 crisis revealed in stark detail just how much sovereignty they had given up when they joined the eurozone and accepted the euro as their sole legitimate currency.

Initially they had been drawn to the abstract ideal of European integration and the utilitarian attractions of belonging to a pan-continental free-trade area that was growing incrementally in terms of economic power and global influence. With a highly efficient and technologically advanced German economy at its centre, they could be forgiven for assuming that economic growth and improved consumer lifestyles were almost guaranteed. For years standards of living did indeed appear to rise.

Understandably enough, when times were good there was little interest in what these nations had given up in order to join the club. However, when the 2008 crisis hit, their total reliance on the European Central Bank (ECB) suddenly became obvious. Without the power of a sovereign fiat currency – which we discuss in the following section – they simply did not have access to the liquidity, spending power and debt monetisation they needed to stabilise their national economies and secure the well-being of their citizens. Like Weimar Germany after the First World War, these nations owed debts in what was essentially a foreign currency. The ECB, together with the other institutions that formed the Troika – the International Monetary Fund and the shadowy and unelected European Commission – were, to cut a long story short, unwilling to issue and hand over the euros that would enable these countries to address the collapse of their national economies. Traumatic levels of austerity and fiscal restraint were duly imposed on these nations and, after some brief resistance by SYRIZA in Greece, left-wing parties had no answer to put to their respective electorates.

Let it be

In order to understand the structural economic failures in which the post-war left allowed itself to be embroiled, let's take a moment to investigate the basic economics that underpin neoliberalism's political landscape. A monetarily sovereign nation-state with its own fiat currency can never go broke. 'Fiat' here simply means 'let it be'. The phrase 'fiat currency' describes currencies that are free-floating and not pegged to a particular commodity, like gold, or tied to a foreign currency, usually the US dollar. Financial markets determine the value of fiat currencies.

The 1944 Bretton Woods agreements were conceived as a means of stabilising currencies and international loans as nations sought to rebuild after the Second World War. Until 1971, many Western countries, including Britain and the United States, were tied to what was known as the 'gold standard'. In Britain between 1944 and 1971, for example, the value of the pound was tied to the US dollar, which in turn was tied to the value of gold. The Bretton Woods agreements also tied Britain to a system of fixed exchange rates. The value of the pound in relation to a whole host of other national currencies was fixed by mutual consent. The system of fixed exchange rates had numerous downsides for national economies, especially as international trade began to heat up. National governments found themselves unable to respond productively to trade deficits and balance of payments crises.

The Bretton Woods system meant that national governments were financially constrained and compelled to manage the total amount of currency in circulation. They tended to do this by extracting almost as much tax revenue from the economy as the currency they issued as public spending. This practice appears to have informed the two interconnected myths that have weighed heavily on the left since the dawning of the neoliberal age. The first myth is that governments must tax their populations before they can spend money on public works or services, and the second is that should governments fail to raise enough money in taxation they must cover spending commitments by borrowing on financial markets.

These myths are ubiquitous and structure popular beliefs about what national governments can actually accomplish. Thatcher famously declared that the problem with socialism is that eventually you run out of other people's money. And yet, since the death of Bretton Woods, the only restrictions placed upon public spending have been pragmatic and focused on the management of inflation. In fact, Weimar-style hyper-inflation is very rare and dependent on other factors that predate the issue of currency, such as defeat in war, the collapse of productivity and owing debts payable only in foreign currencies. The United States and all other nations that possess a sovereign fiat currency do not suffer from such problems. They cannot go broke because they are the sole legitimate producer of their own sovereign currency.

Britain and the United States both have the capacity to buy anything that is for sale in their own currencies, including all unused labour. However, to counter this reality, from the 1980s onwards the unrivalled ideological supremacy of neoliberalism ensured that a range of myths about the financial system became entrenched in everyday life. The fundamental popular message is that public spending beyond tax revenue will incur unmanageable debts and deficits, bankrupting nations and leaving our children with an impossible burden. The mainstream left's acceptance of these myths greatly impeded its progress. It also ensured that there was very little difference between the mainstream left's economic policies and those of the neoliberal right.

The fundamental ideological consequence of the left's incorporation into this pervasive mythology is that the majority of ordinary people understand the left's progressive vision solely in terms of its cultural rather than its economic concerns. In recent years, for example, an increasing number believe that the left advocates open borders and other features of cultural progressivism, while the right is more likely to defend borders and the traditional cultures and customs that lie within. Public understanding of what the left has in store for us economically, and how its proposals differ from those of the right, tends to be unclear.

Throughout the neoliberal era, the left and the right largely agreed on economic fundamentals. As we will see in the next chapter, things changed – but only slightly – with the rise of Corbyn, Sanders and other 'left populists'. However, throughout the 'third way' administrations of Clinton, Obama, Blair, Brown and others, the differences between left and right on economic policy were, in the grand scheme of things, quite insignificant. The left and right did, however, often quite starkly disagree on cultural issues, and many concluded that henceforth all major political battles would be fought on the field of culture.

The left's flight from economic antagonism was a deadly blow to its electoral chances. In Britain, the left should have made it absolutely clear to ordinary men and women that national governments do not need to borrow British pounds on financial markets. The state has the capacity to create as many British pounds as it needs to fund whatever projects the government of the day intends to pursue. The British state can spend *up to the nation's productive limit* without spurring a rapid rise in inflation. The same is true of all monetarily sovereign nation-states. Since the beginning of neoliberal outsourcing in the 1980s, Western states have been far short of their productive limits. The idea that the state is financially constrained and can't afford to spend money on what would be very popular public programmes and infrastructural investments quite clearly benefits the neoliberal right, who prefer sovereign currency to be issued through the central bank to licensed private banks, which can lend it out as interest-bearing loans.

This is certainly not to say that monetarily sovereign nations do not borrow money; they do, but they certainly do not borrow their own currencies to fund public spending. Talk of monetarily sovereign nations being crushed by unmanageable debts makes no logical sense. Hyperbolic media commentators who terrify their audience with talk of the gaping hole in the nation's finances and the possibility of the state being declared bankrupt, or our children being burdened with our debts and deficits, display either a remarkable lack of knowledge or a strategic desire to hide the reality of our fiat money system. The United States is not on the verge of defaulting on its debts, because it has an inexhaustible supply of American dollars. The Bank of England can produce electronically as much money as the British state would ever need to service a debt or pay for public works. It is just a matter of pressing a few numbers on a keyboard. The fact that the left has played along with all of this for so long, and continues to do so, should be a major issue for all truly critical leftist intellectuals to ruminate upon.

Leftist political figures helped to propagate this myth either because of ignorance or because they hoped to disguise their own determination to obey the neoliberal command to ensure that spending in the public interest is kept to a minimum. Even John McDonnell – ostensibly the most left-wing shadow chancellor for half a century – dipped into the fantasies that sustain the neoliberal order. Following so many other post-crash political leaders, he likened the national budget to that of an ordinary household and trotted out the standard myths about fiscal probity and living within our means. For McDonnell, of course – who in 2017 contributed to a very popular Labour manifesto that almost saw the party return to power – an increase in public spending was essential for the relief of widespread social distress. However, he also felt it necessary to tell voters that his spending plans would be paid for by cutting spending elsewhere and by extracting more money from the rich in the form of taxes. McDonnell's spending plans looked quite extravagant, and so he was keen to reassure voters that they were fully costed and that by the end of the administration the nation's deficit would be reduced.

It's disappointing that McDonnell bought into the household analogy. It is totally false and should have been assertively rejected by the left decades ago. In accepting the household analogy, leftist politicians agree to play by the rules set by the neoliberal right. The British state is the sole issuer of its sovereign currency.

It and no one else produces British pounds. Households do not have that luxury, and so a comparison between the two is absurd. It makes sense for households to pay down debt, but the same is not necessarily true for nation-states. It makes sense for household members to spend only the money they have available, but the monetarily sovereign nation-state can in effect spend as much money as it wants within the nation's productive capacity. The state can never run out of its own money. Households can and often do run out of money and are then forced to borrow. Monetarily sovereign nation-states are never forced to borrow their own currency and can afford to fund all of their spending commitments. This does not mean that a nation-state with its own sovereign currency can endlessly indulge the whims of its core constituencies, but it does mean governments are not financially constrained in the ways we have been led to believe.

Governments can spend up to the nation's productive capacity without fear of spurring runaway inflation, which is the bogeyman that haunts the dreams of all mainstream economists. This does not mean that taxes are superfluous. They are important, but not in the ways we tend to assume. Governments do not need to tax before they can spend, but they can use the tax system to control inflation, alter spending decisions, redistribute spending money, limit oligarchic power and subtly shape cultural habits in civil society.

Sin taxes – on cigarettes, beer and so on – are an obvious example. Governments around the world impose taxes on particular commodities in order to discourage consumers from buying them. The most commonly cited justification for imposing sin taxes is the effect these commodities have upon public health. A number of national governments have in recent years added sugary drinks and fatty foods to the standard list of 'sinful' commodities, and it seems likely that others will soon follow suit. Red meat may soon join the list. There are, of course, many good reasons for pursuing such a course. Consumers put off by higher prices may decide to curtail their intake of unhealthy consumables, and corporations may seek to avoid taxes by reducing the sugar or saturated fat in their products.

Tax breaks can also be offered to encourage behaviours widely believed to yield a public benefit of some sort. Married couples still often benefit from small tax breaks, and a number of governments now try to encourage those shopping for a new car to go electric. In this way, taxes can be used in the attempt to facilitate positive social outcomes. Taxes can also be used to truncate social inequality. This was done to considerable effect during the social democratic era, but neoliberal administrations appear to have strategically forgotten about this crucial social function. Most people take the ethical position that the rich should be taxed proportionally more than those lower down the social hierarchy.[28] Curtailing the financial power of the mega-rich has a range of real, positive political and social effects alongside the primary ethical reason of fairness.

It is also vital to recognise that governments tend to recoup a significant portion of public spending. Much of the money the state spends is returned to it in the form of tax revenues. This may seem counterintuitive, but to better grasp the reality of our monetary system we must keep in mind the full diversity of ways governments remove liquidity from the economy. Tax is not simply a matter of deductions from wage packets, although most people focus on this aspect of the tax system above all others.

As academics, our wages are, in a roundabout way, paid by the British government. We pay tax on our wages, so the government immediately takes back a significant slice of the money it pays to us each month. Like you, we imagine, we spend the money that remains. But the vast majority of things we might choose to buy, and the various entities we might buy those items from, are also subject to taxes. The driver of the taxi we take to the station must pay income tax. He must pay road tax, and he also pays tax when he fills his car with fuel. The employee who serves our morning coffee must pay tax on her wages, and her employer must pay tax on its profits. The items used to make the coffee have also been bought and sold and are subject to taxation. The train company that transports us to work must pay tax, as must all of its employees, and much that the train company relies upon to deliver its full range of services involves a payment to the Exchequer. Sales taxes. Sin taxes. Import taxes. In Britain and other European states, VAT (value added tax) is imposed. Various forms of local government also impose taxes.[29] In short, a multitude of interlinked economic chains ensure that more money spent by governments than we might imagine finds its way back to the state.

However, throughout the neoliberal era there have been insistent calls to cut taxes. The system's underlying logic suggests that tax cuts can stimulate economic activity and private capital investment. While it is entirely possible that this claim has been used to disguise the real reasons neoliberals call for tax cuts, which is of course to give business leaders a greater share of the spoils, it is certainly true that specific tax cuts can be used to boost economic activity, especially among those sections of society most likely to spend – rather than hoard or invest abroad – money that comes their way. However, if the ultimate goal is to stimulate economic activity within their borders, monetarily sovereign nation-states have a range of far more effective tools at their disposal.

The reality is that tax cuts have tended to benefit those least in need of financial help and most likely to take their money beyond the nation's borders, which of course can reduce aggregate demand and discourage productive investment in the real economy. Neoliberalism has transformed sovereign nations into global competitors forced to attract global investors and multinational corporations. This in turn has reduced levels of corporate tax, which has enriched corporate elites and aided the profitability of the largest and most powerful corporations. If, for example, corporate taxes in the Republic of Ireland are low, global corporations like Google, Amazon or Intel might be attracted to set up shop there. Many argue that pursuing such a course will create jobs, which in turn will reduce the need for governments to spend money on welfare while at the same time boosting consumer spending. Increases in consumer spending will improve aggregate demand, create more jobs and drive market innovation. However, this kind of international competition – trumpeted from the rooftops by neoliberal ideologues on the left and the right – has for many decades resulted in an unseemly race to the bottom that has benefited only multinational corporations already attuned to minimising tax, and the elite executives in those corporations who have been able to command higher wages.[30] Furthermore, the jobs created by offering tax cuts to large multinational corporations have been for the most part few in number and low in quality.[31] The net result has been that the economic and financial power of the state has been used to enrich elites.[32] Throughout the neoliberal era, this aspect of neoliberal governance contributed to widening inequalities and associated social problems.[33]

It is not only multinational corporations that have benefited from the liberal drive to strip away the shackles of taxation. In England, Northern Ireland and Wales, the standard personal tax allowance rose to £12,500 per annum in 2018, meaning that citizens do not pay income tax on the first £12,500 they earn, and citizens who earn £12,500 or less per annum pay no personal income tax at all. This policy move garnered some support on the left, but of course it benefits the very wealthy just as much as it benefits the very poor. Certainly, it is wrong to think that raising tax thresholds in this manner is a useful means of reducing inequality. While the neoliberals trumpeted changes to the tax system as a gift from government to struggling citizens everywhere, the left acquiesced, generally accepted the logic behind the claim, and got caught in the usual trap of endorsing the policy through gritted teeth while claiming it didn't go far enough.

The fundamental point is this: from the dawning of the neoliberal age politicians and technocrats reduced the total amount of tax the state took from national economies, and this in turn has contributed to what economics commentators call 'the deficit'. But, as we hope you can see, the state's deficit is directly proportional to the private sector's surplus. The state doesn't have it because the private sector has it. The state has issued the currency into existence, but it has not recouped enough of this money through taxation. Therefore, the money is still out there in civil society, and disproportionately skewed towards the wealthy elite, whether they have earned it fairly or not.

Some readers will have a proportion of it stored in a savings account. Money that is saved, of course, is no longer in the spending chain and therefore unlikely to either boost demand and create jobs or be recouped by the state. The super-rich have a good share of it hidden in tax havens, and they have it there because they do not wish to pay money back to the state in the form of tax.[34]

The state deficit we hear so much about is directly proportionate to the amount of money held by citizens, businesses and corporations in the form of savings and liquid assets. The existence of the state's deficit means that a surplus exists elsewhere. Leftist political parties should have exposed the deficit myth long ago.[35] If we can accept that the state's deficit is roughly the inverse of the surplus that exists in the private sector, the argument can move on, and we can begin to look in earnest at how this surplus is gleaned and who tends to benefit from state deficits.

Governments could, of course, wipe out the state's deficit quite quickly by withdrawing a greater proportion of money from the economy in the form of tax, but it would make no sense to pursue this course. Should the government reduce the state's deficit to zero, as many governments aspire to do, then the general public would shoulder the burden and the surplus that now sloshes around the economy would quickly dry up.

Of course, the political parties of the left have traditionally argued that the rich should shoulder a far greater tax burden. For us, this is entirely reasonable. The sheer scale of the wealth held by the super-rich is obscene, and it is absurd to suggest that in every case this wealth is somehow proportional to their individual creativity and drive. As Piketty[36] has shown, wealth tends to beget ever greater wealth. The gap between the super-rich, who possess an extraordinary amount of investment capital, and the rest of us, who depend upon ever more precarious incomes, will continue to grow until the problem is addressed by national governments.

Paying tax encourages us all to view the entitlements provided by the state as ours by right, and surety that others are also 'paying into the system' encourages us to accept the justice of universal benefits. However, it is wrong to conclude that our taxes pay for those entitlements. They do not, but the flawed assumption that they do has lingered on for so long and to such damaging effect because it's *something we want to believe*, which makes us susceptible to neoliberal ideology. We like to believe that our talents result in a job, that our labour produces value, that the value we produce in turn produces tax revenues, and that those tax revenues pay for universal goods and services provided by the state to its citizens. This myth encourages a sense that the state relies upon us, the people, rather than the rather ignominious possibility that we rely on the state, a collection of institutions that often strike us as divorced from our daily lives and blithely unaware of our struggles. However, once we accept the fact that the taxation system is not principally concerned with generating income for the state, we can begin to see the reality of our economic system with a little more clarity.

Encouraging people to actually do this should have been a key concern for the left as the consequences of the neoliberal revolution began to bite in the 1980s. Doing so would have prompted the general public to think critically about the forces that shape many of their trials and tribulations, and about what needs to be done to change things. It would have given the left a sturdy platform of knowledge and understanding from which to build the kinds of transformative policy proposals our nations so desperately need. Instead, all too often the left mystified the economic system, accepted neoliberal dogma or abandoned the field of economics entirely as it rushed to address the injustices of the cultural field.

States with their own fiat currency, we must remember, always have the capacity to produce enough of it to free themselves from debt, although doing so might lead to other significant negative consequences. As the shockwaves from the American financial crisis reverberated around the globe, triggering a sovereign debt crisis across the eurozone, Spain, Greece, Ireland and other EU nations were unable to act independently because they did not possess their own sovereign fiat currencies, which they had forfeited to join the euro. Greece, therefore, was unable to assist its banks. It could not intervene in the way the British or US government did when the crisis hit. Instead, these nations and their citizens were totally beholden to the European Central Bank and the European Commission, which, under the watchful eye of the International Monetary Fund, together design and control the economic policies of the eurozone. The ideology that shaped the attitudes of those with the power to make these crucial decisions was there for all to see. The disdain with which those at the centre of the EU's power block treated their European compatriots as they struggled with the debt crisis beggars belief.

Unlike Britain and the United States, Greece can go broke. It can run out of euros. The same is true of Germany, although the likelihood of that happening is very small. In fact, membership of the euro helps the German export economy, because whatever variant of the mark they might return to should the eurozone be dissolved would be valued higher on the currency markets, making their exports less competitive. Greece is in a far more difficult situation. Like all eurozone members, it owes debts in what is essentially a foreign currency. Also, because it cannot issue its own currency, it is entirely reliant upon tax revenues or loans from the European Central Bank. The former quickly dried up as the crisis worsened and the latter inevitably increased the country's 'foreign debt' problem.

Britain and the United States' federal government do not need to tax before they spend. In fact, the situation is rather the opposite. Britain creates the initial demand for British pounds and gives the currency initial value by levying taxes in British pounds. It then spends money into existence, and in so doing provides the money ordinary people and business entities use to conduct transactions and pay tax. Greece could neither issue currency nor raise the money it needed by taxing its population, so it was forced to borrow. By this time, of course, rates of interest had risen, and Greece found itself with only two choices. It could have dropped out of the euro, reintroduced the drachma, inflated away from its debts and used its sovereign currency to address the social crisis that had unfolded across its territory. Given that Greece is largely dependent upon foreign imports, adopting this strategy would have resulted in a good deal of pain. Greece would have been forced to transform its economy and quickly develop national supply chains. The other choice, of course, was to go cap in hand to the Troika and beg to be bailed out.

Initially, the Greeks refused to accept the unenviable position in which the nation found itself.[37] They did not want austerity. Nor did they want to leave the family of European member states. In the end, of course, and despite their wishes, the Greeks got austerity. It was regretfully delivered by a supposedly radical leftist political party that was more committed to retaining the euro than it was to the well-being of the Greek people.[38]

The EU was and still is committed to ensure that member nations maintain a balanced budget. Even when faced with genuine human suffering, its institutions were unwilling to create the money troubled nations needed to purchase assets, provide immediate liquidity to banks and generally stabilise their national economies before setting out to create employment and return their economies to growth. The European Central Bank did launch its own continental stimulus package, but at no stage was the Troika willing to cede control of the creation of euros to member states themselves. The best the Troika would do was lend money to these troubled nations and, in order to get their hands on this money, national governments would have to agree to slash government spending and do everything in their power to reduce deficits.

The neoliberal drive to ensure nations pursue a policy of 'balancing the budget' can be seen quite clearly in the EU's constitution. This commitment is occasionally clear and occasionally opaque, but it is always there. In the EU's constitution, neoliberalism moves from being simply a raft of pro-business policies pursued by national governments to a new, coherent and potent supranational authority.

The EU's commitment to balanced budgets works its magic behind the scenes, ensuring that democratically elected governments across the continent do not spend lavishly in the public interest or invest too much in domestic industries and infrastructure. In order to join the euro, nations must demonstrate a commitment to ensuring that state spending does not radically outstrip the 'income' the state receives in terms of taxation. Member states must also accept the primacy of the private sector and promise not to interfere too much in national or continental markets. The EU's commitment to boosting the private sector and restricting the economic mandate of sovereign nation-states is written clearly into its constitution. It can also be seen in detail in the responses of its various institutions to the sovereign debt crisis of 2008. Despite this transparency, the EU's fundamental commitment to a key tenet of neoliberal orthodoxy seems to operate behind the scenes because it has somehow managed to escape the notice of huge swathes of the left.

The flight from economic reality

The EU continues to be seen by the left across the continent as generally 'progressive', and often preferable to democratically elected national governments, principally because the field of economics has been mystified and the field of culture accepted as the site of all key political battles. The EU's commitment to the free movement of people across its territories has been read by many as an indicator of its inclusivity and commitment to social justice. The primacy given to such cultural aspects of EU governance, and the general ignorance shown to the EU's deep and broad commitment to neoliberal economic doctrine, is a useful indication of precisely how the left changed in the decades after the Second World War and why it has fared so poorly since the dawning of the neoliberal age.

Picking up on what appears to be a commitment to European cosmopolitanism while ignoring the EU's long history of weak and ineffective responses to crises, many on the British left regard the EU as a pan-continental defence mechanism protecting us all from the perennial threat that European nations will drift towards aggressive, ethnocentric nationalism. Much of today's politics is based not on rationality or clear visions of the future, but on a deep, objective and assiduously reproduced fear that unwanted aspects of the cultural past might soon return.

The pro-EU left in Britain will be explored in more detail in Chapter 9, but we should perhaps at this stage acknowledge that the contemporary cult of Europhilia in Britain is often connected to a general dissatisfaction with Britain itself. At work here is a twin-track process of idealisation and demonisation that bears no relation to reality. The European Union has been idealised and somehow cleansed of its manifold faults at least in part because the nation has been demonised and presented as incorrigibly insular, racist and backward-looking. As we will see, the left has overlooked the many wonders of our nations. It has also disavowed the enduring power of the nation-state and imagines the only institutions, politics and cultural values capable of slowing the nation's slow march to right-wing nationalism exist beyond its borders.

Many of the more radical leftist media commentators fought hard to ensure that Britain remained part of a continental free-trade zone founded on neoliberal principles. Many more displayed contempt for those who, in the 2016 referendum, voted to leave the EU, before voting for the Conservative Party to ensure the result of the referendum was acted upon.[39] This created a strange situation in which radical leftists were fighting hard to maintain a status quo that quite clearly did not benefit those most in need of the left's support.

Some middle-class leftists even dipped into the language of revolution to call pro-EU activists out onto the streets in the hope of preventing a democratically elected government from enacting the results of a national referendum. These leftists ultimately wanted the nation to remain part of a neoliberal free-trade area that in its economic policies had made the poor poorer and the rich richer.

There are few clearer examples of the left's strange transformation as it journeyed through a kaleidoscope of libertarian and postmodern thinking. Up was down, left was right. The working class was the hostile right-wing establishment. Liberal, middle-class, university-educated pro-EU activists were an oppressed proletariat spilling onto the street to fight for freedom. The radical left promised to bravely fight the evildoers, ironically through the state's own legal system, to maintain the neoliberal status quo in the interests of the workers who suffered as a result of it. Had it not been so tragic it would have been funny.

Critical denunciation of the nation has, of course, been a key feature of leftist discourse for generations. However, for the most part it has been geared towards securing, defending and sharing more equitably what was good about the nation, and freeing those who suffered unjustly under the yoke of tyranny and money power. Such traditional leftist critique did not decry as evil incarnate those depoliticised or conservative men and women who refused to adopt the left's increasingly incoherent ideals. Leftist critics of the nation sought to convince, recruit and absorb into its own community those who had in the past, against their own interests, accepted the centre or the right's account of the world. Ordinary men and women could – through rational and respectful debate, and with the aid of logic, evidence and positive rhetoric – be made to see the utility of the left's drive to curb the power of economic elites and use the offices of the state to manage unstable market economies and ensure fairness, justice, equality and peace. Always, without question, the left clung onto what was still beautiful in the nation, no matter how tarnished it had become.

The sentiments and the logic behind this approach were perfectly straightforward. These traditional leftist critics did not hate the nation. Rather, they loved it enough to think it worth fighting for. As we will see, many of those active on the left today cannot bring themselves to accept that the majority of the nation's working class enjoy national cultures and traditions, remain moderately patriotic, and are still committed to the regional cultures of their birth. The liberal left seems sure that there is nothing positive about the nation. Its history of war, injustice and colonial conquest are such that it cannot be redeemed or rehabilitated. Nothing positive remains. The refusal of the working class to accept the liberal left's tutelage drives further division and has inspired some leftists to abandon traditional protocols and denounce the working class as irredeemably atavistic.

Never before in our lifetimes have we witnessed so many leftists denounce ordinary working people. In academia, media and some elements of leftist politics, it is now common to identify two basic social groups: those who have been educated to recognise and appreciate the benefits of cosmopolitanism, and those who are uneducated and thus pathologically attached to the environments they call home.

Any commitment to the region or nation of one's birth increasingly seems to be decoded by today's left as a commitment to nationalism, which of course can never be benignly patriotic and is always just a short step from fascism. Being told that it is wrong to love one's place in the world, or that it is narrow-minded to feel attached and committed to the locale, region and nation of one's birth, is unlikely to inspire support. Alienating millions of ordinary people is not a strategy likely to lead to success at the ballot box, but then, for many on the left, that no longer seems to be the principal aim. They do not hope to transform the nation by achieving electoral success and managing economic processes in the interests of stability and fairness. Nor, it seems, do they hope to recruit and persuade. For many on the left, especially in supposedly 'radical' circles, those days are gone. Revolutionary cultural conflict has been identified as the platform from which they can launch a great leap into the future.

Many leftists we have met and listened to in recent years quite clearly imagine themselves to be ethical, knowledgeable, intelligent and capable of thoughtfully appraising truth claims. Nevertheless, they seem remarkably comfortable denouncing working-class Brexit voters as a thoughtless bovine herd that stupidly accepted right-wing lies. Educated liberals are capable of critical thought and judgement, but Brexit voters clearly aren't.

In many respects, the traditional model of class and political alignment has been flipped on its head. The broad working class – especially those who happen to have been born with white skin – are assumed to be incorrigibly right-wing by those on the left, while the left is increasingly considered 'upper class' by members of the working class. The Labour Party is now a party of graduates, which tends to mean it is also a party of liberals, and its cultural and political leadership increasingly comes from the educated middle class. Members of the working class are recruited, but usually in subordinate roles after they have sworn allegiance to the realisation of the liberal vision of cultural progress.[40] While there are notable differences, a similar process of change can be discerned in the Democratic Party in the United States. As we will see, these changes are important and revealing. It fills us with regret to acknowledge it, but the liberal goal of creating a left without the working class is close to realisation.

As the edifice of twentieth-century liberalism continues to teeter wildly – and seems sure, at long last, to crash into the dust – what counts as 'right wing' and 'left wing' is undergoing radical change. Away from the spotlight, cultural conservatism seems to be making some progress among ordinary people.

This is certainly not to say that conservatism was until recently absent from working-class cultures.[41] Rather, it is to claim that this underlying cultural conservatism has come to the fore in voting decisions as so many working-class men and women now see clearly that the main left-of-centre political parties no longer represent their interests.

The progress conservatism has made in areas once judged solidly left of centre is not the result of an orchestrated campaign. Rather, an organic, nameless, chimerical conservatism is becoming more prominent among ordinary people who find themselves ill-disposed to rapid and relentless cultural change over which they have no control, and mildly nostalgic for a world in which they felt more at home.

However, quite often this cultural conservatism sits alongside quite radical attitudes to economic management and the unyielding belief that the rich benefit too much from the present economic model. Many firmly believe that more must be done to ensure that the majority have more security and a better standard of living. The conservatism of these voters is also far more nuanced than many leftist commentators care to understand. Many are 'conservative' on an assortment of issues, such as patriotism, the general pace of cultural change and mass immigration, but they can also be quite liberal on many others, for example homosexuality or having a child marry a man or woman from a different ethnic or religious background.[42]

Nuanced contradictions also exist on the left. Many appear unperturbed by the staggering concentrated power wielded by global financial elites, and the central role they play in keeping some people poor. Despite their loud hostility towards the nation and the state, they rail against the state's refusal to address climate change, racism, sexism, hate crime and a whole host of often quite bespoke cultural themes that they believe structure social injustice. Theirs is a socialism not of economics and economic justice but of culture and cultural justice in an unchanging economic context they make little attempt to understand.

Their fight for cultural justice is often admirable, but they are generally unconcerned with class, and do not see it as a broad and potentially unifying category that cuts across all cultural identities. Many involved with the activist left are, truth be told, not really leftists at all. They are radical liberals, and, as a large proportion of young people are processed through the unwaveringly liberal university system, their numbers appear to be growing. These two groups now look set to butt heads regularly in the years to come.

With a modicum of forethought, a focused strategy and a willingness to engage in reflexive self-critique, the left could have profited greatly from this evolution. It could have broken down barriers, focused on the betterment and enrichment of all, identified the neoliberal economy as a fundamental source of disunity and social suffering, and placed an appealing, comprehensible and feasible alternative before electorates. Instead, the left managed to get everything wrong. It alienated its core constituencies, failed to unify minorities, disregarded the interests of majorities and, as nations were thrust deeper into an unforgivingly competitive global economy, turned away from economic management and historical economic storytelling to focus solely on cultural injustice. And, for us the clearest indicator of its terminal decline, it adopted the haughty, holier-than-thou image of moral and cultural superiority it once lampooned in the haute bourgeoisie.

The economic question, unanswered

In the wake of the 2008 global financial crisis, an unholy concoction of myths, evasive fudging and outright lies, sprinkled with a liberal helping of ignorance and arrogance, sloshed out from central government and leftist political parties alike. Dutifully broadcast by the mainstream media, it permeated the living rooms of ordinary voters who deserved so much better. As we have seen, to bail out the banks, anxious governments had fortuitously managed to locate the magic money tree, but as soon as the dirty deed had been done, they lost it again. Even the great hope of liberal America, Barack Obama, trotted out the lie that the state was broke – it had run out of money, and to meet its commitments it needed to borrow ever-increasing sums of US dollars from financial markets. The nation had to learn to live within its means. A huge proportion of the nation's wealth was being used to cover interest payments, and logic dictated that everything must now be done to pay off debts, reduce the deficit and balance the books.

Ordinary people would ultimately be the victims of the state's subsequent cost-cutting. Young people attempting to establish themselves in a secure career. The poorest and those most in need of medical help. Couples setting up home together and thinking about starting a family. In some countries, older people in receipt of pensions were victims. Homeowners, families, ordinary people totally divorced from the financialised economy, everyday people who had no direct experience of business investments, men and women who didn't care about the wealth that could be earned on Wall Street or in the City of London. The burden of responsibility did not fall on those who had played an active role in causing the crisis. Those with the least power and minimal access to worthwhile political representation suffered most.

Across the West the story was the same. The Democrats in the United States, the Labour Party in Britain, and virtually all mainstream leftist political parties across Europe were enslaved by deficit fetishism. They might have liked to spend public money to invest in their economies and put people back to work, but they could not. If they did not display sufficient fiscal probity, they warned the public, future generations would be saddled with a crushing debt.

As we hope you can see, it is all nonsense. However, the story was so ubiquitous it was accepted as truth. The neoliberals argued that spending must be slashed. The liberals who had taken control of the leftist parties basically agreed but tried to sustain the myth of political antagonism by arguing that spending should be cut at a marginally slower rate. Politics took on a deathly pallor. Millions were struggling and scarcely a voice was raised in opposition. The left slashed spending as deeply and enthusiastically as the neoliberal right. Both wings of this strange post-political pantomime agreed on the fundamentals, and what passed for debate addressed the pointless minutiae that no one really cared about. The conclusion had been reached. It would be austerity for all, apart from the rich.

The mainstream left's adoption of austerity produced a range of intertwined effects that are immediately conspicuous but also hard to measure. The old assumption that the left would look after those who struggled financially was finally put to bed. The poorest would no longer gravitate towards the left, unless the poorest believed the left's multipolar cultural agenda would pay off economically for them further down the line. For hundreds of millions of ordinary voters across the West, the left's political parties had become indistinguishable from the neoliberal right in basic economic matters.

The left has been successful only when it encouraged the people of a nation to dream about a future that surpassed the present. As the post-crash era developed, the left should have created an image of a brighter future together with a feasible means of reaching it. This would be a future in which ordinary people would be valued and able to live happily, safely, cooperatively and with dignity. Unfortunately, the liberalised left's vision – a future in which all individuals would be granted the freedom to be who or what they choose to be – failed to either inspire or reassure populations suffering declining living standards and perennial anxieties about their capacity to sustain themselves financially.

Many dropped out and refused to vote, but the real damage was to the nation's faith in democratic politics. People continued to vote because voting was the only thing one could do. They hoped but did not believe that the act of voting would change things. And of course, many who had throughout their lives voted left began to contemplate voting rightwards. They had not suddenly begun to subscribe to fascist doctrine, and they had not been tricked into voting for the right by posts on Facebook[43] or the apparently titanic ideological power and incisiveness of the right-wing press.[44] Others, left uninspired and cynical after years of drab neoliberal centrism, shed their commitment to the left to swell the ranks of the pragmatic 'floating voter' unaligned to any established political position.

The left had become a serial loser, but a minority of activists received some quite valuable consolation prizes. The new cultural radicals of the metropole were to play an increasingly important role in the left's local and national operations. Groups on the outskirts of the left during the social democratic era moved centre-stage. Most of these groups accepted neoliberalism as a given. In the few cases where they did not, they tended to display minimal understanding of neoliberalism's economic framework and offered hastily formulated replacement packages divorced from reality. The field of culture was their focus, while identity and subjectivity displaced class and political economy as the field of social transformation.

In some of the neighbourhoods we visited in our role as social scientists, a general, unspecified anger was palpable. It often fused with desperation as chronically insecure people who had very little before the crisis were forced to get by with even less. History needed to move forward, but a zombie neoliberalism continued to limp on unopposed, propped up by state institutions staffed by a pseudo-technocratic liberal elite deeply committed to market ideology. It was inevitable that there would be a return to politics. Nature abhors a vacuum. The populist moment had arrived.

2

Democracy, without the people?
The rise and fall of left populism

During the period of austerity that followed the financial crash, new antagonisms rooted in shifting material reality began to emerge, while older antagonisms rooted in class and culture evolved and became gradually more acute. The ongoing fragmentation of society during these years became normalised. Some on the left continued to persevere with accounts of unity, but increasingly they seemed to be talking about temporary truces and concessions between irreconcilable fragments rather than the incorporation of all groups of working people in a grand project of solidarity. The traditional focus of left-wing social and political analysis – the class system and its foundation in economic exploitation and political exclusion – receded further into the background.

Action was moving at speed from universalism to particularism; from things all people share to things specific to distinct cultural groups. Old-fashioned ideas around collective life and shared identities, goals, ideals and beliefs were discarded. Those who clung to such ideas were mercilessly mocked for their inability to understand or appreciate the scale of human diversity and the true course of progress. Those at the centre could never understand those on the margins. Those born with white skin could never understand those born with black skin. A heterosexual man could never understand the plight of a homosexual woman. Only those who had fully lived and experienced a marginalised identity should be allowed to 'speak their truth'.

The entire idea of community – the product of material functions, practical alliances, sentimental attachments, histories

52

of trust and shared interests, and once a crucial foundation stone of the left – became contentious. Community was reframed as 'imaginary' rather than material and practical.[1] People who long ago agreed that they had little choice but to get on together were persuaded that they had every reason not to.

The politics of anti-racism was transformed. Since the 1960s, anti-racism had sought to overcome segregation and break down barriers through education and the enforcement of equality through legislation. All races needed to acknowledge that racial distinctions were illusory. The colour of one's skin did not and should never matter. All impediments to integration should be removed and forms of overt and covert discrimination should be mercilessly eliminated.

And yet anti-racism in the twenty-first century seemed to move in a different direction. A dystopian vision of eternal and insurmountable discrimination became standardised and broadly accepted. Even when white people consciously accept the principle of equality between ethnic groups, many campaigners suggested that they retain unconscious biases that subtly preserve white supremacy. For some, the drive to disaggregate social groups was inverted, to the extent that obvious distinctions between groups of white people, especially in relation to class, were judged irrelevant. All ethnic and religious groups were assumed to possess shared interests. A growing number of the left's activists agreed that all institutions were racist, and all white people were beneficiaries of a system founded on 'whiteness', even those queuing at foodbanks or sleeping in shop doorways.

Cultural leftists expended a huge amount of energy attempting to convince their audience that, for example, black people were always worse off than their white-skinned peers. Black CEOs were worse off than white CEOs, black homeless people were worse off than white homeless people, and so on. Yes, they admitted, poor white people existed, but they still had it better than poor black people. Traditionally, the left had sought to direct the ire of the multi-ethnic working class upwards towards financial and business elites, or towards the capitalist system itself. The principal strategy was to overlook minor cultural differences and focus on shared experiences and interests. Only when the working class was united would it be able to change the world for the better. Now many on the cultural left seem to be arguing that the opposite is the case.

Some among this new generation of anti-racism activists and scholars came to the sad conclusion that discrimination would never be vanquished. White people – even those committed to racial equality – would always seek to secure the privileges of their own ethnic group. Such critique neatly complemented the neoliberal political system. Social competition was accepted as inevitable, and the prizes on offer for those who ascended the social hierarchy were accepted as indisputable sources of value. The problem was that some people from minority backgrounds were being systematically impeded as they tried to compete to the best of their ability. Many of this new generation of radicals were not against privilege or unforgiving competition as such; rather they wanted privilege to be earned in the here and now as part of a fair competitive process.

There was also an accompanying move from objectivity to subjectivity, from the careful, value-free analysis of generalisable conditions and trends to an acceptance that the particularities of social experience belonged to the encultured individual alone and could never be generalised or fully comprehended by people from other cultures.[2] In the social sciences, for example, far less emphasis was placed upon gathering objective evidence and developing a convincing explanatory schema, while far more was placed upon simply gathering testimony and allowing individuals to register their feelings, emotions and personal views. The standard expectation that an audience of critical academics would then attempt to identify flaws and build alternative explanatory systems in a dialectical process fell out of fashion.

Subjective knowledge became just as fixed and righteous as it was fragmented. Increasingly, academic audiences were expected to sit quietly and simply digest these indisputable subjective testimonies, in the hope of identifying more clearly how their own personal failures, privileges and biases had contributed to the suffering of others. Where traditional socialist strategy involved a systematic attempt to understand and overcome shared negative experiences, now the emphasis was on 'giving voice' to specific micro-communities beset by the oppressive majority's constant bigotry and prejudice. As time passed, an ever-diminishing number of life's trials and tribulations were regarded as common to all, and even the economic issues that were undeniably shared by many were identified and ranked as exclusive identitarian variants.

It was no longer enough to claim that poverty and grotesque economic inequality were unconscionable and must be immediately remedied. One had to acknowledge that those who possessed specific identities suffered more than others. The central questions became why these particular groups suffered more, and how the left might effectively fight against such injustices. The poverty, desperation and political powerlessness that cut across ethnic groups could be neither acknowledged nor politicised. Generalised accounts of exploitation and oppression, which for the left in the modern age had afflicted huge numbers of wage-dependent people from a variety of cultural backgrounds, were replaced by intersectional accounts of 'oppression' suffered by specific cultural groups and individuals who identified with them.

Sleeping giants awaken?

Despite the cultural field's proliferating antagonisms, the global financial crisis and its effects did seem to momentarily stir the silent majority. However, most left-leaning academics and journalists glossed over systemic critique and quickly moved on to note how the crisis's intersectional effects were differentiated, weighing more heavily on those who suffered multiple forms of disadvantage and discrimination.[3] No unifying politics emerged on the left and it was difficult to detect such a political will within the population – millions, especially those getting by on low incomes, had dropped out of politics and saw little point in voting.[4]

But as the crisis begin to bite, things began to change. There was not an immediate and concerted move back to mainstream politics, but anger and dissatisfaction gradually became more pronounced. People began to look around for explanations and analyses that might identify and explain the root causes of their troubles. And here the left failed yet again, allowing the neoliberals to continue by default. The people wanted change. Even those who remained politically disconnected seemed to want it. Many seemed unsure of the sources of their problems or the type of change they wanted and were open to persuasion, which was the traditional left's role. However, all mainstream politics could offer was the appearance of change – swapping one set of neoliberals for another – so that nothing fundamental had to change. This constant avoidance of underlying structural contexts opened the door for the nationalist right to stroll in and reprise its traditional story of a nation bravely struggling to cope with the problems caused by its external enemies, and the need to secure what remained of its traditional culture.

At first these changes were quite subtle. At long last, people began to think again about politics. Much of this thinking was inspired by dissatisfaction and a measure of what we have called 'objectless anxiety'.[5] Many began to think about the implications of government policies and, in most cases, this involved a growing recognition that the system as it stood did not work for them or people like them. Corruption seemed to be everywhere. Christophe Guilluy,[6] addressing the post-crash political context in France, claims that 72 per cent of French citizens believe that politicians are corrupt; 89 per cent believe that politicians are concerned only with their own personal interests, and 87 per cent feel that governments of both left and right take no interest in 'people like them'. French citizens were not alone in feeling this way about their elected representatives. For years, many across the West had assumed that corruption of all kinds was the norm. Everyone seemed to have their hands out. Everyone seemed to be out for whatever they could get, and few seemed to possess the moral fibre – especially a sense of duty to the collective – once considered integral to public service. Many formed the view that this corruption had brought the entire system to the brink of collapse. Clearly, something must be done. The elites had become too greedy. They had overreached, and now everyone was suffering.

Growing numbers of people momentarily separated themselves from the media matrix and took a long, hard look at the world around them. Inevitably, they saw multiple threats opening up – to their livelihoods, homes, jobs and the life chances of their children. There was also a general feeling that new threats awaited them just a little further along the road. Beyond these threats they could discern a murky backdrop of decline, often manifested in material ruination and the withdrawal of industries and once reliable services.

Many also thought about decline in more abstract ways. Culture, community sentiments and feelings of comfort and security seemed to be slowly draining out of everyday experience. Many across the broad multi-ethnic working class concluded that important aspects of their everyday lives had been getting progressively worse for some time. Things of great value had fallen into obsolescence. Where once the majority saw progress in terms of material lifestyles, education, health and freedom, now there was a prevailing sense of diminishment and lack. What seems to have rankled most – aside from the obvious decline in incomes, job security and consumer lifestyles – was the sense that something less tangible but perhaps even more important was being left to wither and die; something valuable had been mismanaged and in some cases degraded and abandoned. Many seemed unsure what this was, but it had been present in their early life and now it was gone. The inevitable conclusion was that something needed to be done, and those at the centre of the system – politicians of all kinds, and media and corporate elites – simply couldn't be trusted to come up with or enact the system changes that would give the majority feasible opportunities to acquire the security and prosperity they desired.

By this time modern institutional forms of political alignment had died out. When politics returned it did so in an organic form. Anger and frustration did not suddenly reanimate mainstream political parties, and nor did they lead to a surge in union membership. Many had assumed that when ordinary people returned to politics, support for the left would surge. The organised left, of course, had traditionally striven to be the voice of the people, and in politics and academia many leftists blithely assumed that a newly politicised demos would fall into line and accept the greatly revised agenda imposed on them by a thoroughly liberalised and increasingly middle-class left. However, in many cases the opposite was true. Since the 2008 global financial crisis, right-wing populists have made the most headway. Populist leaders have been remarkably successful in drawing upon popular dissatisfaction and presenting themselves as the natural defenders of the people, but their successes are predicated on the failure of the left to step forward and seize this mantle for itself. Clearly, the right has prospered in the gap left by the disappearance of the left from the life-worlds of ordinary people.

A new populist moment

Today in the West, almost every politician and popular political commentator seems sure that populism is wholly and indisputably bad.[7] The same is true in academia.[8] All seem to believe that the rise of populism is a threat to the otherwise orderly reproduction of everyday life. The word now tends to describe a politics deprived of complexity and animated only by the reductive and dangerous passions of the uneducated mob. Liberal media elites often portray grassroots populist movements as inexorably anti-democratic and potentially authoritarian. These elites regard those who have voted for nationalist political parties as either incorrigible fascists or ideological dupes manipulated by malevolent forces. They seem unable to grasp the fact that a significant proportion of ordinary people no longer accept their intellectual and political leadership. It's far easier to identify far-left or far-right bogeymen who can be blamed for stripping the people of their senses and dragging them into new populist political movements that will inevitably make things worse.

If we are to evaluate this calmly and rationally, we should keep in mind that what is denounced as populism today was once considered the very essence of a vibrant democracy. Populism emboldened the passive masses to take an active interest in politics, to ensure that their concerns were listened to and addressed by the technocratic elites who pulled the strings. Now, perversely, this raw form of democracy is presented as anti-democratic. For anyone not consumed by fear and loathing of the common people, populism is best understood as an eruption of the raw energy from which democracy can be fashioned. However, if the basic shape of things is to continue as it is, established elites must continue to make all the key decisions while the people should be politely ushered away from issues that really should not concern them. Popular involvement in politics should be restricted to marking a ballot paper in support of one of the approved political parties every five years or so, or perhaps heading out on a peaceful but ultimately futile protest to register dissatisfaction with some small facet of parliamentary capitalism or the cultures that sit alongside it.

Some of the elite's commentary on the new populism was wrapped in almost eugenicist overtones. The people were stupid, racist and backward-looking, and democracy needed to be saved from such vulgarity.[9] Those who lent their support to populist movements were on occasion portrayed as small-minded, parochial and angered by the declining geopolitical power of their nation.[10] The core message seems to be that clever liberal technocrats should rule, and the hoi polloi should return to their silly distractions.[11] In the years following the global financial crisis, the gap between these elites and the people became wider than it had been since *La Belle Époque*. The reappearance of this social chasm fed into the desire of ordinary people to reject the current leadership and seek change.[12]

In the broadsheet press and on the university campus, populism signalled the rise of dark, menacing political passions. Of course, popular political passions have always troubled elites, and elites have always moved to quieten or redirect these passions in one way or another. The depoliticisation and commodification of everyday life, a process that accompanied the rise of technocratic neoliberalism, was very effective at cordoning off the privileges of elites and shielding them from popular scrutiny. It is generally assumed that elite technocrats have the expertise and experience to lead in the interests of all. Throughout modern history in the West, this is precisely what has happened. At least for the most part. However, the ability of the people to disturb the usual order of things has always existed as a latent power, and the elites' awareness of it is the primary reason why so many containment strategies exist to ensure the people do not become overly animated by their own experience of significant economic change. People must be persuaded to respect the competence of elites and the justice of their rule, while remaining steadfast in the belief that our present democratic systems are the best means of representing the will and ensuring the prosperity of the people.

It would be wrong to present the populist movements that developed between 2008 and 2019 as universally positive, but the general desire of the people to free themselves from the confines of mainstream politics certainly seemed to indicate that positive change could occur. Huge numbers of ordinary men and women wanted to break free from neoliberalism's dour post-political consensus and drive popular change. That some of these people chose to follow the far right is regrettable but, given the paucity of innovative political thinking on the left and the huge gap that had opened up between the working class and the left-liberal elite, it was hardly surprising. Populist movements were flawed on many levels, which made it impossible for the majority to fully endorse any one of them. However, when taken as a whole, their rise suggested a growing popular awareness of the globalised neoliberal system's failures, and a general dissatisfaction with mainstream liberal politics.

These movements also tried to represent and respond to the pervasive sense of decline that seemed to have fallen over large expanses of Western culture. In almost all cases they failed in this task, but at least an attempt was made. The mainstream, of course, made little attempt and rumbled on in the usual manner. Some mainstream parties began to listen and adjust their policies in the hope that those who had voted for populist parties could be persuaded to return to the fold. Many changes were cosmetic, but some were quite significant and partially effective.

In Britain, the Conservative Party prospered by doubling down on its commitment to Brexit and promising to invest heavily in long-forgotten deindustrialised zones. As the COVID-19 pandemic unfolded, they made significant policy changes, which were either ignored or dismissed as cosmetic by the cultural left. Out went the old commitment to fiscal probity and balancing the books. A handful of individuals close to real institutional power began to admit in public that the state was not financially constrained in the way many people had been led to believe over the past four decades. To appease the private investment banks, Rishi Sunak, the Chancellor of the Exchequer, stressed in public that the 'borrowed money' would have to be paid back and the deficit reduced, but to soften the contradictory clash in his narrative he was vague about when and how.

A staggering amount of currency was issued through the Bank of England to pay for the furlough scheme, which allowed millions of workers to remain in receipt of 80 per cent of their wages while whole sectors of the economy were locked down in response to the contagion. The magic money tree, lost in 2010, had been miraculously found again. And, contrary to the usual neoliberal scaremongering, huge state spending did not cause hyperinflation or thrust millions into penury. Recently rising inflation in Western countries, now moderating in late May 2022, is the product of exogenous factors such as supply chain disruption, weather changes, war, and post-pandemic economic recovery encouraging consumer spending and price gouging. There was also significant investment elsewhere in the real economy.

In 2020 the Tory government released a National Infrastructure Strategy, which looks likely to cost far more than initial estimates, and a National Investment Bank to make up for shortfalls in private investment as the UK tries to lever itself onto the cutting edge of what the corporations are now calling 'the energy transition'.[13] Not only had the Tories rediscovered the magic money tree, they were also prepared to rather coyly shake it whilst continuing to deny its existence.

It seems likely that, when the lockdowns recede, the Conservatives will return to the standard neoliberal narrative of balancing the books in order to lower public expectations and appease the investment bankers. However, it will be difficult to keep up the pretence that money is in short supply, and the nation cannot afford to pay for public services and badly needed infrastructural investment. But, unless a complete ideological cover-up operation succeeds, it is clear that the traditional political spectrum has been redefined. Increasingly, the mainstream left in Europe expresses needless concern about balancing the budget while championing cultural equality, diversity and inclusion, and the nationalist right – which, in the European context, might be characterised by France's Le Pen, Hungary's Orbán and Poland's Duda – is concerned with providing citizens with economic security and championing the nation and its history.[14] Up is down, left is right.

It may be that the new populist movements' sole impact will be to force change upon the mainstream. However, considerable momentum still exists in some populist movements, which suggests that the game is far from over. National populism, in particular, remains a potent force, and it is certainly not beyond the bounds of possibility that nationalist movements at the core and periphery of the European Union might see some success as they attempt to prise their nations free from the EU's commitment to a now outdated and intellectually threadbare neoliberal consensus.

The populist movements of the post-crash era are a symptom of a deep, underlying malady that runs right to the core of our present way of life. The claims they make about the world deserve to be taken seriously, even though their solutions should arouse caution. However, this book is not a paean to populism. Populist movements ignore or misconstrue the fundamental issues at stake. They focus on symptoms, rather than contexts and causes, and generate their moral and political energy by identifying specific groups they claim have spoilt or corrupted the nation, its culture and its economic and political systems.

From the dawning of the capitalist era until the latter half of the twentieth century, left-wing populism tended to identify various manifestations of the global business elite as the enemy. Lazy, entitled, rapacious, and immoral, the business elite enriched itself and left many ordinary men and women to struggle by in desperate circumstances. Right-wing populism tended to take a nationalist-nativist position, focusing its anger upon immigrants or specific ethnic groups who are presented as disruptive, instrumental and keen to deprive citizens of the security once provided by traditional culture and the benefits of a stable national economy. Populism, then, tends to accept the legitimacy of the system and focus its attention upon parasitic or opportunistic groups accused of disrupting what would otherwise be its smooth functioning.

Herein lies the problem for the left. There is much to be said for a genuine mass movement that hopes to curtail the wealth of the elite, truncate inequality and equip ordinary people with the ability to build decent lives. However, as the philosopher Slavoj Žižek[15] might suggest, such movements can often appear to radically disrupt the status quo, but in leaving the underlying system itself intact, and no matter what they manage to achieve in practical terms, they are inevitably *not quite radical enough.* They fail to question the legitimacy of the system and, for the most part, fail to identify an appealing alternative. For them, the central question is how the combined economic and cultural systems can be stabilised and how the spoils are distributed, rather than whether the system itself should be replaced or go through a process of significant modification. In the same way that Marx saw the reality of global capitalism expressed in its periodic crises and Freud saw the roots of hysteria in normative social experience, the things left-wing populists tend to dislike – greed, corruption, inequality, injustice, desperate poverty side-by-side with ostentatious wealth – are not indications of the system being polluted, dragged off course or breaking down; rather, they are the inevitable outcomes of the system's *normal operation.*

Right-wing populism always ignores the true source of social antagonism. No matter who it blames, it misidentifies the causes of social suffering and cultural diminishment. It accepts the fragmentation of the social body into warring cultural groups, and rallies some against others, rather than rallying all in a shared cause to build a society free from incessant conflict and antagonism. As we shall see, left-wing populism is more complex. However, one thing is clear; the liberal left's preoccupation with the horrors of right-wing populism is nondialectical and totally ignores fundamental issues. The left's true antagonist is neoliberalism – minimally regulated global capitalism – and it is in this political struggle that the left must make progress or die out.

The misfiring engine of history

Whilst for us as academics these issues remain fascinating and provoke us to think deeply about the constitution of reality and the reproduction of our present way of life, for those involved in the practical world of politics, and those struggling to make ends meet, they are understandably of little importance. To intervene in history and set society on a new and better path is no small matter, and it is vital to think through carefully what can be achieved within the present system. Certainly, as history shows, it is possible to manage capitalism's raw, amoral drives in ways that render them far less disruptive and injurious. As we hope to show, it is also possible to distribute money, opportunities, freedoms and entitlements far more widely among the population, just as it is possible to guarantee all citizens an illuminating and edifying education, cutting-edge healthcare, and well-paid and socially valuable jobs. However, the fact that all of this is possible within the system as it stands should not preclude us from taking up the demanding task of thinking through and designing achievable alternatives that might at some point be brought into being.

Carl Schmitt, a German political philosopher writing in both the pre- and post-war period, claimed that true politics is only possible when consensus is dispensed with and battle lines drawn between those deemed friends and those deemed enemies.[16] Schmitt's political theory came in for a hammering in the years following the Second World War. He was an active supporter of Nazism, and his work appears to have lent a degree of intellectual heft to the Nazis' uncompromising Manichean account of the embattled German *volk* and the need to rid the nation of the corrupting influence of Jews and other parasitic infiltrators. However, many contemporary leftist philosophers and political theorists have returned to Schmitt's work and, in particular, to his claim that the friend/enemy distinction represents the fundamental essence of all politics.

As the project of neoliberal globalisation established itself as an orthodoxy and all credible alternatives gradually disappeared from the political stage, many political philosophers settled on the belief that history had ground to a halt. Francis Fukuyama,[17] perhaps the most noted advocate of the 'end of history' thesis, achieved a good deal of renown and approbation for his claim that liberal democracy coupled with free-market capitalism represented the pinnacle of human organisation. All conceivable alternatives had fallen out of history and could no longer return. While there may be a little disruption here and there, the future,

Fukuyama believed, would unfold within the general framework provided by liberal democracy and capitalism. Because this system represented the best that humanity could hope for, and because it integrated all social groups into its corpus, it would endure. Nothing external to this framework was capable of intervening to set history on a new course. History had thus ended. The future would be the present, save for a few minor adjustments.

Fukuyama quickly became the academic other academics loved to hate. What they hated was the suggestion that the way things are is as good as it gets. Academics mindful of the great diversity of human suffering found the entire thesis discomforting and rushed to assert that things can and must improve. The problem was that, as the years passed, the general thrust of Fukuyama's thesis seemed to be right on the money. History had indeed stopped. Mainstream political parties became indistinguishable. All roughly agreed on the basics, and politics descended into the mere administration of what already existed. Communism, capitalism's last great adversary, had become so tarnished in the eyes of the majority that it could never make a comeback. It was impossible to identify any coherent political ideology that stood even a slim a chance of dislodging parliamentary capitalism from its lofty perch.

However, if Fukuyama was indeed right, he was right for the wrong reasons. It was ridiculous to claim that the neoliberal era was as good as it could ever get. Things could improve. The problem was that they did not. Despite its injustices, parliamentary capitalism endured, and there were few advocates for genuine revolution or deep political intervention in economic matters. Of course, many advocated piecemeal social and economic reform, but such reforms could be endlessly assimilated by the system without the need to change its fundamental structure.

In the absence of a viable ideological adversary, the system simply rolled forwards unchallenged. Capitalism and democracy had won, and everyone seemed to accept this reality. In the shadow of communist crimes, the bulk of the radical leftist intelligentsia abandoned all hope of a future socialist utopia. Liberal democracy seemed to be history's terminus, the final earthly embodiment of eternal truths and verities. History had stalled. To restart it the field of politics had to be brought back to life. A new enemy must lock horns with the capitalism/democracy dyad to move history beyond the prevailing consensus.

However, real enemies are quite rare. Our political history is characterised by long periods of consensus punctuated only by infrequent and very brief moments of transformative conflict. These moments tend to establish the shape and constitution of the consensus that follows. We have already discussed the post-war social democratic settlement; it lasted for a little under 40 years and was eventually overturned by the return to prominence of free-market thinking, especially in the field of economics. It would be an over-simplification to conclude that this moment of change was peaceful and represented the will of the people. It was not. Organised politics had to be changed and ideological pressure applied through numerous institutional channels. The old social democratic polity was rudely ushered out and a new and energetic neoliberal polity installed. Collective entitlements and social expectations were withdrawn and replaced with a broad range of anti-collectivist sentiments that complemented the new atomised market society. Eventually a new consensus took hold and much of the remaining opposition was silenced. That consensus – the neoliberal era – has thus far endured just over 40 years. The global financial crisis and the rise of a new populism at first seemed to signal that neoliberalism was coming to an end, but throughout much of the West it somehow managed to stumble forwards.

Now, as we write these words in early 2021, there are again signs that the consensus is coming to an end. However, if this proves to be the case, it is not because a new ideological opponent capable of attracting popular support has been found. Schmitt's theory of eternal and indispensable antagonism seems to have had its day, for the time being at least. Rather, it seems that the established elites have deemed it wise to dispense with key aspects of neoliberal dogma and adopt strategies and policies that might quieten the masses and assist in securing the system's continuity in a significantly modified form – precisely how significant, and whether the modified system can still rightfully be called neoliberalism, is what we need to understand. Certainly, if we appraise state responses to the global COVID-19 pandemic, many of the standard neoliberal shibboleths seem to have been dispensed with, at least for now. However, while there have been a number of important political changes, a new consensus has yet to emerge. Western states are beginning to display a new commitment to making a more environmentally sustainable world safe for oligarchs and large global corporations. There also seems to be a new willingness to make better use of the gargantuan financial power of central banks. We continue to occupy a strange historical interregnum, an indistinct space between a comprehensible and reasonably coherent historical epoch and whatever lies ahead.

Alain Badiou,[18] one of the left's most revered philosophers, claims that true politics occurs not during periods of consensus but in history's moments of great change. It is in these moments that battles are waged over the future, about what type of society we will live in, how we will relate to one another and what will be included in the rights and responsibilities of citizenship. It is in these moments that history can be forced in a new direction. Those involved in these great battles may not fully grasp what is at stake and in their heart of hearts they may be unsure about what, in practical terms, they are striving for. However, for Badiou, it is vital to maintain one's fidelity to the event or, to put it simply, to believe in and keep believing in the ideals that lie at the core of one's politics, to stay the course, see it through and never give in, equivocate or compromise. For Badiou, true politics has two key elements. First, we must identify and name what we believe and what it is we are fighting for. And second, we must identify our enemy.

The first element – identifying and naming our politics – has been kicked into the long grass and forgotten by those who have taken charge of the new left. Many in the left's main political parties have either decided for themselves, or been told by powerful elements within their parties, that the traditional features of leftist political discourse no longer fly with voters. In Britain – a society with social class antagonism etched into its long history, and a society in which class continues to pattern behaviour, expectations, ambitions, attitudes and demeanour –

virtually all members of the Parliamentary Labour Party refuse to utter the words 'working class'.

The refusal of prominent mainstream leftists to use what is a standard and hugely important symbolic feature of their own political discourse often verges on the comedic. The lengths some mainstream politicians will go to as they try to avoid uttering these words truly beggars belief. Their weird refusal clearly reflects a general faith that class-based political antagonism is archaic and fails to reflect the lives of today's voters. It also seems to indicate the degenerative assumption that the best way to win political office is to talk confidently about bland abstractions but exercise extreme caution when talking about substantive principles, issues and policies so as not to alienate potential voters from allegedly disparate cultural groups. The inevitable result is that politicians now talk loudly about nothing of any real significance, while hoping that their opponents perform the same range of exercises less ably.

In many respects, this descent characterised the Labour Party from Blair up to the election of Corbyn as leader. Labour politicians didn't want to dissuade voters who considered themselves middle class from voting for the party, so they replaced the 'working class' with a range of hollow phrases that further alienated its core constituency. Those on the Labour Party's front bench continued to talk about fairness and justice, but the general sense was that these words had become merely buzz phrases without genuine substance. How precisely did these politicians plan to make Britain fair or more just? As time passed, it was clear that the best that could be hoped for was a few small measures here and there, all of which accepted the continuity of neoliberalism as a *fait accompli*. Members of the Parliamentary Labour Party instead latched onto substitutes for the historical term that could no longer be uttered. The Labour Party, they said, would do what they could to help 'working people'. Clearly, they wanted to draw a line under Britain's long history of class antagonism and drive the neoliberal bandwagon forward. They wanted to convey to the electorate that they would try to assist those who strive and are keen to improve their personal marketability in a transformed labour market dominated by poorly paid, unstable and non-unionised work.

The discomfort caused by the phrase 'working class' made it clear that the party had once and for all cast aside its history and ideological foundations. It wanted to be something else. It had accepted the coordinates of neoliberalism and was perfectly happy to work within them. As part of this rejection of the old and adoption of the new, the party accepted uncritically the liberal doctrine of meritocracy. There were no longer classes of people. Society was like a ladder, and individuals should be free to climb as high as they could. To aid their endeavours, the Labour Party would take on the never-ending task of identifying and removing whatever might impede their progress.

Identifying and analysing the details of liberal meritocracy's absurd pantomime is really a distraction and should not detain us for too long. It is, however, crucial to note that, in accepting meritocracy and portraying it as something the left should commit to and strive to realise, the Labour Party had left behind traditional notions of community, solidarity, togetherness and equality and replaced them with an unabashed faith in progressive liberal individualism. The Labour Party had moved from an understanding of society as composed of groups of people who suffered or profited from a range of objective social processes to an understanding of society as a multitude of self-interested individuals who strive to achieve for themselves as much as their talents and luck will allow. The traditional left in Britain, rooted in the labour movement from which the party took its name, aspired to improve the living standards of the entire working class, who would move upwards together. No one would be left behind. All would move away from poverty and insecurity, and every citizen would be equipped with rights and entitlements that would allow the great unspoken need of all human beings – security – to take hold and act as the foundation for future flourishing. The new goal was quite clear – help for talented individuals to fight their way free from their backgrounds, leaving behind families and friends and those judged less talented, to climb the corporate or institutional ladder and secure the glittering prizes that were on offer in the consumer economy.

When asked about her greatest achievement, Margaret Thatcher quickly and unequivocally identified Tony Blair and New Labour. Her main political opponents had accepted her dogma on the economy and the state and, for her, this was her crowning glory. There were many good reasons for her to think this way. Thatcher was at first considered an anomaly. Once she was dispensed with, it was assumed that the old consensus would reassert itself. But it did not. Thatcher established the foundations for a new consensus, and in many ways her key opponents were as committed to this consensus as she was.

When the Labour Party finally returned to office under Tony Blair, key figures in New Labour refused to acknowledge that their economic policies accepted or extended the key tenets of Thatcherism. Instead, they preferred to couch their hardcore neoliberalism in the terminology of economic pragmatism. By this stage, everyone seemed to accept that markets must be deregulated so they could work their magic. Everyone seemed to accept that there exists a finite group of super-talented wealth creators upon whom the rest of us depend. By the late 1990s, hardly a voice was raised in opposition to policies that sought to make the national economy as attractive as possible to bankers, speculators, international business interests and global conglomerates on the lookout for highly profitable investment opportunities. Blair and others could not bring themselves to acknowledge that Thatcher had won the economic argument, but the facts were there for all to see.

However, the extent of Thatcher's victory may have been even greater than we tend to assume. Thatcher had not simply won the economic argument. She had also won the social argument. 'There's no such thing as society',[19] she famously averred. The Labour Party seemed to first accept and eventually champion this dismal creed. To win elections, the party needed to appeal to the instrumentalism of post-social consumer citizens.[20] There were no longer any grand ideals to rally around; only the prospect of personal enrichment and freedom was believed to hold any allure for voters. Or at least that is how it appeared. The traditional leftist concern with collective interests was gone.

It was not only the term 'working class' that was abandoned by the left. In the United States, of course, it remains almost impossible to use the words 'communism' and 'socialism' honestly and accurately. It is clear that these words have been cloaked in the symbols of absolute evil and cannot yet be rehabilitated. The word 'socialism' has suffered a slightly different fate in Britain. Rather than being eschewed entirely, it has been diluted until it became meaningless. Individuals from virtually every bespoke political position, from the Trotskyite far left through the postmodern culturalists to the neoliberal centrists of Change UK, including committed free-market neoliberal Tony Blair, feel comfortable identifying themselves as socialists.

While it is certainly true to say that 'socialism' has always been a rather woolly phrase, subject to a considerable diversity of definitions, identifying yourself as a socialist in Great Britain today is unlikely to communicate to others that you are committed to common ownership, or to mean that you believe the state should restrict some forms of private enterprise and take a significant role at the very centre of the formal economy. 'Socialism' is used today to signal that one is vaguely interested in equality across the intersectional lines of one's choosing, usually in accordance with one's own interests. Socialism, therefore, seems to mean whatever one wants it to mean. It has lost its traditional symbolic substance.

In Schmitt's dark account of political philosophy, human beings are essentially self-interested and amoral creatures who will join together to form functional and moral communities only when they identify an enemy. Copious anthropological and archaeological evidence suggests that the earliest human communities were first brought together by the identification of a shared threat.[21] Only a shared threat can submerge self-interest and persuade people to accept the rules and purposes of community life. And so it is with the state. The nation-state is, for Schmitt, an outcome of this process of negative identification. The sense of unity and purpose needed to build and maintain it is created not by some shared commitment to a grand ideal but by the identification of an external enemy and the need for protection. The actual substance of this antagonist is for Schmitt quite unimportant.

It is quite easy to see how this framework might have been considered useful for the Nazis during the 1930s and 1940s. The identification of an internal enemy was, for them, a key component of their rise to power, and the identification of multiple external enemies served to further bond the nation together during wartime. The allied nations also profited from the clear identification of an enemy. Doing so created a powerful sense of shared endeavour and interdependence. Populist political movements from across the globe and across the political spectrum have also profited greatly by identifying an enemy to overcome. Friendship also appears to have its roots in a mutual commitment to defend against a common enemy. Even our most popular sports successfully marshal the power of enmity and unflinching competition.

In times of consensus, the identification of an enemy tends to fall out of mainstream politics. While our main political parties seem to butt heads on our news broadcasts each night, it is difficult not to form the view that this is all for show, and the jousting between Republicans and Democrats or Labour and Conservatives is nothing more than post-political theatrics of little or no consequence. Our interest in mainstream politics sags in consensual times. No matter how much our politicians scream at each other, it is difficult to remain invested in politics when the main political issue of the day is whether interest rates should be raised by 0.25 per cent or 0.5 per cent. But we become more interested and attuned when we sense a genuine and growing enmity between key political groups.

Throughout the post-political era, the emotional attraction of enmity shifted from the policy domain to the domain of 'personality'. As with so many other features of social life during these years, depth and substance were replaced by shallow presentation. Material issues were replaced by symbolic issues. The shallow politics of personality continue to play a central role in what passes for politics today. Because mainstream neoliberal parties tend to agree on the fundamentals, personality clashes, smear campaigns and character assassinations have become more important in determining the popularity of parties and their leaders. Political parties became virtually indistinguishable in policy terms; therefore, voters look to the personalities and comparative moral rectitude of those who head the main parties.

However, from the 1990s onwards, we have seen the rise of often quite brash and morally questionable politicians capable of commanding the attention of an audience. These roguish characters never entirely replaced the grey technocrats who continued to wield considerable influence in the background, but the rise of Silvio Berlusconi, Nigel Farage, Boris Johnson and, of course, Donald Trump seems indicative of this general trend. However, even quite uninspiring politicians have sought to distinguish themselves in the eyes of voters and supporters by actively soliciting clashes with their more notable antagonists. There was no longer any great enmity in policy terms, but politicians could still secure media coverage by displaying anger at the claims of their opponent or by criticising their opponent's personal life. Red-faced fulminating at some perceived slight or policy failure created an impression of seriousness and played well in front of an audience deprived of genuine political antagonism.

While many angry personality clashes seemed staged, or at least strategically inflated for effect, these politicians still appeared to capture a small measure of the political power of enmity. Hillary Clinton's obvious hatred of Donald Trump played well in front of liberal, educated women, but much less so in front of rural traditionalists who were unlikely to vote for her in any case. Donald Trump profited greatly from his theatrical disdain for Clinton's metropolitan elitism and corporate connections. Of course, beneath the hostility, there was little difference between Clinton and Trump in terms of core policies. While populist leaders have profited from marshalling the politics of personal enmity, the new populism also suggested that we could see a return to a far deeper and more productive form of political enmity.

Security and insecurity form an important part of this picture. When we identify significant threats and genuine cause for concern, we shake off our lethargy and re-engage with politics. We listen closely to those who attempt to explain our situation, and we weigh up the claims they make in relation to our experiences of everyday life. Of course, the broad and long-lasting triumph of philosophical, economic and social liberalism across the West means that our elites and many ordinary people would prefer not to identify an enemy. When enmity appears on the rise, we are now taught that it is our responsibility to seek conciliation.

It was certainly not always thus. In previous epochs, super-ego restraints and inducements encouraged us to defend our honour, retain pride and secure social standing. These concerns still shape our responses to potential conflict, but rather than driving us to a violent defence of the symbolic self, we are more likely to seek the same ends by other means. Today, a willingness to negotiate and compromise is essential, and for the majority a peaceful middle ground is always preferable to open hostility. We are encouraged to attenuate righteous anger and indignation, despite that fact that, as Freud recognised, permanently repressing basic drives – especially, we would add, in such anxious, uncertain times when we crave clear sight of the true source of our anxiety – can have far-reaching and occasionally highly disruptive consequences.

While it might be reasonable to suggest that a shock of violence might jolt the public awake and enliven the realm of political contestation, our politicians are forced to sublimate the urge to violence, stick to the unstated rules and, instead, behind the scenes, stretch every sinew to secure a victory over their ostensible opponent while also working hard in front of their audience to create an image of themselves as committed, intelligent and morally superior to their adversary. The artificial inflation and theatrical presentation of political squabbles therefore tends to be entirely cynical. In most cases, real enmity is attenuated or hidden from view and replaced by a proliferation of manufactured substitutes, the function of which is to draw the approval of supporters and undecided voters.

The liberal drive to seek conciliation and avoid conflict is now established as a durable norm in Western culture, yet these cultural characteristics mask the fundamental duplicity of contemporary liberalism. Enmity persists despite the emphasis placed upon conciliation. And this is what we see bubbling to the surface in post-crash populism. Intense but confused political passions rise as our sense of security recedes. Populism is always reactive, in the sense that it tends to grow in historical eras defined by falling living standards, fears about the future, and anger at the injustices of the present. The populism of the post-crash era was, in all its forms, set against a backdrop of economic crisis, injustice and a prevailing sense that things were heading downhill fast. The same is true with regard to the rise of the Nazis in Germany during the 1920s and 1930s. Of course, the Nazis misdiagnosed the causes of crisis, as right-wing populists are wont to do, but the fundamental point is this: contrary to the diagnoses of many media commentators, populist movements do not arise out of nowhere or from some timeless psychological wellspring of prejudice. Populist movements most certainly arise from somewhere, and those 'somewheres' always reference a deep desire to arrest decline, transcend fear and rebuild on firm foundations.

Populist political movements, then, seek to explain and channel popular passions rooted in feelings of insecurity. To varying degrees, all genuinely populist movements take the crucial step of identifying an enemy. The Five Star movement in Italy directed its ire at the corrupt political class. The United Kingdom Independence Party, and the Brexit Party that followed, were, on the surface, singularly concerned with taking the UK out of the hated European Union, which, they argued, had corrupted British national identity, placed a range of downward pressures upon the British economy, stolen British sovereignty and assisted the movement of millions of European immigrants into Britain. The Occupy Movement, which responded directly to the global financial crisis, captured the crux of traditional socialist collectivism with its apt slogan, 'We are the 99%'. Here, all trivial differences were set aside to assert the shared interests of the majority against the parasitic 1 per cent.

It is true that, in each of these cases, focusing attention on an enemy that corrupts the system meant that the system itself tended to escape critical attention and remained firmly in place. However, in asking for concessions and changes that should be deliverable in a system that prides itself on its open democracy and the adaptability of its market economy, populist political movements reveal a crucial hidden truth: even ostensibly minor changes with widespread popular support cannot be delivered by the system as it stands. Sometimes, even to deliver what appear to be quite minor changes, the system itself must undergo fundamental change.

Jeremy Corbyn: the British left's last chance?

One politician who once might have been committed to fundamental change is Jeremy Corbyn. We watched his career in the Labour Party for some time before he was abruptly shoved to the centre stage of British politics. A committed follower of Tony Benn, one of the great figures of the post-war Labour Party and an advocate of deep intervention in the capitalist economy, Corbyn was an outsider for most of his parliamentary career. As the years rolled by, his political insignificance seemed only to grow as Blair's neoliberal revolution stripped the party of any remaining socialist ambitions. Corbyn was part of a tiny band of left-wing MPs who doggedly clung on, apparently steadfast in their belief that the Labour Party needed to better represent the interests of the exploited, downtrodden and underprivileged.

Corbyn has always been the quintessential 'conviction politician'. Looking back over his long career in parliament, he seems even more so because he has been surrounded by the careerist weathervanes of the Parliamentary Labour Party. It is difficult even for his most strident ideological opponents to deny that he has proven himself again and again willing to fight for the principles that drew him to politics in the first place. The principled stances that so many voters crave and neoliberal technocrats attempt to counterfeit came naturally to Corbyn.

While traditionally associated with the British working class, the Labour Party has always been influenced by the professional middle classes. Corbyn's background of affluence and private education is not unusual. However, the beginnings of his career were modest. He first became a reporter at a small local newspaper and then took up a series of minor roles on the periphery of the trade union movement.[22] Both of his parents were interested in politics, and Jeremy appears to have been a committed socialist from a young age.

Although many lose their radicalism as they age, this was not the case with Corbyn. He still seems driven to fight injustice wherever he finds it, and, if he has learnt to accept those things he cannot change, he remains committed to at least going through the ritual of publicly expressing his opposition to them. He has refused to simply go with the flow and there is little evidence that he has capitulated to pressure from either his party or his peers. These facts made his ascent to party leader all the more remarkable. The movement of Corbyn's brand of English middle-class liberal socialism – a long tradition stretching from

Beatrice and Sidney Webb and R.H. Tawney to Tony Benn – to the forefront of British politics suggested that change was possible. For a brief moment it seemed that history could be restarted and British society could move in a different direction. That it did not is an indication of the flaws inherent in Corbyn's project as well as the huge power and scale of the opposition to it.

While still quite young, Corbyn campaigned for the Labour Party in London, the city he had made his home. Eventually, after working in the background for some years, he became the party's parliamentary candidate for Islington North. He won the seat in the general election of 1983. He became a committed constituency MP and for years fought against war and racism of all kinds. He campaigned for gay rights. He fought for nuclear disarmament. He campaigned against apartheid in South Africa and was arrested for doing so. He supported the miners' cause in the great strike of 1984–85 and campaigned energetically on their behalf. He fought against the poll tax. Corbyn stuck to his guns, often against overwhelming enemy fire. It is difficult for us not to admire him.

Despite his reputation as a firebrand, it seems in his personal life he has always been polite, respectful and accommodating. Much of the critical commentary that came his way when he became leader portrayed him as weak, ineffectual and inept, and there certainly appears to be some truth in this portrayal. While it would be wrong to underestimate the administrative impediments he faced, his failure to truly take control of the party's apparatus meant that he was often deprived of the support that might have driven his project forward at greater speed. Many party employees were dedicated Blairites who worked behind the scenes to unseat him at the earliest opportunity. The scale of this opposition was such that many within the party were effectively campaigning for a Tory victory.

The perception of Corbyn as weak and ineffectual was also electorally significant. Few voters believed that he possessed the gravitas to lead the nation, while many others worried about his much-discussed 'radicalism' and the feasibility of his plans. However, that he was not a strongman, a talented bureaucrat or a savvy media operator really should have been no surprise. Before securing the party's leadership in 2015, Corbyn had for

32 years focused on assisting his constituents and the various progressive causes to which he had attached himself. Unlike so many others, he did not try to enrich himself or claim expenses to which he was not entitled. He appears to have nurtured no grand desire to thrust himself to the forefront of British politics. He despised the gamesmanship of party politics and regularly voted against the party whip, which, of course, did little to endear him to his colleagues.

At first his candidacy for the Labour leadership appears to have been merely representational. Traditionally, a member of the Socialist Campaign Group put themselves forward for the job. Corbyn's two great friends in that group, Diane Abbott and John McDonnell, had given it a go in 2010 and 2007 respectively, and now it was Corbyn's turn. Few paid his candidacy much attention. He was a rank outsider and expected to fall at the first hurdle. The fact that he went on to win the contest, and then a further contest prompted by a challenge to his leadership from the dominant Blairite faction, was quite remarkable. Clearly, there was a desire within the party's broader membership for genuine change. Blairism was dead in the water. Austerity was a millstone around the party's neck, and those who gave up their time to knock on doors and persuade cynical voters to give their support to Labour longed to be free of it. Labour's strategic pseudo-centrism no longer reassured voters. Many potential Labour voters believed that if both of the main parties stayed on their course, things would continue to get tougher. Something needed to change, and many were open to new ideas. Corbyn rode this widespread desire for change to the party leadership and, in 2017, almost became the country's first socialist Prime Minister for half a century.

Many jaded leftists, young and old, were jolted awake by Corbyn's candidacy in 2015. We are not ashamed to admit that for a brief moment we numbered among that group. Membership of the party shot up to over half a million, making Labour the largest political party in Western Europe. Flush with the fees paid by its members, a new day seemed imminent. After decades of austerity and pathetic soundbite politics, it was good to hear talk about fundamental economic issues such as the establishment of a national investment bank orientated to infrastructure and the productive economy, and the renationalisation of public utilities.

However, as time passed our enthusiasm waned. Some of the meetings we attended were dominated by middle-class, university-educated cultural activists who projected their yearning for some vague cultural revolution onto Corbyn's project. Where some we encountered were committed to helping the underprivileged and generously gave up their time to help out wherever they could, others simply wanted to push their pet projects into the limelight for a brief time and showed little interest in economic renewal or the more practical concerns of traditional Labour voters.

We also encountered bellicose class bigotry, especially when discussions moved towards the thorny issue of Brexit. In some locales, the fact that the local population had voted to leave the European Union was taken as evidence that the local white working class were incorrigibly racist and needed to be politically re-educated. Here were radical Labour activists who appeared to despise many white working-class men and women – or were at least morally opposed to what they imagined to be their regrettable beliefs – yet viewed themselves as committed leftists and the natural representatives of that very same class.

It quickly became clear that Corbynism was a project far too open to the left-leaning, liberal middle classes, despite the fact that some admirable and dedicated socialists and social democrats rushed to become involved in it. At this early stage it became clear that, yet again, the practical concerns of the working class would be left to one side while the cultural concerns of liberal middle class would be pushed to the forefront. However, we should not simply assume that this move was made primarily on behalf of minority ethnic groups. In keeping with the long history of the left in Britain, the primary objective was that the irredeemably populist working class would once again be put back in their box and limited to playing only a supporting role in what was supposed to be their movement. The multi-ethnic working class would not be given the opportunity to understand themselves as a potential political unity that could represent themselves, their concerns and their interests in Britain's major political and cultural institutions. The liberal middle classes would once again occupy the bridge and command the ship. They would be the intellectual leaders of the project. They would identify priorities and draft policies. Working-class intellectuals could either fall into line and accept the ideas of their middle-class superiors or leave. At no stage was Corbynism a movement of the working class.

It would be wrong to suggest that Corbyn himself was simply a blank screen onto which various interest groups could project their nuanced desires for change, but there is little doubt that many of his supporters imagined that his ascendancy would further their own niche interests. The traditional shared commitment to class advancement had fractured into a dizzying proliferation of bespoke cultural movements. Temporary unity could be discerned in the drive to get Corbyn elected, but ultimately it was a convenience. The only shared commitment was to individual freedom and the ascendancy of approved micro-communities. And, of course, a shared commitment to multiple self-interests leads inevitably to conflict.

Some on the left have responded to this apparent conundrum by outlining a hierarchy of suffering. Once the new political day has dawned, those who have suffered most should be first in the queue for benefits and freedoms. Those who benefit from current arrangements must go to the back of the queue, while those perceived to have been in the driving seat throughout much of history should be prepared to suffer in remorse and compensate for the horrors their ancestors unleashed upon the world. Inevitably, arguments crop up about the supposed justice of the new hierarchy. Should a recently arrived upper middle-class immigrant from India be placed more highly than a white working-class woman? What if that immigrant is a well-paid academic from a Brahmin background? Should a middle-class white woman be considered advantaged or disadvantaged relative to, say, a black Caribbean male doctor? Complexities, contradictions and conflicts abound while a genuine sense of shared interests and destiny is notable only by its absence.

A unity of purpose – to break free and establish in reality a new cultural order free from the bigotries of the past and the present – could exist, but it is always fragile and liable to break out into open hostility as soon as one group achieves a goal at the expense of another. Proliferating internal contradictions and conflicts are divisive in their own right, but, externally, they are grist to the mill of conservative lampooning and only further discredit the left in the eyes of everyday people.

The new cultural radicals who drove Corbyn's project forward were more interested in establishing new intersectional pecking orders than in building equality and class solidarity. Of course, Corbyn had always been a dedicated campaigner for cultural equality. He had always bristled at injustice and tried to help those who found themselves, through no fault of their own, in desperate circumstances. This bearing seemed to make him a natural ally of the new cultural left, even though some of his longstanding views clashed with the latest edicts from the group that eventually became known colloquially as 'the Woke'.

In its early days, Corbyn's project seemed keen to create a new and inclusive economic framework that some more experienced leftists saw as the essential bedrock on which advances in cultural justice could be achieved. However, as it developed, he increasingly dismissed or gave wrong or ambiguous messages on many issues of vital importance to working-class voters. Certainly, voters did not hear enough about reindustrialisation, job creation, wage levels and job security, and as time passed it became increasingly clear that he commanded little respect amongst the majority. Corbyn and his entourage seemed blithely unaware of the huge global economic changes implied by the current 'energy transition',[23] and what they could mean for restarting British manufacturing freed from EU competition, state subsidy and fiscal credibility restrictions.

Many voters, rather unfairly in our view, saw continuity rather than change in Corbyn's politics. He was, for some inhabitants of the deindustrialised north, just another liberal middle-class metropolitan who knew nothing of their struggles. Others viewed him as a dedicated multiculturalist who despised the patriotism that clung on so doggedly among many of the country's poorest citizens. He was tarnished by his alleged support for terrorist causes, and finally brought low by his capitulation to his own party base, most of whom were either conscious or unwitting neoliberals who believed the Labour Party should fight hard to ensure the UK remained part of the EU.

Corbyn himself appears not to have been a great supporter of the EU, and with good reason. There is not a scrap, not a scintilla, of socialism in the EU, and throughout Corbyn's time as party leader, there was barely a shadow of social democracy to be seen there either. However, his supporters were sure that the progressive route forward was back towards the EU's reductive market fundamentalism. They were not concerned with EU rules on fiscal deficits and state involvement in the economy. The EU's commitment to the free movement of people was central to its wildly exaggerated positive image. The fact that this was underpinned by the free movement of capital and labour – a fundamental neoliberal principle – was neatly disavowed.

Certainly, Corbyn's merry band of EU-supporting progressive neoliberals were comfortable talking about the cultural benefits of moving across the continent without impediment. Precisely what was liberating and beneficial about impoverished young Eastern Europeans feeling compelled to cut their ties to their families, communities and nations in order to travel across the continent to take up poorly paid, exploitative and insecure work at the bottom of Britain's service sector was rarely discussed. Few seemed to care that the EU's pan-continental economic framework had fomented the huge economic disparities that drove mass migration. Stranger still, many EU-supporting leftists in Britain assumed that those who moved from the East to the West shared their values and were liberal cosmopolitans with little connection to their homelands.

Some of the commentary on social media indicated how far things had fallen. Labour-voting activists wanted a divorce from what they imagined was the nation's racist white working class so they could take up with what they assumed was an inclusive, liberal and cosmopolitan new population of EU migrants. Their deep faith in the superiority of their own ideology seemed to submerge any lingering sense of doubt. It was either cosmopolitan liberalism or a new fascist authoritarianism; pick a side.

Corbyn's project hit the rocks on Brexit. The Labour Party fudged and equivocated, but it was clear to many traditional voters that the party was committed to remaining in the EU. In taking this position, it alienated many in the heartlands who had voted to leave while at the same time annoying many who simply wanted the issue resolved so the nation could move on to address the multitude of other matters atrophying in the background. That the Labour leadership refused to unequivocally come out against Brexit didn't help matters. If the issue had been put to the party's membership, the vast majority would have wanted the party to push for a second referendum and then campaign hard to remain in the EU.

This was undoubtedly a difficult position for Corbyn. Before Brexit, he had huge support among the party membership. In the early days of his leadership, his Euroscepticism had been unimportant. Now it was a problem. Back Remain and lose the support of many traditional Labour voters who had voted to leave. Back Leave and lose the support of the party membership who had carried him to power. In time-honoured fashion, he and those around him decided that they would try not to alienate anyone, and in so doing alienated everyone.

Corbyn's team tried to adopt a position of objective analysis and critique, underpinned by a desire to protect the British economy and the interests of its workers. However, this was a Remain position in all but name. They wanted to remain in the customs union – because they appeared to believe that leaving it would result in economic devastation – and this meant that the country would be forced to accept the continuation of the EU's commitment to free movement which, of course, was the one EU policy Leave voters most wanted to be rid of.

Still, this was not enough for Labour's hardcore Remainers. The remaining Blairites in the party, who as dedicated neoliberals were committed to the EU, had found a large stick to beat Corbyn with. In the run-up to the 2019 election, they seemed to take great pleasure in making it clear that they would do everything in their power to prevent Brexit from happening. Of course, this went down well in the southern seats and university towns that had voted Remain, but not so well in those seats in the provinces that had voted Leave. In retrospect, it would have been better for Corbyn to pick a side and campaign on that basis. But it would have been even better had he stuck to his guns and chosen to follow Tony Benn and Peter Shore's lead by talking passionately and persuasively about the potential benefits of leaving the EU on a social democratic programme based on public investment and industrial renewal.

While it once seemed to us that Corbyn was a true conviction politician, on the crucial era-defining issue of Brexit, he suppressed his convictions and meekly capitulated to the views of those who surrounded him. He did not unequivocally back Remain, but that decision seemed to be driven by an expedient desire not to alienate Leave voters and otherwise supportive Labour MPs fighting to retain Leave-voting seats. It didn't work. The majority of Labour MPs were in favour of remaining in the EU. Many indulged in absurd dystopian fantasies about the effect of Brexit upon the nation's economy and clung on to membership of an organisation dedicated to the rule of markets as if it were a comfort blanket. Many in Corbyn's inner circle were also in favour of Remain, and so was the vast majority of the party's membership, which was bigger than it had ever been. However, the views of party membership were not reflective of the views of the nation, and nor were they reflective of the views of the working class.

For a short time, it seemed as though Corbyn enjoyed huge support across the nation. He would be greeted by chants of "Oh! Jeremy Corbyn!" wherever he appeared. But as time passed it became increasingly clear that the huge support Corbyn enjoyed within the party and among the university-educated middle class was not shared by other diverse social groups, which ranged from working-class whites to culturally conservative British Asians. The party was not the nation, and the evangelical support Corbyn received in some quarters was matched amongst traditional Red Wall voters by a quiet but growing dissatisfaction with his leadership and the party's response to the Brexit crisis, and a dawning realisation of his project's liberal metropolitan nature. Corbyn seemed keen to dodge the limelight and keep his views on Brexit to himself. If pressed, he would present Labour's 'five demands' – which were basically five barriers to actually delivering the Brexit that Leave voters wanted – and repeat his standard line about wanting to secure the interests of workers. His performance didn't impress.

Maddeningly, there was talk of another potentially ruinous referendum. Leftist media commentators suggested that the referendum result had been stolen by the far right, who wanted to lower wage levels and workplace protections in order to boost the profits of already incredibly large and powerful corporations. Some suggested that many who had voted Leave felt they had been tricked by the Leave campaign and had now switched their allegiance to Remain. Overturning a democratic vote, they said, would be a triumph for democracy. The media followed every aspect of the road to Brexit and often seemed transfixed by the left's shouty faux-radicals, who stretched every sinew to protect the political and economic status quo. The blanket coverage of every feature of the process, and the sheer amount of airtime given to the pro-EU left often made it seem as if they were in the ascendency and heading for victory.

However, in reality, most people were sick of the whole charade. The gap between the hyperbolic metropolitan mediascape and the rest of the UK had, during the Brexit debacle, become even deeper and wider than the gap between the liberal elite and the working class. The liberal media commentariat and the left's vociferous advocates for Remain did not understand the country, and the rest of the country could not understand them. They were living in different worlds. Labour's Remainers imagined the people were behind them. They believed that the power of their rhetoric and the force of their arguments would convince those who were wavering. They thought that the majority shared their values, and they were convinced their values were the only ones that mattered.

Ordinary people, meanwhile, were getting on with their lives. They were focused on jobs, wages, bills, debts, family members and friends. They wanted the security and stability that would allow them to rebuild and move forward. They were also concerned about the decay of their neighbourhoods and the break-up of their communities. Certainly, many traditional Labour voters were alienated by the hardcore Remainerism of the party, and distinctly underwhelmed by Corbyn's leadership and apparent unwillingness to accept the result of a democratic referendum.

The Brexit fiasco was to be Corbyn's undoing. Ultimately, despite all of the enthusiasm and promise, Corbyn's revolution in the Labour Party proved not to be a democratic socialist revolution at all. There were certainly elements of traditional socialism in there, but in the eyes of the electorate the Labour Party had become an organ of the metropolitan, university-educated middle class. Popular policies, such as taking key utilities back into public ownership, were overshadowed by proposals that seemed set to attract only minority interest. Labour no longer seemed to stand for anything concrete. It was a rudderless, listless weathervane, pulled towards whichever cultural issue had received the benefit of media amplification, and drifting further and further away from its traditional commitment to the broad working class.

If there was a force driving Labour at all it was a small but pugnacious and growing cabal of radical liberal idealists, who seemed to possess quite remarkable self-confidence and a strange, secular yet pious sense of devotion to their own hyper-morality and vision of the future. Variants of this subset had existed within Labour's ranks since its earliest days and, as the Corbyn project got up and running, it seemed like the right time to have its rather esoteric collection of policy demands shunted centre stage. Both the left-wing and right-wing factions of the party's mainstream seemed to accept the moral superiority of this subset and ushered more and more of its members into positions of power, both in the parliamentary party and in the provinces beyond.

Ordinary voters simply weren't getting the message. Adding to the Brexit fiasco, some of the policy proposals whirling around the Labour Party – for example, the commitment of many Corbyn supporters to the goal of open borders – seemed crazy even to those who accepted a steady, controlled flow of immigration: the politics of the student union bar rather than the politics of a government-in-waiting keen to advance the interests of the nation. The rise and fall of Corbyn ultimately reflected the fundamental cleavages that for decades had been deepening and widening on the left and threatened to drag the whole endeavour into the abyss. These cleavages remain and, indeed, have deepened further since Corbyn's departure from the front line of British politics.

Corbyn: endgame

As Corbyn edged nervously towards the disastrous 2019 general election, his party was caught up in a controversy that drew attention away from its ambitious manifesto. Labour's 2019 manifesto included the abolition of Universal Credit and the overhaul of the welfare system; tax rises for the wealthiest 1 per cent of the population; a massive increase in funding for the healthcare system and the introduction of universal social care; the renationalisation of the rail system, Royal Mail and the water companies; a commitment to build 100,000 homes per year, and removal of the charitable status of fee-paying schools. There was also a promise to deliver free broadband to every home and business in the country. Many media commentators scoffed at these ambitions, but many potential Labour voters were behind the general thrust of Corbyn's economic programme. If Labour MPs had been willing to argue vociferously in support of these measures across all public forums and make it clear that they were eminently achievable, many floating voters and abstainers might well have been attracted. It was the cultural aspect, and Corbyn himself and his leadership team, they found less convincing. That these popular policies were overshadowed by the Brexit debacle was a great shame, but it was one of Labour's own making.

The media had also got hold of a new scandal, and they were not willing to let it go. Labour was accused of being institutionally anti-Semitic. For Corbyn and his inner circle, these allegations were preposterous and appeared to have been cynically manufactured by opponents in his own party and further afield. While there is a whiff of paranoia in this response, there were in fact many good reasons for Corbyn and his team to feel assailed by plots and threats.

One of the most remarkable things about Corbyn's time at the centre of British politics was the extent to which virtually every aspect of the British establishment mobilised to demonise him in the eyes of the electorate. He was openly mocked by journalists who were supposed to remain objective and impartial. He was subjected to a barrage of baseless rumours and allegations. For the most part, the right-wing media tended to mock Corbyn and present his politics as juvenile, but some on the right took

Corbyn's rise more seriously and did all they could to portray him as a dangerous communist and terrorist sympathiser who hated freedom.

However, if anything, the left-wing media were more vociferous in their criticism. *The Guardian*, for example, certainly Britain's most prestigious left-leaning newspaper, posted editorial after editorial attacking Corbyn from every angle. He was a weak-willed imbecile who was leading the left to certain doom. He was a splitter who would ensure decades of Tory rule. Everything Corbyn had ever said or written was dredged up and reassessed in the hope that it might provide the ammunition for yet another salvo in a remorseless war to unseat him as party leader. It must have been difficult for Corbyn to cope with such a barrage of scurrilous lies and mischaracterisations. Some supposedly impartial TV news programmes even mocked up an image of Corbyn as if he were a leader from Soviet-era Russia. The neoliberal establishment – both its left and right wings – was unrelenting in its crude demonisation and scaremongering.

The ultimate goal, of course, was to move the party back to the centre ground but, by this advanced stage in the neoliberal era, the centre ground of British politics had been moved firmly to what used to be recognised as the right. Corbyn's standard social democratic economic programme seemed radical only when set against the background of compulsory neoliberalism. The programme would have been considered unacceptably cautious and quite conservative during the years of public investment and economic growth that followed the Second World War. If we broaden the scope of our analysis beyond the neoliberal years of market fundamentalism, Corbyn's ostensible radicalism was really quite conventional.

Corbyn's economic programme may not have been particularly radical by the standards of the twentieth century, but there can be little doubt that it prompted a concerted backlash from a diverse range of actors committed to the continuation of neoliberalism's global economic system. Of course, many Corbynites believed his cultural programme – rooted as it was in a deep commitment to tear down existing cultural hierarchies – threatened the status quo and inspired determined opposition, but this is not the case at all.

That Corbyn's inner circle initially assumed that the anti-Semitism scandal which engulfed the party in the run up to the 2019 election had been manufactured by his opponents was understandable. However, it gradually became clear that the issue was slightly more complicated than they first imagined. Throughout his time as a Labour MP, Corbyn had been a defender of the Palestinian cause and an unswerving critic of Israel's conduct on the West Bank, in Gaza and elsewhere. Of course, Corbyn was sure that it was not anti-Semitic to criticise the state of Israel, and many of those who flooded into the party to lend him their support felt the same way.

Some Jewish organisations within the Labour Party suggested that anti-Semitism in the party was on the rise, while some Labour MPs with Jewish roots also announced that they had had enough of Corbyn's refusal to address Labour's obvious and growing problem. Luciana Berger pushed Corbyn to explain a comment he had written on Facebook in 2012, which appeared to offer support for a street artist who faced having his work painted over by Tower Hamlets Council. Apparently, the artwork contained stereotypical images of Jewish bankers controlling the global economy. Corbyn later apologised and suggested he had not looked closely at the work before posting his supportive comments.

Certainly, it seems odd to portray Corbyn as a racist. He had spent much of his life fighting racism, and his record is hardly in dispute. However, some Jewish Labour MPs claimed that Corbyn was comfortable with the presence of anti-Semites within the party. Anti-Semites felt emboldened, and full-blooded public criticism of Israel made some Jewish MPs and party members nervous. However, this was not the core issue. Corbyn's detractors claimed that many of his supporters were using the Jewish diaspora as a symbolic proxy for the global capitalist class. Jews, they claimed, were increasingly demonised by some party members with a shaky understanding of history and a warped understanding of capitalist enterprise. And despite repeated calls, Corbyn refused to take the problem seriously.

Some Jewish groups within the party, especially Jewish Voice for Labour, backed Corbyn and maintained that the issue had been cynically manufactured and used as a stick to beat Corbyn by those keen to see him jettisoned from frontline politics and the party's neoliberal centrism restored. The scandal soon became a staple of the broadsheet press and the broadcast media. Corbyn's numerous and diverse opponents could now argue that removing him as party leader was a morally justifiable thing to do. It was strange to watch so many of his opponents who, since his election as party leader, had argued that he should be deposed for pragmatic reasons – in particular to make the party more electable – suddenly claim the moral high ground by arguing that he should go because he had systematically failed a historically oppressed minority.

Corbyn's team tried to quell the increasingly strong winds, but they were rapidly turning into a storm. Corbyn spoke out against racism and anti-Semitism, but it was nowhere near enough. He was pushed to adopt the International Holocaust Remembrance Association's (IHRA) definition of anti-Semitism into the party's code of conduct. The definition itself was not particularly controversial and had already been accepted by the party. However, the Board of Deputies and the Jewish Leadership Council wanted Labour to go further and adopt the IHRA's eleven illustrative examples of anti-Semitism. This was the sticking point. Corbyn was willing to adopt seven of the eleven but unwilling to adopt those which related to the Israeli state's policies. He saw no logical reason why criticism of Israel should be considered anti-Semitic. Which other state anywhere in the world was afforded such a luxury? Why should Palestinians and their supporters be denied the right to legitimately critique the existence or the behaviour of the Israeli state? For Corbyn and many of those close to him, the IHRA definition of anti-Semitism threatened to restrict the rights of Palestinians and could therefore not be adopted in full.

Corbyn attempted to adapt the examples, but for the most part his attempts to find middle ground were lost in the media frenzy. Some Jewish Labour activists close to him made the point that those members of the Jewish community pushing for the adoption of the IHRA in full were on the political right and not representative of all British Jews. Capitulating to the Jewish right on this crucial issue would ensure that, going forward, it was the Jewish right who were the 'official' spokespeople for the entirety of British Jews.[24]

Corbyn drew sustenance from his Jewish contacts in Islington and elsewhere. There was no legitimate reason for him to apologise – he was not a racist, and it would be absurd to suggest otherwise. The party, Corbyn seemed to believe, would immediately act upon any firm evidence suggesting a party member had behaved in an anti-Semitic manner or voiced anti-Semitic views. For Corbyn, it was that simple. Everything else was just conspiratorial nonsense trotted out by those who were willing to use any possible means to ensure his downfall.

There are between a quarter of a million and three hundred thousand Jews in Britain today.[25] The overall population of this sceptred isle runs to around sixty-eight million. The Jewish Labour Movement, the Labour Party's largest Jewish organisation, has somewhere in the region of one thousand members. There are smaller Jewish organisations in the party too. Overall, the party remains the largest in Western Europe, with around half a million members. We do not want to diminish the experiences of those Jews who have encountered anti-Semitism, and nor do we deny the existence of anti-Semitism in Labour or in the wider British population. However, as a recent YouGov poll shows,[26] negative feelings towards Jews among the wider British population are really quite uncommon. Other minority ethnic groups in Britain today suffer far more. As a social group, gypsies are most likely to inspire the animus of the broader population, and it is worth noting that the hardships of gypsies have not provoked a strong response from left-wing activists. Researchers working for Institute for Jewish Policy Research (JPR) in 2017 noted that:

> [L]evels of antisemitism in Great Britain are among the lowest in the world. British Jews constitute a religious and ethnic group that is seen overwhelmingly positively by an absolute majority of the British population: about 70% of the population of Great Britain have a favourable opinion of Jews and do not entertain any antisemitic ideas or views at all.[27]

Jews are also unlikely to be held back by their religious commitments and ethnic background. As a whole, they perform well in education, and a significant proportion of young Jews progress into professional and managerial jobs.[28] This is not to suggest that Jews have it easy or that, as a group, they can be considered one of the key beneficiaries of our present social and economic system. However, these points should serve to reinforce the point that, while Corbyn and the Labour Party scurried around trying to placate the media and the Jewish Board of Deputies, the rest of the country did not feel particularly invested in the issue or its resolution.

Labour is, quite clearly, an anti-racist political party. It campaigns with a great deal of energy on anti-racist issues. There may be a higher degree of anti-Semitism in the Labour membership relative to the broader population, but the available evidence is not conclusive. It is entirely conceivable that leftist radicals in the Labour Party overstepped the mark and, rather than criticising the state of Israel, criticised Jews as a broad religious group. It is also possible that Corbyn's enemies skilfully manufactured a scandal in an attempt to derail his project and put an end to his leadership.

While the 24-hour news channels talked incessantly about the issue, millions around the country gradually began to change their views on Corbyn. There was a good deal of support for his economic policies, but the party seemed incapable of placing these policies front and centre. There was gradually less talk of real, secure, well-paid and satisfying jobs and how Corbyn's economic policies might breathe new life into the dying post-industrial regions. Many broadcasters assumed that the anti-Semitism affair would be a death knell for Corbyn, and in some respects they were correct. But it was not that voters were turned off by an alleged anti-Semite. Rather, the anti-Semitism scandal distracted everyone's attention away from the universal issues that can attract support and swing elections. Corbyn, when he did appear on the mainstream media, was bombarded with questions about anti-Semitism. He was given no chance to talk about renationalising core industries, or building 100,000 new homes per year, or overhauling the welfare system, or taxing the super-rich more ... these and other potentially vote-winning policies simply disappeared from public view.

In truth, Corbyn himself contributed to the mess. There was measured support among the general public for Labour's economic policies, but this support declined markedly as soon as it was made clear that they were, in fact, Corbyn's policies. The politics of personality had rendered him remarkably unpopular. His economic programme was overshadowed not just by Brexit and the anti-Semitism debacle but also by a diverse range of flaws that were highlighted and used to reconstruct his public image – he became a weak liberal multiculturalist, an ageing student radical, a scruffy bleeding heart from the big city keen to open the country's borders to uncontrolled immigration and deaf to the interests of his party's traditional base. Much of this was unfair, but certainly he did not do enough to defend himself.

Corbyn's ultimate failure came in the 2019 general election. The 2017 election had been the undoubted high point: Corbyn's Labour Party had surpassed most informed expectations and came very close to forming a government. Despite what many commentators – and Labour MPs – said, countless voters were willing to countenance a significant deviation away from the neoliberal consensus. Corbyn could win popular support, and this success gave him licence to overhaul the Labour Party while waiting for the snap election many believed was imminent. But it was pretty much downhill from then on. Labour succeeded in alienating both the main warring tribes on Brexit, and the party received a huge amount of negative coverage as the anti-Semitism scandal broke. But to really get to the heart of the matter, we need to dig deeper.

Labour is now a middle-class party. Its membership is predominantly middle class. Labour has made a great deal of headway with younger voters who have been through the university system, and the party's power base is now London, a world away from its roots in the industrial heartlands. Labour can also rely on the continued support of university towns and cities, and other areas where the liberal middle classes cluster.

As we write, Labour is about neck and neck with the Conservatives in terms of support among middle-class voters.

However, it has for many years been haemorrhaging working-class support. Despite Johnson's questionable handling of the pandemic, in 2021 the Conservative Party had a remarkable 16 per cent lead over the Labour Party among working-class voters.[29] The 'Red Wall' seats lost by Labour in the 2019 election are, of course, areas dominated by the working class.

Many working-class voters found themselves gradually becoming more sympathetic towards the Tories ahead of the 2019 election. The Brexit saga had served to quicken the movement of many working-class voters from the mainstream left to the mainstream right, but the Tories were also now willing to talk about investing in post-industrial areas, building homes and creating meaningful jobs. The fall of the Red Wall was a key historical turning point. Some notable Conservatives spoke sensibly of the need to secure the long-term support of those who in 2019 had voted Tory for the first time. However, by early 2022, most of the Tories' grand promises to bring post-industrial regions back to life had failed to materialise and, engulfed by a series of scandals, support for the Conservatives began to decline.

The Labour leader, Sir Keir Starmer, a member of the neoliberal Trilateral Commission[30] and a supporter of fiscal responsibility, has certainly not experienced the concerted negative media coverage experienced by his predecessor, and he has prospered by staying silent on policy matters as the Tories busied themselves destroying their reputation in the eyes of the electorate. Rather than attempt to secure a future election victory by offering voters a compelling and original policy programme, Starmer seems happy to accept the negative aspect of contemporary politics and simply wait until a majority of voters become so disgusted with the Tories that they are again willing to countenance a Labour government.

Bernie Sanders: a momentary return of radicalism in the Democratic Party?

There are many parallels between the rise and fall of Corbyn in Britain and that of Sanders in the United States. Both men came to prominence late in their careers, after decades as outsiders.

Both were committed to social democracy and opposed to economic policies that enriched a small and increasingly powerful elite at the expense of the majority. The fundamental principle behind their opposition to the neoliberal world order was clear: a small number of individuals in possession of more wealth than entire nations was unconscionable, especially when some citizens could barely afford to feed themselves. Wealth, they agreed, should be more evenly distributed throughout the population. Economies should be organised to maximise satisfying and reasonably remunerative employment.

They also shared the belief that obscene wealth held in a tiny number of hands indicates ongoing policy failure. Economies work best when the vast majority of citizens have a stake in a shared project that fairly rewards effort, skill and commitment. Since the dawning of the capitalist age, the continuous reinvestment of capital has been considered essential to economic growth and the expansion of labour markets. Money atrophies when it is taken out of circulation and stored in offshore tax havens. Corbyn and Sanders also agreed that tax avoidance deprives the state of the revenue it needs to invest in infrastructure, employment and other public goods, and erodes popular belief in the fairness of the tax system and the principles of citizenship and collective endeavour. As we have seen, the idea that tax is needed for spending is technically incorrect, but such old-school ideas, well-intentioned and once normal, became radical in the neoliberal age. Corbyn and Sanders' fidelity to them set the stage for their elevation close to the pinnacle of political power.

Both inspired great devotion among their core supporters, not simply because of their attractive policy agendas or the power of their oratory. Many were clearly attracted to these ageing radicals because they appeared to possess the commitment and sincerity that would allow them to push through genuine change. In an age of pervasive cynicism, they inspired many to believe that it was indeed possible to use the existing democratic system to steer the nation towards a better future. It was too hasty to assume that the hundreds of thousands who joined the Labour Party to vote for Corbyn in the party's leadership elections indicated a deep wellspring of untapped leftist radicalism among the people. It did indicate, however, that many, even members of the professional middle class, wanted to rescue history from the soul-crushing banality of mainstream neoliberal politics. Similarly, those whose support almost carried Sanders to the Democratic nomination in 2016 clearly saw him as a man who would fight to improve the lot of ordinary Americans.

Overall, Corbyn and Sanders seemed like truthful, decent and committed guys. Part of their initial appeal was that they seemed starkly at odds with so many of their contemporaries in the Labour and Democratic parties. They were not vapid, narcissistic careerists out to become famous. They did not aspire to five boring years in office before earning a fortune on the after-dinner speaking circuit. They wanted to change things for the better. Corbyn and Sanders embodied the return of the virtue that had been lost from public life, and in that sense seemed to represent the last throw of the dice for the left in their respective countries. However, despite their honesty and the brief flurry of support they received, they also seemed to alienate some voters and inspire a number of worrying stereotypes about what the contemporary left would mean for ordinary people should it achieve political office.

It is comforting to think that Sanders and Corbyn failed because their projects elicited fear at the core of the system. Corbyn, in particular, received a huge amount of negative media coverage, but we should keep in mind that despite this hostility he came very close to victory in 2017. This is not without precedent – centre-left figures such as Roosevelt, Attlee, Kennedy and Wilson had achieved victories with interventionist economic policies in the face of relentlessly hostile sections of the mass media. Sanders, too, especially in the early days, suffered at the hands of the corporate media but, again, this did not prevent him just missing out on the Democratic nomination in 2016. And neither man can realistically claim to have received a harder time from the mainstream media than Donald Trump, who defied the pollsters and established groups within his own party to secure the presidency in 2017. Despite what some left-leaning academics continue to claim, an electorally significant number of ordinary people are capable of forming their own views about politics and where they want their countries to go.

They do not unthinkingly accept the views of the mainstream media commentariat and what they might have seen on Facebook or written on the side of a bus.

Both Corbyn and Sanders enjoyed high-profile support, and both benefited from powerful campaign teams. They were particularly popular among younger voters. They had huge support online, both in terms of formal support systems tied to their official campaigns and unofficial campaigners who took it upon themselves to extol their virtues to anyone listening. Joe Biden, who defeated Sanders in 2020 in the race for the Democratic nomination before unseating Donald Trump to become the forty-sixth President of the United States, could only dream of inspiring the kinds of support enjoyed by Sanders on Facebook, Twitter and YouTube. Sanders also had far more boots on the ground than the other candidates. He headed up the 'biggest activist and volunteer network … in American electoral history' and 'raised more money in just the month of February ($447.6 million) than Biden spent in five months combined'.[31] Sanders may have been a rank outsider in 2016, but he was a frontrunner in the race for the Democratic nomination in 2020. So, what went wrong for Sanders? At the beginning, his image was that of a principled outsider who for years had been ignored and ill used by his party. Just a few years later, when he was the main challenger to Joe Biden for the Democratic nomination and Donald Trump was about to start campaigning for his second term, this image had changed.

While Sanders' supporters tend to point towards the consistency of his political views, there can be little doubt that he lost sight of what worked in 2016 and listened too much to those who had rushed to offer him support in 2020. In 2016, his grounded approach and clear focus on the issues that mattered most to ordinary people had taken him close to success. He was generally understood to be a principled, ordinary guy – slightly outside the usual parameters of mainstream politics but not threateningly so – who talked sense about things that matter to the majority. However, his 2020 campaign had a markedly different tone.

He spoke far less about bringing jobs back to the American heartlands. Displacing this theme was the new left's standard list of cultural preoccupations. It is not clear whether Sanders' personal views changed as he engaged with his new supporter base of university-educated radical liberals, whether they pushed him to change tack, or whether he independently came to the view that it was strategically important to signal his determination to fight sexism, racism and discrimination against sexual minorities, which now included the rapidly growing number of people who identified as trans.

In 2016 he benefited from the popular view that his economic policies were achievable, but in 2020 a large proportion of voters began to see him predominantly as a cultural radical who had put his economic policies on the backburner in order to prioritise the new left's niche interests. These interests, of course, were of huge importance to those around him, and indeed *are* important in their own right but, in relation to secure livelihoods and the conservation of at least the ethical core of traditional ways of life, they mattered far less to the ordinary people whose support Sanders needed to win. Prioritising jobs, improving living standards, reintroducing essential values and stabilising community life appeals to the vast majority of US citizens. However, rather than focus on issues that have the potential to appeal to all, Sanders and his team moved in the opposite direction.

It's true that some universally compelling policy proposals formed part of his 2020 campaign. He promised to provide Medicare for all, raise the minimum wage and implement a job-generating 'green new deal'. He made other promises: a free college education to a far greater proportion of the general public, and a cap on student loan debts; the expansion and solidification of work-based rights; the expansion of social security benefits; building 10 million permanently affordable housing units; an end to the involvement of for-profit businesses in the criminal justice system; an end to the war on drugs by legalising marijuana and expunging past convictions, as well as cutting the national prison population in half by abolishing the death penalty, three-strikes laws and mandatory minimum sentences, and expanding the use of alternatives to detention.[32] While perhaps not as transformative as many on the American left hoped, there was much to be admired. However, if this is the case, why did so many blue-collar voters in states that supported Sanders in 2016 overlook these positive aspects of Sanders' agenda and shift their allegiance to another Democratic candidate in 2020?

The fundamental problem is that most voters tend not to carefully analyse the fine details of policy proposals. Since Pericles, mass politics has always rested on a bedrock of gut feelings and roughly adumbrated perceptions. Voters pay attention to headline proposals that represent clusters of policies in broad categories – such as 'the economy' or 'crime' – that help them to get the rough measure of each candidate. Voters then draw upon general feelings about their character, trustworthiness and so on. The balance has to be just right.

In 2016, Sanders announced he did not want to focus on 'identity politics' because he saw it as a distraction from the 'real issues'. Broadly speaking, he did not present himself – and neither was he presented by the media – as being the champion of the cultural left. He spoke passionately, but broadly and briefly, of the need to increase the representation of minorities and acknowledged that racism and sexism were genuine problems that needed to be quickly addressed, but he clearly wanted to dig beneath the fragile sensitivities of 'identity politics' and talk about how the Democrats might build a fairer society for all. In pursuing this course, Sanders seemed to offer a more palatable form of change that focused on improving the lot of ordinary people while simultaneously reining in the enormous and growing power of the super-rich. He seemed serious. Considered but ambitious. A practical and committed man, rather than a shouty ideologue. He wanted to focus on the practical issues that mattered most to ordinary people, and, crucially, his plans seemed achievable without being overly disruptive.

However, by 2020, Sanders' disdain for 'identity politics' had waned. He again spoke passionately about ending racial and gender injustice, but he failed to identify concrete and easily comprehensible policy proposals. For many watching at home, it wasn't clear what he planned to do to fight racial injustice, save for condemning racists and bolstering the protections already offered by the state and its legal system. For the most part, voters were told only of his plans to fight discrimination, rather than precisely how he intended to fight it and how his performance in that fight might be assessed.

Sanders spoke passionately about cultural issues, but his solutions lacked both detail and clarity. But this wasn't the main problem. Most blue-collar voters were against racial and gender injustice but didn't want these concerns to be paramount. They didn't want universal issues, especially fundamentals such economic justice, prosperity and security, to be crowded out.

As the 2020 campaign continued, many came to the view that Sanders had switched track and was first and foremost a champion of identity politics. Identity politics seemed to project an image of division and instability, bringing to the surface difficult emotions centred around guilt, atonement and revenge. As he was at pains to point out in 2016, it also tended to treat the 'real issues' as secondary. In the 2020 campaign, Sanders seemed to contradict himself by presenting identity politics itself as the 'real issue'. Only by prioritising and advancing the causes of specific cultural groups could the whole nation advance.

In 2020 the Sanders campaign prioritised the equality, diversity and inclusion agenda and, somewhat strangely, seemed to think of it as an inherent good and an obvious vote-winner. This general perception of Sanders and his campaign appears to have prompted many of those who voted for him in 2016 to look more closely at other candidates. Joe Biden, who many saw as an establishment candidate associated with the economic status quo, managed to capture far more blue-collar voters than expected. In many cases, these were votes that had been swept up by Sanders in 2016. These blue-collar Democrats, it seems, looked past Sanders' economic programme and instead saw his vague cultural programme as being at the core of his candidacy. Clear promises that might benefit the many had been displaced by vague promises that might benefit a few. The balance was wrong.

Cultural activists tried to press the claim that the injustices associated with race, gender and sexuality *were* actually the fundamental issues that affected the many. However, the majority seem to have disagreed. This general understanding – that Sanders had changed course and was now first and foremost a determined supporter of the cultural left's constantly evolving agenda of niche issues – seems to have been reinforced by the nature of his on-the-ground campaigning.

At the start of his 2020 campaign, he apologised for his 2016 campaign having been 'too white and too male-orientated'.[33] To make up for his previous failures, and perhaps in the hope of preventing future attacks by the activist left, Sanders ensured that his 2020 campaign was sufficiently 'diversified'. Angela Nagle and Michael Tracey interviewed staffers involved in Sanders' campaign for the Democratic nomination. Some spoke of shocking levels of ineptitude, complacency, waste and even fraud. These failures appear to have been overlooked because the principal commitment of the campaign was to diversity rather than competence.

In South Carolina, a crucial state for Sanders that he eventually lost by 29 points, these problems appear to have been particularly severe. According to some staffers, even the most elementary features of political campaigning were ignored. Jessica Bright, who acted as state director, was singled out for strong criticism. Nagle and Tracey suggest that Bright 'was hired in large part because her mother had filled the seat of Clementa Pinckney – the state senator killed in the 2015 Charleston church shooting. The idea was that such a transactional arrangement might compel the mother to endorse Sanders.'

In any case, it didn't work. Bright's mother ended up endorsing Biden, and Bright herself lacked the qualities needed to boost support for Sanders among Democrat voters in South Carolina. One staffer claimed that Bright couldn't spell or speak coherently, but that was the least of it. Phone-banking and canvassing data were, multiple staffers allege, outright fabricated, giving central campaign headquarters a misleading impression of Sanders' standing in the state.

The general climate of the campaign in South Carolina also appears to have been problematic. Rallies for Sanders were attended mostly by white people, but the campaign staff were overwhelmingly black. It wasn't clear that there existed any sense of solidarity or mutual interests between the staff group and what appears to have been their core support. Some staffers felt stifled and unable to speak up because to do so would be interpreted as a sign of racism. The majority of campaigners were, of course, radicals attached to the activist left. Despite having had absolutely no practical experience of campaigning, they displayed the astounding levels of moral superiority and intellectual self-confidence that are hallmarks of this influential political and cultural group. They brooked no dissent and were impervious to the advice offered by more seasoned campaigners.

One might imagine that Sanders' embrace of identity politics at least boosted his appeal among black and other minority ethnic voters. However, there is no evidence to suggest this was the case. If we look closely at the statistics, in the United States and across the Western world, we can see that simply talking loudly about racial injustices and hiring an ethnically diverse staff doesn't necessarily attract minority ethnic voters. Despite Sanders' efforts to make his campaign feel, sound and look more diverse in 2020, he lost ground in southern states with higher proportions of such voters. In 2016 these voters had been more interested in his focus on economic justice than they were in his dedication to the cause of racial justice in 2020.

We should also note that, despite his divisive rhetoric and policy agenda, Trump was more popular with minority ethnic voters in 2020 than he had been in 2016. Black men, when taken as an undifferentiated group, appear to have increased their support for him by around 6 per cent, and Asian and other ethnicities by around 7 per cent.[34] In the UK's divisive Brexit referendum, we can also see that minority ethnic support for the supposedly progressive side of the argument was not cut and dried. Around 30 per cent of Asian and Black voters gave their support to Leave,[35] despite what some academics claim was a racist campaign focused on the preservation of 'white supremacy'.[36] Conservative and centrist people of colour simply do not show up on the new left's faulty political radar.

Ultimately, Sanders and his team got the balance between economics and culture wrong enough to lose. A good deal of popular support for left-of-centre economic policies continues to exist in the United States, and throughout much of the Western world. Many voters want their politicians to prioritise good jobs and full employment. They want to be free of economic insecurities so that they can plan for the future with confidence and enjoy life a little more. They want a solid base upon which to build and sustain their families. Given the other significant advantages he enjoyed, had Sanders continued where he left off in 2016, there are good reasons to believe he could have secured the nomination and beaten Donald Trump. However, while it is certainly true that Sanders' campaign promises did include what would have been significant and achievable policy advances, many voters withdrew their support because the campaign seemed to be more about fighting cultural injustices than equipping all Americans with a sturdy economic platform.

We are not suggesting that blue-collar Democratic voters are against racial and gender equality. There is more than enough evidence to suggest that most Democrats believe more needs to be done to improve the life chances of women and ethnic minorities.[37] However, we should also note that, in cultural terms, large expanses of US cultural life continue to be really quite conservative, despite what appears to be a surge of support for cultural liberalism among key demographic groups. What these voters were against was not gender and racial equality but the warp-speed advance of cultural liberalism in the Democratic Party, and the Sanders campaign in particular.

By embracing identity politics, Sanders boxed himself into a corner and left the other candidates too much room for manoeuvre. Biden's eventual victory was not a matter of having the most appealing policies, and nor did voters believe that Biden would do better than Sanders against Trump. It wasn't even that Biden's campaign was free of any sign of cultural liberalism. While a number of issues caused Sanders to lose ground among blue-collar Democrats, the dominant one seems to have been his rapid and conspicuous adoption of the language of the activist left.

The inevitable conclusion isn't that Biden won, but that Sanders lost. The crucial shift in emphasis appears to have pushed potential supporters to disengage and look elsewhere. The old saying, 'by their friends shall ye know them', seems apt here. Sanders' dramatic shift to a closer association with the activist left in 2020 dissuaded voters, even though some of his stated policies seemed sensible and his opponents' campaigns were uninspiring. His departure from the political scene and the resurgence of technocratic corporatism offer us yet another disheartening example of the left's ability to bravely snatch defeat from the jaws of victory.

The declining significance of left populism

The projects of Sanders and Corbyn failed because they did not close the growing gap between the dominant liberal left and potential voters among ordinary working people. While there was much to admire in their policy proposals, the overall impression of both men was that they had allowed themselves to be browbeaten into becoming figureheads for an activist left focused upon rapidly changing cultural attitudes but lacking any feasible plan for positive economic change. As we have said, in some respects this view of Sanders and Corbyn is unfair, but the fact that so many people were persuaded to adopt it is of great significance.

Sanders' failure, of course, left the door open for Joe Biden. At the time of writing, it is difficult to see how Biden's presidency can be anything other than a return to the fundaments of neoliberalism, softened by a patina of cultural liberalism and a few symbolically important attempts to address racial injustice. He is likely to get an easy ride from the liberal mainstream media, simply because he is not Donald Trump. He will shake hands, smile at the camera and be treated by much of the press as a statesman the nation can be proud of. And yet nothing much will change in policy terms. Perhaps Biden and his entourage will learn that if he is to avoid being a one-term president he must use the colossal power of the federal state's fiat currency to drive the economy back to sustained growth, rebuild the nation's shattered industrial base, and create secure livelihoods for ordinary people – especially those without college degrees – in the aftermath of the pandemic. Perhaps he will take the historic opportunity to remake the nation by ditching the well-worn neoliberal policy playbook, ignoring the stolid economics commentators who drone on incessantly about the 'national debt', and forge a new path by offering all Americans the chance to take a reasonably well-paid and meaningful job that contributes to the well-being of the nation and its people. Or perhaps not.

Corbyn's demise opened the door to Sir Keir Starmer who, despite his rather serious demeanour and much discussed attention to detail, appears to be unencumbered by any firm political commitments. He has so far shown little interest in reaching out to the voters the party lost in the old industrial heartlands, and he and his entourage continue to accept and occasionally champion the cultural politics of the activist class. He has been largely silent on economic matters. When the economy is discussed, Starmer and his front-bench team have been at pains to stress Labour's fiscal probity and commitment to balancing the budget. At the time of writing, Labour seems even more liberal and metrocentric than it was under Corbyn.

There is, for us, a sad aspect to all of this. There were positive signs in the left populism of Corbyn and Sanders, but ultimately this positivity was shouted down by an alliance forged between dispiritingly cautious apologists for neoliberal economics and the deeply divided liberal left. In the face of this strange chimera, the multi-ethnic mass of everyday people disengaged.

While the left stubbornly perseveres with its 'broad church' mythology, the fact is that to move forward with purpose it must split. The resulting splintered groups must redefine their commitments and their missions. If the left does not take on this painful task, a paralysing lack of clarity will continue to militate against genuine forward movement. Voters must know what the left is for, what it is committed to and how its success will affect their lives. Certainly, those who still believe the left should be principally concerned with advancing the economic and social interests of the multi-ethnic working class must move away quickly from both the neoliberal centrists and the cultural left, whose concerns have come to define the entirety of the left in the popular imagination. Only by cutting itself free from the left's decaying corpse can such a group stay true to the things that really matter in leftist politics.

3

Wrong turns

The rise of post-crash populism has been far more significant to the political right than the left. The vast majority of left populist movements that arose after the 2008 financial crisis have now petered out. Sanders failed, Corbyn failed, while Podemos in Spain and SYRIZA in Greece seem spent forces. Many of Europe's old, centre-left parties continue to haemorrhage support. Only the political right has gained electoral mileage from the aftermath of the global financial crisis, which reinforces the point that where the left still exists in an organised form it has grown accustomed to electoral failure and has lost touch with the very communities its parties and key institutions were initially formed to protect.

The right has shifted and evolved a great deal in a relatively short period of time. Numerous right-wing populist movements that arose after the global financial crisis continue to exert considerable influence. While the appearance of new and renewed forms of nationalism and racism are part of this picture, they are not the sole causes of the right's success. The right has fared particularly well by doing what the liberalised left refuses to do. While left-liberal commentators tediously repeat the Rawlsian plea to ignore the material realm and remain true to liberal ideals, the right has adapted its approach by closely observing shifting economic trends and learning from the strategies of its opponents.

Some elements of the new right have adopted the language of the counterculture and depict the left as an authoritarian establishment set to deprive the people of their freedoms. They present their own ideas as edgy and subversive and pour scorn on the edicts of the stuffy, sanctimonious and censorious leftist establishment. Again, up is down, left is right.

The new right is not yet achieving electoral success, but it has succeeded in two important ways: first, it has swayed many swing voters over to established right-wing parties; and, second, it has injected new life into the elements of cultural conservatism that, despite more than 40 years of global neoliberalism, linger throughout civil society. The liberal left's total commitment to cosmopolitanism, in particular, clashes against the fact that many people remain emotionally attached to the regions and nations of their birth. They are unconvinced by the logic of boundless, freewheeling, global migration, and many remain quite fixed in their views despite constant attempts to present the further liberalisation of cultural forms as inevitable, progressive and intrinsically beneficial.

The acid test, of course, lies in the experience of reality. Many, especially among the working class, see decline rather than progress. They see no positive change at all in the economic, social and communal dimensions of everyday life, and they often have significant fears about what may lie ahead. They also see the stark diminishment of public services and the built environment, and the gradual falling away of valued features of their cultural lives. If the ubiquitous narratives of cosmopolitan progress could somehow align with what ordinary people see in the world around them – even in the most general sense – there would be a much greater chance of acceptance and support. But the chasm is deep and wide.

Feeling affection for the region of one's birth does not necessarily mean one is antagonistic to difference, and nor does it mean one hopes to keep its wonders solely for long-term inhabitants. Loving the region of one's birth often means one is keen to show to others what it is that inspires affection. We rarely regard our place as perfect, but it nonetheless remains ours. We belong to it, and it to us. We feel a sense of familiarity and ease in our place, in part because our own personal biographies remain tied to the environs that acted as the backdrop for key events that shaped our lives. Dissatisfaction with our particular place is very common, but this dissatisfaction is productive in the sense that it provides the impetus to maintain, change and improve it over time.

This conditional love for our particular place allows one to understand why others might also love their own particular place in the world. Knowing what it is to love a place, its history and its customs is crucial preparation for developing the ability to feel respect for other distinct cultures. When visiting another culture, we are outsiders and cannot love it in the same way as its members, but we can appreciate that its members do indeed love it and wish for it to remain intact. One of the principal joys of travel is watching, appreciating and trying to understand others as they enjoy their culture. However, while travel can open doors to wonderful new places, for most the joy of travel is tied in subtle ways to the pleasures of returning home.

Contemporary liberal cosmopolitanism encourages all of us to see this process differently. Rather than accept our position as an outsider, enjoying other cultures as external observers and visitors, all should be free to move to and seek membership of any culture that appeals to our tastes and sensibilities. Constant circulation is said to improve individuals. It exposes them to new ideas, beliefs and ways of being. We should accept that all cultural change is progressive. Obligations to the past are ultimately meaningless and tend to be regressive and exclusionary. We can improvise brand new cultures as we go along by relinquishing outmoded attachments and joining with others to build something new that reflects the always evolving reality of our transformed place.

In committing fully to liberal cosmopolitanism, we can again see how the policies and politics of the liberal left and the neoliberal right tend to complement each other. The basic narrative of liberal cosmopolitanism puts a positive spin of the neoliberal right's drive to ensure that investment capital can flow across borders to exploit opportunities for profit wherever they can be found. The neoliberal right is keen to force all local, regional and national cultures, and the individuals who inhabit them, into the global marketplace. And this is certainly what we have seen throughout the neoliberal era.

We were told that globalisation would inspire diversity, encourage creative hybridisation and open up myriad opportunities for personal pleasure and freedom. However, beneath the shiny veneer of cultural heterogeneity lies the soulless homogeneity of the market. The sociologist George Ritzer neatly captured this process with his 'McDonaldization' thesis.[1] Despite the emphasis that is placed on diversity, globalisation led to banal standardisation. The unique cultural characteristics of Sunderland, Singapore, Stockholm and Sao Paulo were falling away as the uniformity of the market advanced. It is true that this project is especially advanced in the West, but now every region in the world has been affected.

Should we claim that indigenous tribes in South America should be stripped of their illusions and open themselves up to the great benefits that come with deforestation and commercial logging? Should we tell them that the arrival of McDonald's is a sign of progress? Should these men and women be encouraged to accept cosmopolitanism, discard their traditions and accept that their new corporate neighbours have something valuable to contribute to their culture? Shall we tell them that their existing culture is backward-looking and founded upon myths, and that they should rejoice and dash towards the new freedoms of the market? Perhaps they might appreciate the benefits of global movement and eventually decide that moving to the other side of the world would be right for them?

As true inhabitants disappear into the morass of global consumer culture, their remaining traditions and artefacts can be commodified, copied, mass produced and sold to tourists. This process has happened and is still happening around the world. Genuine cultures and traditions eventually dissolve, to be replaced not by creative heterogeneity but hollow, commodified facsimiles.

The liberal left constantly asserts that cosmopolitanism is an absolute good while attachment to place and heritage is inherently bad. But if this is true, why are some traditional communities spared critique and others not? Here we encounter another of the liberal left's weird ethical dualities: for the left it seems entirely reasonable that, for example, African immigrants hope to hang on to their traditional culture and remain emotionally connected to the regions and nations of their birth. However, when white post-Christian populations in the West seek to cling on to their cultural inheritance, the left tends to see things differently. What seems like a preposterous double standard is routinely justified by recourse to the great evils of Eurocentrism, colonialism and empire. Those who make such an argument, however, tend to tacitly endorse the rather simplistic and exceptionally punitive view that all can be held to account for the sins of their ancestors. Empire has left white Europeans and their heritage irreparably tainted while others from elsewhere in the world are judged eternal victims in need of financial restitution and constant support and sympathy.

This is not to say that all of those judged by the liberal left to be worthy of sympathy have not suffered and do not need support. It is rather to suggest that the ways we tend to measure suffering seem to have been cut adrift from reality, and devoid of any acknowledgement of the role of corporate markets in creating and sustaining both wealth and privilege alongside poverty and desperation. What sense does it make to proclaim white people to be inherently privileged, when so many white people suffer terribly? What sense does it make to proclaim all Asians to be victims of white supremacy and colonialism, when some Asians have accumulated vast wealth and actively seek to exploit others? The standard riposte to such questions is to suggest that, no matter where they find themselves in the social hierarchy, they inevitably fair worse than equivalent white people.

Of course, those who make this argument are attempting to draw our eye towards subtle forms of cultural bias, but in doing so they distract us from the fundamental issues at stake. The subtle forms of cultural inequality that may exist between a poor white man and a poor black man are unimportant in relation to the things that they share as a result of their socioeconomic position. And perhaps more to the point, rather than engage in unproductive squabbling about who suffers most and whether or not poor white people can be considered privileged, why is it no longer considered incumbent on the left to silence such discussion, focus on what is shared, and direct our attention upwards, towards the upper echelons of our class system, where true privilege and concentrated decision-making power are to be found?

Such simplistic forms of critique inevitably alienate huge swathes of the population who cannot see the utility of the liberal left's reconfigured stereotypes. The traditional left would have insisted that a poor white man has more in common with a poor black man than he does with a rich white man. A Muslim billionaire has more in common with a white post-Christian billionaire than any of the Muslim workers she exploited to become a billionaire. Such things were once broadly accepted on the left, but they are no more. That the left continues to head down this road – having previously abandoned class as a framework capable of explaining the dynamics of privilege, wealth and exploitation – seems to be at least partly a reflection of the refusal of generations of leftist leaders to anchor critique of social injustice in reality, preferring instead to fight the good fight in the realm of abstract idealism and 'identity'.

Such forms of idealistic critique also leave the door wide open for the liberal right to make the point that categorising all members of ethnic minority groups as victims destined for a life of desperation and dependence demeans these groups and strips individuals of their agency and particularity. Of course, some men and women from ethnic minorities do achieve high office. Instances abound of such men and women leading political parties, large corporations and key public institutions. When they do so, popular discussion tends to play into the hands of the neoliberal right rather than the socially liberal left: rather than assume that such people have had to work twice as hard as their white competitors, most seem to assume that the system is broadly fair, and that those with 'talent', drive and a little luck can indeed succeed in the system as it stands.

What is missing is a grounded account of the socioeconomic and political processes that keep the poor poor and the rich rich, irrespective of their cultural background. What is missing is a real-world analysis of the failures of our productive industries, our labour markets, our schools, our welfare systems and our communities, and an inspiring account of how these things can be rebuilt and set to the task of improving the lives of all. What is missing is a powerful challenge to the deeply embedded reverence of money wealth, and an insistent call to find value elsewhere in our lives. What is missing is a detailed critical understanding of the processes of credit issue and financial investment, under which whole regions or nations can prosper or decline. And, of course, what is missing is a compelling vision of the future; a vision that includes all by right, and in which every individual is equipped with the entitlements and opportunities they need to build a good and satisfying life.

In pursuing this course, the left has tended to get everything back to front. Rather than holding cultural identity on high, the left should have pushed it into the background and reiterated the core claim of unity and common interests. Once, on the left, difference was considered dialectical. It was assumed that differences could be brought together to produce a higher unity. Now, on the left, accounts of difference so often fall into the trap of relativism. There are no truths, no objective measures, no universal values: all we have are 'differences', which must be respected for what they are.

And how has the liberal left's unwavering support for cosmopolitanism worked out in the context of global neoliberalism? Their dismissal of all Western people attached to a specific place as small-minded, regressive and bigoted tends to run parallel with their willingness to countenance, and occasionally endorse, the commodification of the entire globe. The free movement of labour, goods and capital across borders is, of course, an integral part of this process. During the deindustrialisation process in the 1980s, many traditional industries in the West were abruptly and unsentimentally discarded as it became clear to investors that greater profits could be generated elsewhere. To many working people in the West, especially those from the former agricultural and industrial heartlands, the liberal ideal of untethered free movement has become indelibly associated with dereliction and ruin.

The liberal left has, generally speaking, displayed very little sympathy for communities adversely affected by fluctuations in global labour markets. Some among the left's activist class have gone so far as announcing that they are happy to see the back of the inward-looking, bigoted and exclusionary cultures they imagine grew alongside traditional industries. Such views reflect what has been for over a hundred years a carefully hidden class antagonism. However, flushed out and animated by Brexit, Trump and the emergence of national populism, many on the liberal left have now dispensed with the pretence that they are motivated by a desire to defend and advance working-class interests. They appear to feel justified in dropping their advocacy at least partly because they believe a working class deprived of the cultural education they offer will be incorrigibly regressive and illiberal.

It is very difficult to imagine how the great gulf between the working class and the middle-class liberals who now dominate the left can be closed. The differences appear too great. Large sections of the white working class are scornful of the middle-class left's assumed intellectual leadership. They consider the liberal left to be disinterested in their struggles and uncomfortable with their cultural concerns. Ethnic minority groups within the working class appear only instrumentally and tenuously engaged with the liberal left's identity politics. Of course, many of these groups are far more culturally conservative than the liberal left is willing to countenance, and it is highly likely that class dynamics – especially the common liberal middle-class assumption that they should lead, and the multi-ethnic working class follow – will unsettle the rather tense and conditional relationship between the two. Culturally conservative members of ethnic minorities do not seem particularly keen to dissolve those aspects of their traditional culture the liberal left disapproves of, and it seems inevitable that further fragmentation and conflict lie ahead.

Deaptative cultures

The liberal left refuses to accept the legitimacy of all alternative ethics and political programmes. Opposition to the liberal left's cultural agenda never results in a productive exchange of views. Empirical evidence and traditional accounts of reason are of little use. The liberal left's position is simply assertive: it is sure that its values and politics are beyond logical or ethical dispute. To disagree on any issue – the value of cosmopolitanism, the deleterious consequences of Brexit, systemic white racism – indicates only stupidity, bigotry or both. The liberal left has brought dialogue to a standstill by demanding that only when its ethics are unconditionally accepted can there be any true progress.

To view oneself and one's politics as incontrovertibly superior to all others is to deny Kant's categorical imperative and transform those around us into a means of achieving desired ends, rather than ends in themselves. For some on the cultural left, the consequences of deindustrialisation are considered collateral damage on the road to a better future, free from the working class's residual bigotry. Only those capable of crawling from the wreckage to adopt the doctrines of the liberal left and take up arms in the fight for 'social justice' are worthy of a place in the new world.

Some sections of the traditional working class are now experiencing a process of deaptation, a concept developed by the philosopher Adrian Johnston.[2] As one might imagine, deaptation is essentially the opposite of adaptation. Cultures and ideologies that once had a purpose and a clear place in the world are often left behind as mainstream civil society moves forward. Continued subscription to these dead or dying cultures and ideologies results in deaptation – by simply continuing to be him or herself, the individual becomes gradually more distant from the cultural mainstream.

First, many of the traditional working class were told their skills were redundant. To find a job and an income, they would have to change. However, the change required to thrive in the new economy was not simply a matter of updating one's skills. Often, one was required to change one's identity and demeanour too, to become more biddable, personable and marketable as a service worker or entrepreneur. One needed to let go of the past and commit to the transitory logic of the present, while also remaining agile and ready to adapt again as markets continued to remake the world.

It also became clear that these men and women could no longer count on the unequivocal support of the liberal left and its institutions. Union membership shrank alongside the benefits of membership as the ideological gap between the workers and their senior representatives began to grow. This gap was even wider in the main centre-left political parties. Most politicians had their eyes focused on floating voters in the middle class, and all but a tiny minority had accepted and begun to champion the supremacy of the global market system that had stripped the working class of traditional forms of industrial employment, status and security.

Then it seemed that the working class's attachment to traditional neighbourhoods, towns, regions and nations was considered atavistic and unsuited to the new cosmopolitan era. Over time, many began to feel increasingly alienated from popular culture. The great consumer prizes on offer there were out of reach, and there seemed to be increasingly little in the popular entertainment sphere that spoke to their own attitudes and experiences.

The outcome is that those who subscribe to deaptative cultures and ideologies feel set apart from the world. The world often seems unusual or unrecognisable. They no longer have a practical function to fulfil. They look on as the engine of history motors into the future, knowing that, whatever the destination, it is not for them.

One might assume that deaptation is simply about ageing. Over time, older people inevitably feel separated from a world that continues to change and move forward. However, this assumption tends to overlook the fact that, throughout the world, young people continue to be socialised into what are essentially deaptative cultures. Parents pass on to their children skills, attitudes, beliefs, values and norms that in truth will not be of great service to them if their goal is to move into corporate employment and find a place in the new cosmopolitan, technologically mediated cultural mainstream. To turn things around they must ditch their deaptative cultural inheritance and commit to the process of adaptation. But, of course, abandoning what one is in one's bones in order to become something more suited to our imperfect and increasingly unstable world is not at all straightforward, and nor is it without political significance.

Emotivism

Rather than engage in a productive discussion when questioned on any aspect of its broad cultural vision, the liberal left responds immediately with what Alisdair MacIntyre[3] called 'emotivism'. The liberal left believes its strength of feeling should carry the day, and its depth of commitment to its mission should immediately silence dissenting voices. Emotivism is inherently manipulative. Protagonists will talk about how your dissent offends, scares or harms them, or how rationality and basic moral decency require you to curtail your critique and accept their superior logic and moral probity. The reaction is instant *ad hominem* – they will ignore the actual argument itself, make immediate assumptions about the evil motives driving it, and ruthlessly mock and condemn the person making it. For example, only a racist would question the cultural left's commitment to open borders, and there is no sense in debating a racist. Therefore, the actual substance of your argument can be immediately disregarded without so much as a cursory inspection.

It is not solely the liberal left who draw upon emotivism. For MacIntyre, the ubiquity of emotivism suggests that we have lost our shared commitment to universal morality and logic, which, of course, are the products of engaging in dialogue to sift consequential evidence and appraise sentiments, arguments and intellectual positions from across the political spectrum. Consider, for example, the ongoing debate about abortion. This debate has become entirely non-dialectical. It is stuck at the level of mere assertion and cannot move forward because there is no shared commitment to universal rationality or morality. There is no longer a universally accepted yardstick by which to measure the veracity of an argument, and consequently both sides have succumbed to emotivism. No concessions, compromises or progress can be made, and both sides wage an endless war of mutual defamation.

At a fundamental level, both sides are right, at least in the terms they themselves have set. Yes, every human life should be treated as intrinsically valuable. To dispense with one human life because it threatens to impede the freedom of another is wrong. And yes, women should have the right to determine what happens to their bodies. It is tragic that so many women feel compelled to continue with an unwanted pregnancy, and the diverse forms of misery and harm that often result should never be minimised or ignored. Some women are subject to sustained sexual violence, and to be forced to carry the resulting child to term is a terrifying imposition. And, yes, many pregnancies result from simple mistakes, and to ask very young women to shoulder the burden of raising an unwanted child also breaches common decency.

Attempts to identify a final, convincing piece of evidence that will at long last bring the argument to a close – for example, debates about the development of the foetus in the womb and at what stage the foetus can feel pain or be described as fully 'human' – generally tend to ignore the fundamental paradox by burrowing deeper into already established arguments. In the absence of a universal morality, the argument about abortion simply cannot be brought to a satisfactory conclusion. All that can be done is for an authority to identify one side as the winner.

The degradation of universal morality and logic prevents us from communicating with each other and moving forward as a collective using reason, evidence and honest evaluation to guide us as we develop fundamental ethics and practices. Instead, we preach to each other like clerics representing a profusion of unassailable bespoke positions that cannot be brought together in constructive tension. Thus, politics today tends to be about winning, and when victory is achieved, the interests of one alliance of communities tend to advance at the expense of another. As one might imagine, MacIntyre's preference is for a politics that advances the interests of all people, free from the forms of emotive antagonism pushing Western society deeper into a new Dark Age.

Paradoxes

The liberal left, then, has meekly accepted the neoliberal right's economic model and papered over the harms of neoliberal socioeconomic transformation with the perceived benefits of cosmopolitanism, free movement, cultural fluidity and personal freedom. Commitment to cosmopolitanism requires acceptance that anyone should be free to move around the globe to wherever they can find a job that pays an adequate income. In Britain, we see this concretely in the liberal left's dedication to the EU's free movement of labour policy. However, this dedication to an abstract ideal glosses over a whole series of awkward facts. Perhaps one of the most significant and consistently overlooked is the relative poverty and lack of investment that blights EU migrants' homelands and drives many non-professionals to what in the more affluent member states is a subsistence income in the service economy.

Instead, many on the liberal left assume that such migration is driven by the individual's desire to expand his or her horizons, experience other cultures and exercise the inalienable rights of individual freedom and choice. Few appear willing to think about the negative effect that outward migration has upon the countries of origin. Even if we restrict our discussion to practicalities, it is perfectly clear that consumer demand and productivity fall as talented people of working age leave. Outward migration thus damages the economic health of countries that already lag behind neighbouring EU states.

Left-liberals are quick to identify key industries that rely on the labour of immigrants to make the point that immigrants make a significant contribution to our economy. However, in making this argument, they inevitably ignore the obvious fact that high levels of migrant labour in the larger economies of Western Europe tend to deprive the smaller economies of Eastern Europe of both skilled and unskilled workers. The same is true when the liberal left highlights the number of doctors and nurses from Africa and Asia working in the NHS. We in Britain can, of course, be grateful for the contributions of these workers, but we must also note that, because they are here, they are not there. Many parts of Africa and Asia sorely need healthcare workers, and it seems regressively nationalistic to assume that the exportation of highly skilled workers to an already large and diversified economy such as Britain's should be considered a positive process, especially given Britain has the capacity to train large numbers of healthcare workers should it choose to do so.

Wouldn't it make more sense for left-liberals to claim that Britain should be urgently training doctors with a view to despatching them around the world to assist nations with far less training capacity? Of course, such issues tend not to be considered because despite its injustices the consequential logic of the global marketplace is considered unchallengeable and therefore not worth discussing. Doctors move from Africa to Britain because they can secure a much better wage. The same cannot be said for British doctors open to the prospect of moving to Africa to practise their calling. Underneath cosmopolitan culture lies personal instrumentalism and the great and often unacknowledged power of capital investment.

Worse, some on the liberal left suggest that, because British workers are not willing to accept the low wages that predominate in the lower reaches of the service sector, we need foreign workers to keep these industries operational. That such arguments are made by professed leftists really beggars belief. Often, there is an implied critique of the lazy 'native' working class – now multi-ethnic for close to four generations – who prefer the mythical comforts of unemployment to the prospect of taking up a job at the bottom of the service sector, which seems to justify ongoing calls to import a low-wage workforce.

When labour shortages exist in a large and highly diversified economy like Britain's, it tends to mean employers are not willing to pay the proper market rate. Of course, if they were to raise wages, employers would not struggle to attract applicants. Businesses that rely on incredibly low wage rates are, in reality, contributing very little of value to our economy and culture. The traditional left never hesitated to say so. Perhaps today's left should open itself up to the possibility that in some instances wages have been kept artificially low in order to facilitate higher profits and attract inward investment, and migrant workers are mere pawns on this board. That criticism tends to fall upon the native working class who refuse to take up such jobs should give us all pause for thought. This sort of belief should occasion the left to reflect upon a fundamental relation that it has avoided for at least four decades – the hidden ties that bind the liberal left and the neoliberal right.

Neoliberalism's transformation of Western labour markets stripped many working-class communities of the partial security offered during the modern industrial age. As the wealth gap widened while real wages and job security declined, the disproportionate influence of the rich could be felt in every sphere of social life, whereas the voices of the poor could scarcely be heard at all. This profoundly negative story of neoliberal economic change sits alongside the liberal left's positive story of the onward march of tolerance, openness, freedom and progressive cultural change.

The superficial compromise is to weigh the perceived benefits of neoliberalism against its perceived negativities, before reaching the common-sense conclusion that, on balance, the present order has some good points and some bad points, but it certainly isn't all bad. Competition and insecurity have increased, but we do have new technological devices and the transitory pleasures of the consumer sphere. Problems and injustices abound, but we are generally more tolerant of 'otherness'. The nasty right-wingers are in office at the moment, but in five years' time we will have the opportunity to change things.

Liberalism has turned the left into a relativistic utilitarian calculator of the least-worst consequences. As populations were encouraged to divide themselves into competing victim-claimant groups, the fundamental objective of political struggle shifted from the founding of a fairer socioeconomic system to the quest for a guarantee that a greater share of the system's benefits will be given to one's chosen micro-community. As we have seen, the traditional realm of antagonistic politics died out as the left's ambitions shifted, fragmented and shrank.

While typically overlooked in academic research and in popular political commentary, we must note that the liberal left and the neoliberal right have a shared heritage in liberal ideology. The neoliberal right, at a fundamental level, seeks to advance the economic freedoms of the global investment and corporate business class, whereas the liberal left tries to advance the freedoms of minority groups who suffer under the yoke of Western cultural orthodoxies. Unrestrained freedom and rights – not obligation, solidarity, economic security, community cohesion or social betterment – is the fuel that drives both of these political positions, despite the fact that they are regularly presented as opposites.

While they continue to clash theatrically on our news broadcasts and in parliamentary chambers, their ostentatious enmity disguises the broad range of issues upon which they agree. As we have already noted, the liberal left has generally accepted the neoliberal right's economic programme, but that is not all. The neoliberal right's abandonment of any lingering attachment to traditional conservatism has enabled it to endorse the liberal left's cultural programme. For example,

David Cameron's call for a softer, kinder form of conservatism sought to couple together hardcore neoliberalism with cultural progressivism. The ideological ties that bind the liberal left to the neoliberal right are out in the open and obvious for anyone willing to take an honest and objective look for themselves.

In more recent times, perhaps from 2015 onwards, the liberal left flipped the standard account of incremental progress on the field of culture on its head. Still silent on economic matters, key cultural activists now claim that societies are no longer moving away from the bigotries of the past. In fact, there is now more bigotry than ever: racism of all kinds is on the march, 'toxic masculinity' is embedded in every culture and institution, and new bigotries – such as hatred of disabled and transgender people, or even hatred of the activist class itself – are proliferating with frightening rapidity. Therefore, the need to rid the world of regressive attitudes and diverse forms of bigotry is more urgent than ever.

To some extent this claim is valid, but we suspect that it is right for the wrong reasons. The need to unite so that we are better able to face down the problems of the present and the future seems to us perfectly obvious, but for the liberal left unity can only be achieved once the injustices of the cultural field have been brought out into the open, and all accept the central tenets of its ideology. For the moment, at least, and despite evidence that racism and sexism in Western nations continue to decline, there are compelling reasons to believe that we may see cultural antagonisms grow in the years ahead. Of course, the problems of the present result largely from the failures of the past, and not insignificant amongst those failures is the liberal left's wilful disregard for universalism and common interests.

Keeping it simple

The liberal left's cultural approach has limited intellectual and political life by displacing complexity with simplistic single causes. For instance, the emphasis now placed on hatred has drawn attention away from the underpinning contexts and multiple causes of enmity and social division. The discourse that has arisen around hate crime is an obvious example.

The identification of hatred as the principal emotion at work in crimes that target those who display the markers of a minority identity simplifies what is, in reality, a far more complex picture. It puts the analytical cart before the horse, inasmuch as the processual logic of 'hate crime' starts with a conclusion – the crime was caused by hate – rather than the standard exploratory question; what is the fundamental cause of this crime?

We might reasonably speculate that some of the offenders convicted of 'hate crimes' might not have been truly motivated by 'hatred'. Hatred is rarely a fixed emotional state, and it tends to bleed into associated emotions. An accurate account of criminal motivation is far more complex and requires an analysis of immediate contextual stimuli and deeper-lying dispositions, attitudes and beliefs, and the emotions to which such things give rise. If we must identify a basic emotional state as the cause of crimes against individuals displaying the markers of a minority identity, then insecurity is a far more useful starting point for analysis. Isn't such hostility to difference an obvious indicator of insecurity? Why is the offender so offended by the presence of cultural diversity? There is a multitude of questions one might ask here that push us beyond the initial assumption of 'hatred'. We might also speculate that investigating the experience of insecurity should make clear the fundamental need of all individuals to find a secure foundation upon which to build a life. It is only when we are secure – economically, psychologically, culturally and so on – that we can truly begin to push towards the traditional left's conception of a good life based on friendly relations, shared prosperity and a rich common culture.

We have seen, since the parallel rise of neoliberalism and postmodernism, a resolute, ongoing attempt to strip all people of social, economic and psychic security in the name of freedom. The outcomes of this destructive assault have been entirely negative. Western culture is riven by diverse and corrosive forms of insecurity – psychological, cultural, social and economic. The liberal left, and especially those who have embraced liberal postmodernism, have presented traditional sources of security – for example, religious doctrine, community affiliations, steady jobs and fixed identities – as fetters upon freedom. We were enjoined to fight our way free from such attachments.

We were told that we could be whatever we wanted to be. We could transform our identities at a whim, move around the world and finally take control of our own lives by accepting constant change and the insecurities that come with freedom. However, despite the sales pitch, stripping away traditional sources of security, especially in the economic realm, has not resulted in a positive sense of freedom. The working class, for instance, was certainly not freed by the disappearance of reasonably stable and remunerative labour markets, which for many were the durable bedrock of prosperity, identity and community.

Freedom should not be considered a good in itself, but a crucial vehicle for other goods. Freedom can be a thrilling train to ride, but ultimately what counts is that it takes you to an appealing destination. Positioning freedom as our highest cultural value begs obvious yet rarely asked questions. Freedom, yes, but to what end? Where are these supposed new freedoms taking us? What are these freedoms enabling us to do? Why, in the midst of all these freedoms, do so many experience life as restricted, unfulfilling and ultimately hollow? Where are the true freedoms of those chained to mortgages, endlessly recurring bills and student debts, or terrorised by the threat of unemployment, or dependent on drink or drugs, or unhappy about their bodies, or anxious about their personal safety and worried more than ever about how they are perceived by others? What of the freedoms of those growing up in desperate poverty, attending woeful schools, terrorised by perpetual threats, or subjected to the obscene freedom of others? Should liberals tell these people to rejoice because they are free to travel the world, work in any industry and worship a god of their own choosing, free to redefine themselves through their consumer choices and free to build a life for themselves free from the coddling institutions of the old order?

In the absence of all other clearly identifiable and practically attainable ethical goods, the liberal postmodern account of freedom hinges upon the simple claim that we should be able to do whatever we like without having to pause to reflect upon how we may negatively affect others. As we will see later, postmodernism set out to destroy 'truth'. It certainly succeeded in destabilising traditional accounts of justice, fairness and common interests, just as it poured scorn on the sanctity of altruism and our traditional disdain for unrestrained self-interest. Traditional conceptions of morality, reason and decency restricted our freedoms by compelling us to live in the shadow of myths. These things were, postmodernists told us, simply 'constructs' that reflected established systems of power. There was no God. Scientific reason could never be objective. Cultural rules and regulations were impediments to personal freedom. The people were urged to discard all attachments to such constructs and narratives, assert their freedom and decide for themselves.

In the act of freeing us all from traditional restraints, what postmodernists did was to wreck the platforms of security we need to understand ourselves and our place in the world. Feeling valued, understood and secure in our identity and material well-being provides the infrastructure we need to build a satisfying life. The left simply forgot that the continuity of such an infrastructure, although flexible and open to reform over time, is felt by a majority of working people to be essential to their survival, security and sanity. To paraphrase G.K. Chesterton, there is nothing particularly inspiring about having an open mind; the goal of opening the mind, just like opening the mouth, is to close it on something solid. Identifying the things that are solid, that truly matter to ordinary people, and constructing a viable and convincing plan to maintain, revive or bring these things into being, would have allowed the left to address neoliberalism's fundamental flaws and injustices. It was not to be.

Despite ongoing election defeats and the gradual dissolution of its traditional support, the left has made progress on the field of culture. Culture, of course, has been the liberal left's chosen battleground for decades. The liberal left's progress here reflects the huge amount of effort it has applied to displacing the right in key cultural institutions. Leftist academics' traditional denunciation of mainstream media as incorrigibly right-wing – until the 1990s largely correct – neglects the liberal left's recent successes in supplanting the right in many mainstream media outlets.[4] The liberal left has also resoundingly defeated the right to take ideological control of the university, and it seems to be making considerable headway in our schools. The liberal left has won many victories on the field of culture. We must acknowledge, however, that the neoliberal right doesn't seem to care. In fact, it often seems to encourage the liberal left to pursue further cultural victories, secure in the knowledge that these clashes create the impression that real politics continues, and that the system is evolving in line with popular sentiments. The neoliberal right seems remarkably confident that, as long as the liberal left stays away from the field of political economy, its continued supremacy is assured.

Rainbow capitalism

The clearest indicator of the ideological alignment of the liberal left and the neoliberal right is the corporatisation of critical race theory.[5] Bob Iger, who was until recently CEO of the Disney Corporation, can now encourage his staff to 'check their privilege', 'decolonise their bookshelves' and 'pay reparations' while amassing a personal fortune of around $690 million.[6] Lockheed Martin, the United States' largest defence contractor, made somewhere in the region of $60 billion in 2019 alone. Around 70 per cent of the company's income comes from the United States federal government. In fact, Lockheed Martin accounts for 28 per cent of the US Department of Defense's total military procurement budget.[7] Given that the corporation trades in armaments and much of its day-to-day business involves devising new and efficient ways to kill, it is difficult to comprehend precisely why this titan of the military industrial complex and long-time *bête noire* of the activist left might want to associate itself with critical race theory. And yet it now sends white male executives on a diversity training programme aimed at deconstructing their white male culture and having them atone for their white privilege, before sending them back out to develop new weapons systems that are usually aimed at men, women and children with black or brown skin.[8]

Many large American corporations now go out of their way to present themselves as rich patrons and active partners in the struggle for social justice. At the same time, they import low-wage workers, outsource production to low-wage nations, offshore profits to tax havens, hand out redundancy notices and cut workers' pay and benefits wherever possible. The basic message is quite clear. Corporate America can get behind the cause of racial and gender equality and a broad range of LGBTQ+ issues precisely because these cultural causes do not impede profitability. Accepting the cultural agenda of the activist left also allows corporations to launder their reputations for rapacious greed by cultivating an image of politically correct corporate citizenship.

Corporations are now willing to increase the number of women and ethnic minorities in the upper echelons of their institutional structures.[9] They are also happy to do all they can to root out racism and have staff undergo unconscious bias training. However, they do not appear particularly keen to open a dialogue on increasing rates of pay for their most poorly paid employees, some of whom will, of course, come from minority ethnic groups. The corporate adoption of the liberal left's language and cultural concerns is obviously a calculated move driven by material self-interest, but more telling for us is the liberal left's general acceptance of the corporate world's patronage and alliance.

Many on the liberal left are happy to watch as the corporate system again sheds its skin so that it can survive by adapting to new political realities, demographic changes and cultural mores. Rather than see huge global corporations as a source of injustice, they are happy to accept their sponsorship in their ongoing war against the injustices of the racial and gender orders. Of course, the symbolism of cultural progress is considered paramount, and the economic dimension of everyday life is rarely discussed. Corporations have now joined the liberal left in the symbolic fight against racism and sexism, and they are happy to transform themselves into a welcoming environment for the LGBTQ+ community. In return, the liberal left has agreed to remain relatively silent about the negative effects of corporate power.

How did we arrive at this lamentable position? To get to the heart of the matter, we go back to the formation of the modern left.

4

Beginnings

The roots of the left are to be found in the early industrial age. Demands for equality, political representation, rights at work and better care for the poor can be traced further back in recorded history, but it was during this epoch that the left grew in confidence and popularity, taking on many of the characteristics and policies that became synonymous with leftist politics.

The dawning of the industrial age transformed our societies in ways that are difficult to fully appreciate today. Western nations urbanised swiftly during the nineteenth century as the established features of the agrarian economy fell away. Towns and cities that hosted new sites of industrial production grew rapidly as workers from around the country, and sometimes further afield, moved in search of work. Many traditional aspects of pre-industrial culture and identity were lost entirely while others quickly adapted to fit in with the new world.

In both Britain and the United States, industrial production was for some time largely unregulated. Industrial workers were often subjected to extreme danger and exploitation. This is not to say that ordinary men and women lived lives of boundless freedom and fulfilment before the dawning of the industrial age. Child labour, for instance, was entrenched in small-scale manufacturing sites and throughout much of the agricultural system before large-scale factories became a common feature of industrial towns and cities.[1] Industrialism did, however, change the nature and our expectations of work.

The literature on Western industrialism is too voluminous to summarise here. What we want to do is bring into relief the sources of agitation and piecemeal reform that qualitatively improved workers' lives and opened doors through which they could step and exercise at least some influence on politics and economic life. When in the nineteenth century improvements did come, they derived from the agitation of evangelical Christians as much as the activities of trade unions and other sections of the organised left. The power of trade unions grew gradually throughout the nineteenth century, but they were not all animated by the relatively new and growing philosophy of socialism.

Christian campaigners for social reform – the most notable of whom tended to be middle class and endowed with the confidence and eloquence needed to solicit the support of the largely aristocratic political classes – capitalised upon a prevailing sense of *noblesse oblige* among Christian elites. In highlighting, for example, the unchristian degradations suffered by innocent children born into squalor and hardship, evangelical Christian groups used linguistic skills and knowledge of moral codes to implore and shame key members of the political establishment in the direction of reform. They also drew a good deal of public and political attention to particular social causes, often to significant effect. Of course, these evangelical Christian groups tended to have neither a deep technical knowledge of economics or economic history, nor a programmatic or structural approach to social, political and economic change. However, some Christian activists certainly were confirmed socialists who understood their political and religious beliefs to be intertwined.

Roots of the left in Britain

Morgan Phillips, once General Secretary of the Labour Party, is usually identified as the first to have claimed that the development of the British Labour Party owed more to Methodism than to Marxism. This basic observation has been repeated countless times, often in a tongue-in-cheek manner with the goal of delivering a sly dig at the stuffiness and technocratic coldness of the Labour Party, particularly its dominant right wing. But there is also some truth in Phillips' old claim. Methodism grew quickly during the early industrial period. Much of its success can be traced back to its evangelical mission to move beyond the confines of the Anglican Church and reach out to the poor wherever they may be. John Wesley and his followers offered practical as well as spiritual help to those in need. He stressed that all were equal in God's eyes. Every life was valuable, and every individual was loved by God. These most basic of Christian sentiments inspired some among the working class to believe that the power and authority of the capitalist class was unjust. If God loved all people and valued every life, how could an economic system that exploited some to enrich others be allowed to remain intact? Why were such obscene inequalities allowed to stand when all were equal before God?

E.P. Thompson, the famous Marxist historian, saw things differently. Thompson was in many respects a liberal Marxist, if it is possible to imagine such a thing. He was resolutely committed to the humanistic aspect of Marx's work and paid very little attention to the structure and operation of the capitalist economy. Thompson's humanist Marxism prompted in him an unyielding idealism that encouraged him to present the English working class as naturally politicised and antagonistic to injustice, and always ready to rise up against their oppressors. Thompson was an idealist because in his written work he presented the working class as he wished them to be rather than as they were in reality. The working class throughout the industrial epoch were in fact quite variegated in their ethics, political views and social behaviour, and the same is true today.

Thompson saw no value whatsoever in the complex theoretical work undertaken by post-Marxists on the continent. He believed this work to be unnecessarily pessimistic and obscure. While Gramsci and Althusser believed that the working class had been drawn into capitalism's ideological project, Thompson believed that the working class had proven itself capable of rising up against its oppressors on countless occasions. Gramsci and Althusser's complex work on ideology suggested that the working class had accepted the basic parameters of the world as it is presented to them. They accepted the goals of capitalist societies and their economic role and social position as workers. They accepted the established means of social advancement. They accepted that some are rich and some poor, and they learnt to find their pleasures wherever they could. For Gramsci especially, it was the job of leftist intellectuals to rid the world of the gaudy shroud of positivity and inevitability that had been thrown over it, in order to reveal the brutal reality that lay underneath. Workers toiled every day to enrich a class of exploiters who had structured the world to suit their own interests.

For Thompson, to suggest that the working class lacked insight and agency to the extent that they could be hoodwinked in this way was offensive. The life experiences of men and women from the industrial working class meant that they knew the reality of capitalism in a great deal of detail. Thompson spent much of his time as a historian identifying specific instances in which the working class had risen up to fight oppression. He was not short of material, but then history is a rather expansive terrain. Historians who go looking for material that will act as evidence to support their already established ideological preferences are rarely disappointed.

Thompson's focus on the specific events and conjunctures that seemed to him redolent of class conflict inevitably ignored the expansive gaps of time and space in between, when the working class quietly accepted its subordination. His careful, selective empiricism disguised his idealism, and specifically his idealisation of the working class. For Thompson, the working class needed neither an intellectual vanguard nor an ideological blueprint of a better world. They were shrewder and more politically astute than anyone gave them credit for. They would use their latent collective power to defend their interests whenever the capitalist class grabbed too much of the spoils for themselves or encroached too far upon their vibrant, organic cultures.

The Thompsonites won the battle for the soul of British Marxism. The humanist aspect of Marx's work was to take precedence over the grubby business of economic analysis and the intellectually far more taxing terrain of ideology critique. British Marxism remains resolutely idealist, inasmuch as it tends to assume that the working class are autonomous liberal socialists, and that class conflict continues every day on the field of culture. In this way, the total triumph of post-war capitalism can be disavowed, and the tiniest fleeting instance of cultural iconoclasm can be interpreted as a victory for the working class – or more recently, the 'marginalised' – against their historic oppressors. Even today, as we embark upon yet another epochal shift in global capitalist political economy, many British Marxists and socialists continue to assume that all born poor are by nature anti-capitalists and await an opportune moment to spill onto the streets to enact their dream of a classless society.

This division between humanist and materialist Marxists may seem marginal to the development of the left in Britain. It is certainly true that Marxists have failed to achieve as much power on the left as they would have wished, and that their place in the Labour Party and the broader trade union movement has, since the nineteenth century, been quite minimal. However, this basic division – between liberal humanists on one side and materialists and realists on the other – has proven to be quite important for the development of the broader intellectual and cultural environment of the British left. As we shall see later, the New Left of the 1950s and 1960s was greatly influenced by Thompson's humanist Marxism and did in fact influence the general trajectory of the Labour Party during these decades. Similarly, many of the intellectual trends we will outline and criticise in the latter half of the book are rooted in liberal humanism and its disinterest in material reality.

Thompson acknowledged Methodism's influence on the development of left in Britain, but for him it was always dysfunctional. Methodism, like all other religions, encouraged the oppressed to accept the immutability of earthly struggles and focus on freedom in the hereafter. It sapped their oppositional energies, and, while encouraging sympathy for those who struggled, it did little more than provide what Thompson called a 'moral machinery' that complemented and sat alongside the machinery of industrial capitalism.[2] Many other historians of this period disagree with Thompson's analysis. Most seem to concur that Methodism spurred rather than curtailed protest.[3]

Methodism, and other new religious movements of the nineteenth century, encouraged the men and women of the working class to come together and discuss their shared plight, and also provided forums in which they could listen to radical preachers, some of whom possessed considerable pulpit craft and were capable of imparting knowledge, moving the emotions and inspiring people to dream of change. Many of the leftists who developed a significant profile in the early years of socialism in Britain came from a Methodist background, and some had been lay preachers. These men had grown accustomed to public oratory and knew the tricks of the trade. They had a reasonable grasp of what worked when attempting to win support, and there can be little doubt that for them the drive to rid the world of hideous forms of exploitation was deeply felt.

We should not underestimate the role oratorical skill played in the rise of socialism in the nineteenth century. Speakers who possessed a reputation for being able to move an audience with powerful rhetoric attracted eager crowds, and in the intoxicating atmosphere of a political meeting or a stump speech delivered to a crowd of industrial workers, hearts and minds could be won for the cause. In Northern England in particular, socialists who came to national prominence often used religious tropes when speaking to the assembled masses. Themes of redemption, obligation, self-sacrifice, the godly imperative to help one's fellow man and through earthly deeds prove oneself worthy of entering the kingdom of heaven certainly drew in many who had little time for hazy Marxist abstractions. Speeches heavy with religious references and themes tended to be of less use in the South, and especially in London, where the working class appears to have been more secular in its political tastes.

Methodists, and other Christian denominations, were also connected to the temperance movement. The drive to free the working class from the evils of alcohol was a thorny issue for the left, but it was one they could scarcely avoid. Alcohol and recreation in public houses were firmly established as features of male working-class culture, and many early socialists were of the view that the first practical step members of the working class could take to improve their standard of living was to rid themselves of their reliance on alcohol.

The temperance movement in Britain was a creation of the more devout elements of the progressive middle class. It is easy to make the argument that temperance became a part of the early socialist movement in Britain against the wishes of the majority of the working class, who often greatly valued the release and relaxation that came with a drink at the end of a long and exhausting working day. There was great commitment on both sides of the argument. Some leftist political figures, especially in the early days of the Independent Labour Party, were understandably pragmatic and believed that the majority of the working class would not support a political party committed to taking away one of its most valued and longstanding cultural outlets. Others had seen at first hand the damage excessive alcohol could do in working-class families and communities.

Keir Hardie, who in 1892 became the first socialist to sit in the House of Commons and is now considered as the founding father of British socialism, took the pledge to abstain at the age of seventeen. Hardie threw his support behind Gladstone's Liberal Party as it began to move in a concerted manner towards social reform. It was only later that he became a prominent figure in the early Independent Labour Party, winning seats in West Ham South and then Merthyr Tydfil.

Hardie has a reputation as a pragmatist, but very often he persevered with policy proposals that were not supported by his prospective working-class constituents. He seems to have seen the cause of socialism as a series of loosely connected struggles rather than a model for a future society built upon economic justice and inclusivity. He attached himself to causes which seemed redolent of injustice, and he stuck to his guns and refused to yield ground even when many of his fellow socialists were moving in the opposite direction. A Scotsman who received his political education in the trade union movement, he often failed to connect to local populations and acclimatise himself to local working-class customs and traditions as he moved around the country in search of a parliamentary seat. Other notable figures, including Arthur Henderson, George Lansbury and Herbert Morrison, were also determined abstainers and supported legislation to curtail the drinks trade whenever the opportunity arose. Like Hardie, they knew of alcohol's often deleterious impact upon working-class families, and they held the firm view that the negatives of alcohol greatly outweighed its positive cultural qualities.

Of course, many others in the early socialist movement disagreed. The focus upon actually winning office – so that they could enact an ambitious and transformative programme that greatly boosted the living standards of the working class – was such that in the latter decades of the nineteenth century the labour movement seemed to revolve around a dogged pragmatism that resulted from their firm belief in the importance of their mission. However, in order to be in a position to enact the wide-ranging social reform they wanted, they would have to do what needed to be done to win office.

This pragmatism often clashed against the obvious idealism of some in the movement who were committed to fighting against the diverse injustices of industrial society, even if that meant alienating voters and other socialists. From the outset there was a stark cultural divide between those on the left who advocated temperance, religion and socialism's moral mission and those who accepted the place of drink in working-class culture, understood the appeal of patriotism and secularism, and saw socialism as a movement to disempower the elite and advance the material interests of the industrial working class. These two rudimentary factions clashed on a whole series of issues. While the boundaries between them were not always clear or constant, in their clashes they subtly established the internal dynamics of modern British socialism.

A clear example of the cultural antagonisms between these two groups can be seen as the campaign for female suffrage came to a crescendo. In a similar way to the ongoing internal squabbles over temperance, the campaign for female suffrage had a decidedly middle-class feel to it. Most suffragettes were middle class. The suffragettes were willing to align themselves with any political body that promised to assist in their struggle, and while there were connections between the suffragettes and the Independent Labour Party and other leftist institutions, it would be an overstatement to suggest this represented an unambiguous meeting of minds.

The Pankhursts, Richard and Emmeline, were long-time campaigners for a variety of progressive causes before achieving prominence in the campaign for female suffrage. They were certainly not fly-by-night opportunists, keen to exploit the growing political power of the labour movement. However, their early campaigning for social causes fitted very firmly into the long tradition of middle-class liberal benevolentism. This is not to say that the various causes they attached themselves to were inconsequential or that their reformist crusades had not yielded some benefits for working people. However, for some on the left, especially those who hailed from the working class and were principally aligned to the trade union movement, the Pankhursts and other middle- and upper-class progressives were unwelcome interlopers who assumed it was their right to determine the movement's priorities. Their pet projects always seemed to take precedence over the long-term drive to transform the material fortunes of the industrial working class. And they never seemed content to merely contribute or lend support from the side-lines. They wanted to be out at the front and leading, while members of the industrial working class – those who had real 'skin in the game', as the Americans often say – were expected to follow.

The issue rumbled on for some time. Keir Hardie, who had grown very close to Sylvia Pankhurst, was a confirmed supporter of the cause, as was George Lansbury, who as an older man would take on the leadership of the Labour Party. On the other side of the argument was Ramsay MacDonald, who would go on to be Labour's first Prime Minister in 1924. As the actions of the suffragettes became more extreme, MacDonald, who had grown up in poverty in the north of Scotland, dismissed the group as 'pettifogging middle-class damsels'.[4]

The failure of Labour to unequivocally back the suffragettes' cause prompted Lansbury to resign his seat in order to fight a by-election on the issue. Lansbury's seat was Bow and Bromley in the East End of London. He had lived among the urban working class of the East End from an early age, and he is often credited with a great ability to understand the problems and pressures that bore down upon his constituents. He was certainly a deeply committed activist. He went to prison briefly for supporting the direct action of the suffragettes, and he was again locked up in 1921 for his involvement in the Poplar rates revolt. However, on this occasion he seemed not to be particularly in tune with his constituents. He was soundly beaten by a Conservative candidate running on an anti-female-suffrage ticket. Lansbury's actions did not endear him to his Labour colleagues, for whom every Labour seat was of great value in what was a particularly fraught historical moment.

The growing conflict between those on the left who supported the cause and those who believed it to be a strategic minefield best avoided continued to heat up as the suffragettes' tactics became more extreme. Christabel Pankhurst, daughter of Emmeline and Richard, certainly did not help matters. She went as far as to dismiss the Labour Party as the enemy of female suffrage and, despite the fact that the Tories were far from committed to the cause, she encouraged voters in some locales to throw their support behind Conservative Party candidates. Pankhurst's intervention did little to encourage the sympathies of working-class socialists, and animosity deepened towards the suffragettes and others among the middle class who advocated progressive causes divorced from the material interests of the working class.

As members of the trade union movement became more actively involved in the Independent Labour Party and its various satellites, they hoped to dispense with middle-class patronage and define the movement's principal causes on their own terms. However, from very early on it was clear that working-class leftists would struggle to build a movement of their own design and would be forced to accept the presence of middle-class liberals and their various cultural causes at the very centre of their movement. The divide between culturally liberal and culturally conservative leftists cannot be reduced to class alone, and it is vital that we acknowledge the considerable changes that have taken place to what it means to be culturally liberal or culturally conservative over time. However, generally speaking, it is certainly true that those of a more liberal disposition have tended to be middle class and those who are more culturally conservative have tended to be working class. Of course, many members of the working class have been won over to the liberal cause, and the power of liberalism in key institutions has been integral to this process. Today, subscribing to the key tenets of cultural liberalism – or at least successfully feigning one's subscription – has become essential for all members of the working class who attempt to make the journey through the ranks of the professional middle class into positions of political influence.

The campaign for women's suffrage tended to divide the left along these vague but certainly not insignificant lines. Some on the left assumed that votes for women was a matter of conscience and that any opportunity to push the cause forward should be taken, even if that involved working closely with their political opponents. Others were generally in favour of votes for women and believed that all sections of society would be given the vote as soon as the cause of socialism achieved power. However, they did not believe that votes for women should take precedence over the goal of winning a parliamentary majority and forming a government.

At that time, men needed to be property-owners or remain in a single dwelling as the head of a household in order to receive the vote. Of course, this meant that many working-class men, especially in those areas dominated by quite short-term non-unionised work, had yet to receive the vote and so were unable to register their political preferences. The Representation of the People Act 1884 and the Redistribution of Seats Act 1885 together increased the electorate to only a little over half of the adult male population. It was against this background that the campaign for women's suffrage was understood. Equality with men, at least in terms of voting rights, would be of no advantage at all to the vast majority of working-class women, who were even less likely than working-class men to fulfil the established voting criteria. The Labour Party at this time was trying desperately to break through and dislodge one of the two established political parties that dominated British politics. Given Britain's 'first past the post' electoral system, this was a very difficult task that necessitated a Machiavellian approach to political strategy.

While some saw the fight for women's suffrage as a moral issue which required the left's immediate support, others believed the left had little to gain, at least in the short term, by joining the fight. Those women who would be given the vote would be upper- or middle-class property owners and consequently far more likely to vote for the Tories or the Liberals. Only a minuscule number of working-class women would be immediately enfranchised, and so, in practical terms, the party seemed to have more to lose than it had to gain.

Joining the fight for women's suffrage would certainly not lead to an upswing in support for Labour. In fact the opposite appeared to be the case. Working hard to secure a Labour government with a serviceable majority was, for many involved in leftist politics towards the end of the nineteenth century, the best way to ensure that the vote was extended to all people, regardless of their gender or position in the social hierarchy. The answer to the complex problems of political representation wasn't the incremental enlargement of the democratic franchise. The answer was socialism. The quickest and surest route to this destination was the one that should be taken.

For the more culturally conservative elements of the working-class left, it was more important to campaign hard for the interests of the working class, rather than move off course to campaign for the rights of middle-class women. It would be churlish to deny that there was an element of sexism involved in these debates, but again it is vital to consider the context. Gender roles were far clearer and more rigorously enforced in this epoch. The growing radicalism of the suffragettes, especially when it came to the destruction of property, did not fit neatly with the cultural attitudes of the time. However, the distaste of the respectable working class for breaking windows and setting fire to buildings was not simply a reflection of the sexism of the Victorian and Edwardian eras. It also reflected working-class conceptions of value. For an essentially productive class, to destroy things of value, things that took great skill and effort to create, was considered wasteful and pointless. Surely, there were other avenues and opportunities to air one's grievances, especially for these women? And when all was said and done, what did these middle-class women have to complain about, given the horrors that unfolded in the slums, factories and mines every day?

This is not to say that there was no support for women's suffrage among the culturally conservative elements of the working class. Rather, it is to say that many believed the suffragettes' demand for change should be heard after the long and diverse list of material problems experienced by the working class had been addressed. Certainly, if the call had been for *universal* suffrage – that is, votes for all men and all women, regardless of property criteria and the like – there would have been a good deal more support for the cause. While gender is obviously a feature of the left's highly charged debate about political priorities – and the sexism of the time was indeed stark – the crucial issue here is the early establishment of what was to become a growing antipathy between a progressive middle class keen to turn the left to its own evolving cultural agenda and an industrial working class that was just beginning to appoint its own political representatives to address its obvious material needs.

The reform agenda

While the Independent Labour Party was consigned to the margins of British politics with only a small number of MPs, the left could do little to address the social distress clearly exhibited in Britain's industrial towns and cities. However, force was brought to bear on a series of Liberal and Conservative governments who were gradually pushed to address some of the most egregious forms of exploitation exhibited within the new industrial economy. For instance, while the untrammelled exploitation of children could be seen in the cotton mills of the late eighteenth and early nineteenth centuries, throughout the nineteenth century a series of Factory Acts gradually regulated this practice. The Cotton Mills and Factories Act of 1819 made it illegal to employ children under the age of nine and restricted the working hours of children aged nine to sixteen to 12 hours per day. These rights were extended in 1833 to children working in other textile industries, and the working day for children aged over nine years was reduced to ten hours. Of course, many children continued to work in other dangerous and unregulated industries during these years, including mining. It wasn't until 1878, which saw a new Factory and Workshop Act which consolidated existing legislation and extended protections to those who had hitherto fallen through the gaps, that things could truly be said to be moving in the right direction. It became illegal to employ children under the age of ten. Two years later compulsory education was introduced for children aged between five and ten. However, the country had to wait 40 years until the school leaving age was raised to 14. Similar incremental changes benefited working men and women, shortening the working day, guaranteeing lunch breaks and, of course, introducing health and safety protocols that advanced slowly from a very low starting point.

The experiences of the industrial working class in the United States were in many respects quite similar. Industrialism came to the United States a little later and, because of its vast size, older forms of production, exchange and labour exploitation lingered longer. The financial bonanza experienced by the investment and business classes was barely constrained by politicians who were members of those same advantaged social groups. In the shadow of Enlightenment liberalism, the main political parties on both sides of the Atlantic had for many years agreed that the state should not intervene in the private affairs of its citizens. The free hand of the market and the instrumental choices of workers and consumers would provide the growth and relative equilibrium that would in time benefit all.

Against this background, it is little wonder that regulation was slow in coming, despite the obvious hardships experienced by the citizenry. There were small improvements here and there, but it wasn't until the election of Roosevelt and the implementation of his New Deal programme that workers benefited from substantive improvements. The Fair Labor Standards Act of 1938 established the right to a minimum wage, guaranteed 'time-and-a-half' overtime pay for those who clocked up more than 40 hours per week and prohibited the employment of children in most parts of the national economy.[5]

Industrial work was often very dangerous. Workplace deaths were common, and it was not until the twentieth century that compensation for injuries was to be established in law. But deaths were not simply the result of terrible accidents in barely regulated workplaces. A large proportion of deaths resulted from dust and toxins entering the lungs of working men, women and children. John Ruskin, perhaps one of Britain's most prominent nineteenth-century public intellectuals, addressed the effects of industrialism upon the environment in his celebrated book, *The Storm-Cloud of the Nineteenth Century*. The author describes a 'terrible and horrible' thunderstorm observed from his home in the Lake District. The storm left 'one loathsome mass of sultry and foul fog, like smoke' before gradually dissipating, leaving behind the stains of 'Manchester's devil darkness'.[6]

Ruskin had for years observed and written about the natural world, and, without the benefit of scientific evidence, he pointed the finger of blame firmly at the new urban sites of industrial production, the majority of which were powered by coal. At the time, of course, air pollution was poorly understood. However, in places like Manchester, it became gradually more difficult to ignore its corrosive effects. Black sulphurous smoke was often so thick that it blocked out the sun. There was also growing evidence that it destroyed vegetation, corroded buildings, caused public ill-health and, of course, dragged down life expectancy, especially among the working class.

Ruskin's extended commentary is now considered to have presaged the environmental concerns of the late twentieth century and the pugnacious environmentalism of the twenty-first century. He wrote a great deal about the beauty of the natural world and our sacred obligation to defend its wonders. To meekly accept the despoilation of these wonders was a grievous moral offence for which we would pay a heavy price. While Ruskin became more interested in social reform as he aged, and even penned a general critique of classical economics, he was never a true denizen of the left. However, in *The Storm-Cloud of the Nineteenth Century*, he is interested not just in the air pollution but also the moral pollution that followed industrial capitalism, which allowed so many to pursue their own material interests while blithely disregarding their obligations to the natural world and their fellow human beings.

Throughout much of the early unregulated industrial period, many large industrial cities in the UK were enshrouded in thick smoke and smog. It was not until the latter half of the twentieth century that concerted action was taken to reduce industrial air pollution. Even today, the UK government's own statistics suggest it causes between 28,000 and 36,000 deaths each year.[7] For two centuries now, breathlessness and coughing have been common ailments throughout the industrial working class. Many older working-class people today can recall parents or grandparents constantly wheezing and coughing. It was simply a part of life, and for the most part it was met with the stoicism that was reproduced as a key feature of working-class culture.

Steel, iron, textile and shipbuilding workers were greatly affected, but coal miners suffered most.[8] In the 1950s and 1960s, and after years of concerted pressure and gradual improvements to health and safety legislation, more than a thousand British miners continued to die each year as a result of pneumoconiosis alone. Over half a million claims for compensation were made under the British Coal respiratory disease legislation, which closed in 2004, for work-related bronchitis and emphysema. Of course, this number is but a tiny fraction of the overall number of men affected by these debilitating diseases. Most died long before the British state acknowledged the effect of coal mining on the health of workers. McIvor and Johnston claim that 'measured by cumulative mortality and morbidity figures, there is no doubt that occupation-induced respiratory disease in coal mining represented the largest occupational health disaster in British history'.[9]

Other examples of human suffering proliferated as the dash for profit gripped the new industrialised nations. Perhaps one of the most symbolically important was the plight of the 'match girls' – girls and women who worked in the huge and very profitable matchstick-making industry – and the common condition of 'phossy jaw'. Working for long periods with white phosphorous causes the jawbone to rot.[10] The effects were horrific. Annie Besant, a noted socialist and an early campaigner for women's rights, highlighted the plight of the match girls in an article published in 1888 entitled 'White Slavery in London' and led the match workers' strike in that same year. In the article, Besant contrasts the desperate poverty of the match girls with the staggering wealth of the owner of the Bryant and May match works, Theodore Bryant. Besant also made the point that Bryant would have made less money had he used chattel slaves to produce his matches, as slave owners had to cover the cost of feeding and housing their slaves. As things stood, the money Bryant paid his workers to take on this arduous and extremely dangerous work was barely enough for them to feed themselves and a good deal less than the cost of keeping slaves.[11] Besant's point was not lost on her audience. The desperation which often typified working-class experience during the nineteenth century was simply unconscionable. Change had to come. It was against this background that the left developed its political programmes of advocacy and substantive reform on behalf of the working class.

It is common to assume that, as the horrors of the industrial era unfolded, the people became morally opposed to predatory capitalism and began to align themselves with the new socialism. Very often the left in Britain actively cultivates this account of its past, but it is too simplistic for us to accept fully.

In truth, socialism never caught on among the industrial working class to the extent that we would like to assume. The highbrow socialist tradition understandably draws the attention of many contemporary historians, but it did not intrude to any great extent upon the lives of men and women who were by necessity pragmatists and realists. For many years, power on the left continued to lie with the established trade unions – rather than the incipient Labour Party – because their entire reason for being was to defend and advance the material interests of workers.

For much of the nineteenth century trade unions served only a minority of workers, but their place in the developing working-class movement was from the outset clear and unambiguous. Workers could identify the appeal of campaigns for pay rises and paid lunch breaks. Campaigns to shorten the working day or secure compensation for men and women injured at work also had an obvious attraction. The central logic of the trade unionism was clear: if the workers joined together, they could force employers to change. Collective action could produce tangible benefits. The more esoteric visionary goals of various leftist revolutionaries were for the most part given short shrift, and the committed socialists who hoped to achieve the heights of national government in order to enact a transformational policy agenda were often considered worthy but unrealistic. Certainly, grand and idealistic plans for a future socialist society drew only muted support among ordinary men and women forced to carry the burdens of industrial working-class life.

What really hit home was talk of pragmatic changes that would lead to a tangible and immediate boost to lifestyles, and this is why so many members of the industrial working class were slow to align themselves first with the Independent Labour Party and then the British Labour Party. Both parties were, in the broader scheme of things, really quite marginal, and this remained the case until well into the twentieth century. Why give one's vote to a party unlikely to win an election when it was possible to vote for an established Liberal Party that had proven itself, especially after the 1890s, willing to introduce at least some immediately effective practical reforms?

When it came into office in 1905, the Liberal Party introduced free school meals and increased the number of free school places. It also introduced old-age pensions, labour exchanges and some rudimentary medical insurance for the poor. These things were tangible and suggested that working-class life was finally starting to move in the right direction. Of course, these measures did not go far enough, but many working-class voters understandably focused on the fact that, at long last, some progress was indeed being made. They could not see into the future and, in light of their experiences of the recent past, many reached the conclusion that liberal reformers represented the best chance of improving their circumstances. To vote for a minority party with no chance of winning might have meant depriving the reformist liberals of vital votes that – in some marginal seats at least – could keep the Tories at bay.

Towards the end of the nineteenth century, the growth of the fledgling Labour Party was greatly aided by an electoral pact with the Liberal Party. This pact allowed a number of high-profile Labour members a clear run against Tory candidates. In return, Labour agreed not to run against Liberal candidates. While the pact was somewhat informal in nature, it allowed both the Liberals and Labour to pick up seats by ensuring that the anti-Tory vote was not split. While the pact benefited both parties, it would seem the Liberals left more on the table than the far smaller and often quite disorganised Labour Party. Certainly, the withdrawal of Labour candidates ensured that Liberal candidates picked up votes in seats they already had a chance of winning. However, if Labour had not entered the pact with the Liberals and had put up candidates in both Tory and Liberal strongholds, they would have very often finished in third place, and usually by a considerable margin.

The pact allowed Labour to get its members into Parliament, raise its profile and encourage a greater proportion of sympathetic but not yet aligned voters to believe that Labour really could upset the established conventions of Britain's two-party political system. However, the downside was that, by taking the Liberal Party whip and endorsing its social reform programme, many Labour MPs around the turn of the twentieth century, especially those aligned with the trade union movement, often appeared as an only slightly more radical wing of an increasingly reformist Liberal Party. Understandably, those at the centre of the left's attempt to secure democratic power argued vociferously about how Labour could distinguish itself without throwing away the benefits of its close alignment with the new reformist liberalism.

The fact is that many among the industrial working class were far less interested in politics than contemporary historians and political analysts tend to assume. Neither did the majority of the working class immediately throw their electoral support behind the Labour Party as soon as they were given the vote. All men were given the vote in 1918, and all women in 1928. But even after true universal suffrage was achieved, Labour's growth and position as a dominant political party was not entirely assured. Labour improved its position by only 15 seats in the 1918 election, whereas the Conservatives, buoyed by what was seen as an effective contribution to the coalition government during the Great War and the heady combination of victory and relief at the end of it, gained 108 additional seats. It's tempting to assume that huge numbers of working-class men and women were prevented from giving their electoral support to Labour because they had yet to receive the vote. However, this tends to ignore the fact that many members of the working class believed their interests would be best served by either the Liberals or the Tories. The standard account of the incremental growth of class consciousness in Britain, and the concomitant rise of the left, is not entirely accurate.

In the late nineteenth century, the Liberal and Conservative parties set the general tone of political discussion. For the Labour Party to break through it needed to shift the parameters of the debate. Socialism in the nineteenth century was very often filtered through the established policy conventions of the

Liberal and Conservative parties. For example, the appealing effects of socialism tended to be positioned in relation to established policy programmes. Liberals argued that free trade would lower prices and spur economic growth, which would in turn produce more jobs. As jobs were created, wages would rise. The Conservatives tended to take the opposite position. Free trade would allow cheap foreign imports to spill into the country. Prices may fall in the first instance, but jobs would be imperilled. Tariffs needed to be in place to protect British industries. Split on this crucial macroeconomic issue, socialists adopted one of these two basic positions in the belief that such policies would lead to positive 'socialist' outcomes.

Early cultural clashes

There were also quite significant cultural differences within the working class. Those who worked in industries in which the trade union movement was strong tended to possess a different view of socialism, and politics in general, to those who worked in unstable and non-unionised industries. And, of course, there were significant religious differences. In the latter half of the nineteenth century, Labour struggled to deal with the thorny topic of religious education as both Catholics and Protestants fought against the growth of secularism. Extensive Irish immigration also exacerbated ethnic tensions and pushed many of the English working class still further towards populist conservatism. In some locales, unionism clashed against calls for, first, Home Rule and, later, Irish independence.

It is also quite easy to overlook other cultural divides. Many members of what is often called the 'respectable working class' remained attached to religion, forbad drink, sex before marriage and a range of traditional working-class cultural pursuits, and tended to adopt a more formal style of dress and demeanour. The more 'disreputable' elements of the working class were keen to enjoy alcohol, boxing and other popular working-class sports, and were generally less concerned about their outward appearance. It does not always follow that the respectable elements of the working class were better-paid trade unionists, while the disreputable elements of the working class were trapped in poorly paid and non-unionised sectors of the economy. The true picture is more complex. Diverse, regional cultures persisted across the generations and were especially strong in some locales even as the transformative industrial economy forged ahead.

The Labour Party and the broader labour movement did not, generally speaking, seek to challenge and overcome these cultural differences. Rather, the left in Britain tended to vacillate, fudge and mould itself around dominant cultural conventions. The socialists of nineteenth-century Britain attuned themselves to the world as it was, in the vague hope that doing so would equip them with the power to transform the world into what they wished it to be. Although pragmatism and idealism often clashed, especially on the key issues of the day, in the background they often worked hand in glove. The pragmatism of early British socialism focused on getting candidates elected and moving towards a transformative election victory, at which point idealism would attempt to assert itself as strident socialists tested the boundaries of what was achievable within the system as it stood.

There were also significant regional and sectional differences within the British left. The socialism that grew in a haphazard fashion in the working-class enclaves of London was quite different from the socialism that grew in the coalfields of County Durham. The meanings, inferences and associations of essentially universal principles were interpreted and acted upon differently in each regional and cultural context. The drive to secure economic security, much improved lifestyles and better political representation for the working class was inevitably shaped by forms of local knowledge and culture. People cared more about the specific injustices they were subjected to. They cared more about the poverty they themselves experienced. They cared more about the desperation and unfairness they could see around them. They borrowed from local traditions and the cultures of their birth in order to make sense of their position in the world. These local traditions and cultures were also used to bring the abstractions of socialism down to earth where they could be of most use.

The socialism of those who hailed from professional middle-class backgrounds was often quite different from the socialism of working-class trade unionists. From the very outset, it was clear that the middle classes would play a leading role in a movement ostensibly orientated to the practical needs of the working class. Many of these middle-class socialists were deeply committed, and some made important contributions to the movement. However, many working-class socialists were deeply conflicted about the presence of members of the middle class at the very heart of what should have been their movement. Most recognised the benefit of securing allies in the middle and upper classes, and they could see the value of the contributions made by notable middle-class activists. However, it was difficult for many working-class socialists to shake off the feeling that the working-class movement should be led by members of the working class.

As the nineteenth century progressed, there was no shortage of organic working-class intellectuals. Members of the working class held leadership roles in trade unions, and, in the earliest days of the Labour Party, most Labour MPs came from working-class backgrounds. Some of the British left's most skilled orators were born into poverty, and it was their experience of hardship, at least in part, that made them such effective communicators. As an increasing number benefited from formal education, their understanding of their location in the capitalist system deepened and their skills were sharpened further. Surely, the left should be led by talented and committed working-class socialists?

Often, it was assumed that middle-class socialists were motivated principally by a philanthropic desire to help the poorest and those who suffered most. Few doubted their passion and commitment. However, many working-class socialists believed philanthropy should play no part in the movement. Socialism was not about inspiring the nation to adopt a more charitable disposition. Nor was it about feeding hungry mouths or providing beds for the homeless. It was about creating a new economy and society in which *charity wasn't needed*. It was about giving each and every citizen a stake in society and a chance to live a life free from exploitation and insecurity. Philanthropy offered only palliative help when what was needed was a deep intervention to cut off problems at their source.

The socialists of the Fabian Society[12] were few in number but always managed to wield disproportionate influence. They were committed to a programme of gradual reform and were, generally speaking, of the view that the existing democratic system provided the left with all it needed to slowly extinguish the country's most harmful injustices. There was no need for violent revolution, and no great need to radically alter the existing socioeconomic system. Most were social liberals committed to the gradual reform of the capitalist economy and the social relations that sustained it. That is not to say, however, that their suggested reforms were pedestrian, inconsequential and limited to the cultural field.

Around the turn of the twentieth century, there was certainly genuine radicalism in this group, even if their approach to radical outcomes involved recourse to cautious pragmatism. Their desire to alter social reality by winning office and instituting gradual but significant social and economic policies waned over time. The Fabians were often considered the intellectual wing of the labour movement, and it is certainly true that many notable leftists were, at one time or another, attached to it. As one might imagine, they were always rather prescriptive and cautious.

In the aftermath of the Second World War, they abandoned radical reformism to take up a position on the right of the Labour Party. They aligned themselves with the geopolitical interests of the United States and, later, the neoliberal project of global free trade. As time passed, the group functioned as a counterweight to the occasional resurgence of leftist radicalism in the party and became active in suppressing the rise of working-class intellectuals to influential positions. Most of the group's members abandoned all prior commitments to socialism or diluted the meaning of socialism to the extent that it allowed them to advocate reforms that would advantage the 'free market'.

The Social Democratic Federation (SDF) was far more ambitious. Avowedly Marxist and internationalist, it clashed with the reformist Fabians and virtually every other group on the left. The SDF did play a minor role in the establishment of the Labour Party, but very shortly afterwards disappeared from the scene. The SDF's radicalism was quickly marginalised and eventually extinguished by what was always an essentially reformist British left. As it drifted into obsolescence, so did any hope of a radical political intervention that might rid the country of its resolutely capitalist economy. At no stage were the left's small band of revolutionaries capable of attracting significant support among the working class. As we will see in the coming chapters, the possibilities for the radical left shrank still further as the twentieth century unfolded. Leftist politics in Britain was to remain overwhelmingly and unalterably reformist.

As the Labour Party in the twentieth century grew into a truly national party capable of attracting popular support, factional squabbles continued to rage. Sometimes these squabbles were rooted in genuine ideological differences, and sometimes they were quite petty and rooted in personal rivalries and a desire for prestige and power. Generally speaking, these squabbles were pushed into the background as leftists sought cohesion and solidarity around the shared objective of reform. This strategy does appear to have achieved some success, but the factional differences did not disappear entirely. As is so often the case in politics, it was smiles and handshakes frontstage, and muttered oaths and promises of retribution backstage.

Factionalism was complex but rested on a few fundamental differences. The radical liberalism of the late Victorian and early Edwardian era promised to deliver appealing reforms that would improve workers' overall standard of living. Most liberalised socialists believed that free trade was the first step on this journey. Certainly, the prospect of cheap food, which the Liberals trumpeted as an inevitable outcome of free trade, appealed to many newly enfranchised working-class voters. Even some radical socialists tended to argue that it was best to back the Liberals as they pursued their reform agenda. Their muted support, however, tended to be offered only in the belief that the Liberals would eventually run out of steam and die out, whereupon the socialists could then take over and push things further along. However, many who took this position seemed to deny the fundamental outcome of what they imagined would be a temporary and conditional allegiance. For some key figures in the Labour Party, this strategy proved not to be temporary at all. Rather than shunt the liberal reformist agenda over the border towards socialism, they transformed socialism into an extension of reformist social liberalism. One might reasonably claim that socialism in the true sense died there and then, to be replaced by institutionalised liberal philanthropism. However, again, there is more to the story.

In some regions, working-class cultural conservatism was very firmly entrenched. As socialism developed in Britain, it was forced to work within and around this reality. The goal was not to transform cultural traditions. To rid the working class of its patriotism, its discomfort with immigration and immigrants, or its enjoyment of established cultural conventions was too much of a task for a loose political collective whose justifiable foci were, first, campaigning to ameliorate the most obscene forms of exploitation to be found in the industrial economy, and second, taking political power by democratic means. The primary goal was rather to equip working-class conservatives with a clearer understanding of new socialist plans to reform political economy in ways that that worked with rather than against the established cultural environment. Certainly, the socialism that gradually took root in many working-class communities throughout Britain combined a strident critique of economic injustice that reflected class-based interests with an acceptance of cultural beliefs and practices that, since the cultural turn in politics, are now generally understood to align with the political right.

There was also a significant element of instrumentalism involved in this process. It was not simply grand dreams of justice and equality that helped socialism bed down in industrial working-class communities. It was also a clear and comprehensible public commitment that new working-class political organisations would work to improve wage levels and working conditions as the foundations of a general struggle to give the working class a better deal.

Representatives from socialist organisations promised that when they achieved political power they would introduce social protections and other goods that would qualitatively boost the working class's material security and standard of living. Where the middle and upper classes had established political representatives, this new group – the left – presented itself as the representative of the working class. One did not need to fully agree with their policy programme, and nor did one have to be sympathetic towards the diverse array of proclamations made by the left's most notable figures. One simply had to accept that this group represented the interests of the working class, and that they would fight for material improvements to one's security and standard of living.

And so it was as the British left moved with growing purpose into the twentieth century. Socialism – or perhaps more accurately Labourism – did indeed catch on among the working class, but to nowhere near the extent we like to imagine. What truly caught on was the relativistic hope that the Labour Party would try harder than the other parties to advance the working class's material interests. One didn't need to know the various policy positions of the major parties. One didn't even need to know much about politics. Rather, all one really needed to do was identify oneself as a member of the working class and accept that the Labour Party was generally on the side of the working class. Once these rudimentary decisions had been made, the only thing that remained was to vote accordingly.

After the great turbulence of the first third of the twentieth century, we begin to see this more clearly. Whole neighbourhoods, rooted in working-class regional cultures and often dependent upon single industries, aligned themselves with the Labour Party. For the most part, people in these neighbourhoods accepted that they shared with their neighbours many common interests. While they clung on to individuality and the particularities of family life, they accepted that they shared much with those around them. In this way, one could simply ignore what for many was the dull minutiae of political discussion and simply acknowledge that one was, like the vast majority of one's neighbours, 'for Labour'.

Throughout the years of its growth, and as it moved closer to true political power, every single Labour politician accepted the language and symbolism of class. All remained unashamedly committed to advancing working-class interests – there were other peripheral concerns, but these predominantly material interests were paramount. That the Tories were committed to defending the interests of the upper classes was hardly in dispute. As time passed and the new entrepreneurial and professional middle classes began to grow, the Tories stepped forward to present themselves as their defenders and benefactors. In the middle third of the twentieth century, these classes became firmly aligned with their supposed representatives. The working classes tended to vote for Labour and everyone else tended to vote for the Tories.

Despite these tendencies, voting was not rigid or entirely predictable. Some individuals – for various habitual, cultural, pragmatic or idealistic reasons – voted against their class interests. Had they not, the Tory Party would have been in permanent opposition at least until the industrial economy began to die in the 1980s. Clearly, a habitual cultural conservatism that can manifest itself as political support for a Tory Party that promises to defend cultural conventions has been an enduring feature of working-class community life.

The more conservative themes within working-class culture did not necessarily inspire a general fear of and resistance to change, and neither did they encourage hostility to the slow liberalisation of certain aspects of traditional British cultural life. Rather, it was 'conservative' in the sense that it valued the foundational values of late nineteenth-century populist conservatism: patriotism; pride in Empire; appreciation of the pleasures of alcohol and traditional leisure pursuits; and an antagonism towards large-scale immigration.

This antagonism towards immigration was not simply about cultural prejudice. It makes little sense to apply today's cultural conventions to a context entirely different from our own. Popular antagonisms towards immigration had a practical aspect which should not be underestimated. Immigrants increased competition for jobs, and a sudden influx of often quite desperate immigrants into regions yet to establish comprehensive legal protections and an assertive trade union movement also meant that wages tended to fall. These were crucial issues in working-class communities already beset by poverty and a stark lack of state-funded welfare support. We will return to this issue in a moment.

It may strike us as odd that many newly enfranchised working-class voters in the industrial regions threw their support behind a Conservative Party dominated by aristocrats, financiers and industrialists who had done precious little to assist the working class. Some Conservatives did indeed continue to carry with them a sense of *noblesse oblige* but, of course, a charitable disposition to the wretched and downtrodden did not preclude an unflinching faith in their own superiority or a dogged commitment to defend their class interests.

Many socialists and trade unionists did, of course, reject the notion of global free trade and side with the Tories on tariffs, but the overriding appeal of the Conservative Party to members of the working class had more to do with culture and cultural policy. There may have been an element of deference felt towards an aristocracy that some imagined as having achieved great things for the nation. However, it also seems likely that many working-class Tories felt an affinity with the Conservative Party because so many of its MPs were, like them, determined patriots and committed to the pleasures of gambling, drinking, bawdy humour, uninhibited straight-talking, and sport.

In some cases, aristocratic Tories acted as patrons of favoured working-class pastimes and sporting events, mingling with the hoi polloi at race meetings, boxing matches and the like, which the reformist liberal left looked upon with haughty disapproval. There was also a vague sense that the Tories were committed to defending the nation against external or internal threats and would do whatever was needed to preserve its heritage and economic security.

Socialism, then, learned not to threaten but to adapt itself to the existing cultures of the working class. The trade union movement in the nineteenth century grew quickly in regions where working-class conservatism was strong, and many notable trade unionists of the era were quite clearly steadfast economic socialists while also displaying an enduring commitment to some basic features of popular cultural conservatism.

Ben Tillett – one of the great forgotten pioneers of the British left – grew up in poverty in Bristol and played a crucial role in the development and growth of the trade union movement. He is known mostly for his work among London's dockers. Before the rise of dockside trade unions, work was arduous, poorly paid, insecure and dangerous. Of course, Tillett did not singlehandedly transform the industry, but his endeavours certainly helped to curtail the worst forms of exploitation on the docks and establish a firm foundation from which the trade union movement could lobby for further reform. He spoke with great passion about the working-class cause, and there can be little doubt of his deep commitment to socialism. He was at various times in his life a member of the Fabian Society, the Independent Labour Party and the Social Democratic Federation. He ran as a socialist candidate in numerous seats across the country before finally becoming the Labour Member of Parliament for Salford North in 1917.[13]

Tillett was often openly dismissive of the priggish Methodism that had gripped some of his colleagues on the left, and especially those who championed abstinence. He clearly saw himself as a determined defender of working-class culture. His position on economic restructuring changed and developed over time, but for the most part he appears to have been an advocate of syndicalism, inasmuch as he hoped the British trade union movement could collectively disrupt the industrial economy to the extent that it could dictate terms to employers.

Men like Tillett present contemporary historians of the left with something of a challenge. It is difficult to place him on the right of the movement – which today tends to mean accepting the dominance of markets – because his economic analyses and policy suggestions were quite radical. However, in terms of his cultural analyses, he seems very much on the right, especially given that what it tends to mean to be 'on the left' today entails displaying an overt commitment to the progressive cultural causes of the moment. It is difficult, at this historical distance and given the lack of authoritative commentary, to tell whether he deliberately courted controversy or refused to temper views he believed to be in keeping with his various working-class constituencies. Certainly, some of these views upset many of his contemporaries, and, given that so little has been written about Tillett, it seems likely that they are still considered beyond the pale.

Tillett was an unashamed patriot and a staunch supporter of Britain's involvement in the First World War. His support for the war clashed with the pacifism of other notable figures on the left. Nevertheless, he found broad support in the working class, many of whom, at a terrible cost, rallied to the war effort.

However, the cloud that hangs over Tillett's reputation comes not from his advocacy for the war but from his demonisation of Jewish immigrants who had moved into East London to seek work in and around the docks.

Tillett argued that the high numbers of Jewish workers had depressed wages and increased competition for work.[14] Rather than quell popular anxieties and dissatisfaction, as any good leftist is supposed to do, he appears to have fanned the flames. In some of his speeches, he mobilised a range of Jewish stereotypes that did little to foster solidarity among workers. Tillett also appears to have been hostile towards Jews specifically rather than immigrants in general. He had worked to calm tensions between Irish Catholic immigrants and local working-class Protestants in what was at the time a highly charged atmosphere, but he refused to offer Jewish immigrants the same conciliatory support.

Tillett was not alone in his fear of Jewish immigration. Many of his colleagues in the trade union movement also appear to have been of the view that Jewish immigration threatened to undercut pay, especially in poorly regulated industries. Tillett's account of the problem of Jewish immigration also chimed with those of Henry Hyndman, who established the SDF and, later, the British Socialist Party. Hyndman is an unusual figure in the history of British socialism. Born into a well-to-do family, he studied at Cambridge and seemed set for a comfortable life among London's thriving bourgeoisie. However, he became a Marxist after reading the *Communist Manifesto*, and threw himself into London's growing and diversifying leftist political scene. His simplified and popularised account of Marxism, *England for All*, sold well but earned him the eternal enmity of Marx himself. Hyndman remained a Marxist, although quite whether he fully grasped the fundaments of Marxism is a matter of some dispute.

The SDF as a whole seems to have been a rather unusual presence on the left in the late nineteenth century. It was certainly the most significant of the avowedly Marxist organisations of that period. It is not clear how many members the organisation attracted, but it seems likely the overall membership was quite small, especially in comparison to other leftist political organisations. However, given that the SDF and other leftist organisations aimed to represent the working class, and given that whole swathes of the working class could ill afford to formally attach themselves to any political group that solicited fees, the full extent of the SDF's influence is difficult to determine. Certainly, it attracted a significant number of leftist intellectuals, and there is enough evidence to suggest that the group did indeed make some inroads into working-class communities.[15] However, the small number of instances it put up candidates in elections for Parliament ended in failure and controversy, and over time support waned.

Hyndman financed the SDF's pamphlet, *Justice*. In its pages he mobilised the standard, contradictory tropes of modern anti-Semitism. Jews were, for Hyndman, *both* a mobile class of exploitable workers willing to undercut and impoverish indigenous workers *and* the dominant cultural group in the global finance community. Of course, that Hyndman would castigate the profiteers of global finance was to be expected. That he would continually seek to drive home the message that these vulgar profiteers were also predominantly Jews, and that Jews were totally immoral and interested only in their collective advancement, was clearly a step too far.

For trade union leaders focused on the needs of members, the sudden arrival of immigrants willing to accept lower wages weakened their bargaining position, threatened their livelihoods and imperilled both the union and its members. Tillett and Hyndman were simultaneously protecting the material interests of working-class trade union members and spreading dangerous anti-Semitic prejudice. As the trade union movement grew, many within its ranks worried about the disruptive effect immigration would have upon their industries and their ability to organise workers.

It would be easy to present Tillett and Hyndman as outliers whose views did not reflect the far more accommodating attitudes of the industrial working class. However, that seems not to have been the case. Cultural antagonisms and unadorned racism tend to thrive in times of insecurity and competition, and both of these things can be found quite easily among the left throughout the Victorian and Edwardian eras.[16]

There were, of course, many leftists who persevered with the standard account of class universality and sought ways of promoting solidarity. For them, it was vital that the left did what it could to render the ethnic origin of workers irrelevant. What workers had in common was far more important than the issues that set them apart. To move forward, all members of the working class needed to recognise their shared material and cultural interests. All needed to recognise that the many frustrations and hardships they suffered had the same root cause. Together, they could change things. Divided, they would continue to lose.

Of course, the sudden arrival of a large number of immigrants into a particular industry or a part of the city often came as something of a shock, especially given that, overall, the British population was much more ethnically homogenous than it is today. Over time, the shock fades and the idea of universal class interests has a chance to catch on. Barriers begin to break down and inklings of common interests can begin to displace suspicion and prejudice. In many respects, those who present this traditional account of universal class interests continue to clash with identitarians interested in defending only their chosen ethnic constituencies and maintaining clear divisions. Unfortunately, the class universalists are now small in number and appear destined to remain on the losing side for the foreseeable future.

Hyndman's conspiratorial account of a global elite stratum of Jewish financiers intent on exploiting the working class of each nation not only was born of anti-Semitic prejudice but also did not reflect the concerns of an industrial working class anxious about the continuity of their jobs and the meagreness of their wage packets. The workers tended to be pragmatic and focused upon what they could see and understand about the world around them. They were generally unconcerned about the ethnic composition or religious affiliations of a global financial elite, the members of which they would never encounter. What they cared about was their immediate material welfare and that of their families, and when antagonisms arose between established local communities and recently arrived immigrants, this was usually the key issue.

That is not to say that anxieties about one's material welfare and suspicion of incomers cannot be fuelled by traditional cultural prejudices. However, if we hope to develop an accurate understanding of racism on the left throughout the industrial era, we must contextualise the periodic sources of ethnic or religious tension in material and socioeconomic reality. Nor must we deny that suspicion and resentment arising from these tensions, if not replaced by a sense of common interests, can easily become established and culturally reproduced as unthinking prejudice in all cultural groups. Also, of course, such overt prejudice from early socialist leaders convinced many Jewish immigrants that under no circumstances should they support the left.

The twentieth-century false dawn

It is important to keep in mind that until the 1960s there existed no great antagonism between cultural conservatism and the development of socialism in Britain. Many notable socialists managed to be both conservative in their cultural outlook and really quite radical in their approach to the management of the economy. Many were, first and foremost, committed to the interests of the British working class and, for them, a commitment to the economic interests of that class went hand in hand with their ongoing attempts to defend its cultural interests.

Socialism grew slowly in the British trade union movement. For many years, trade union leaders remained focused on the practical interests of their members. These interests were best advanced through negotiation with business leaders mindful of the cohesion of workers, their commitment to the cause and their willingness to engage in strike action. Most trade union leaders supported liberal reformism, but many tended to believe that trade unionism should be separated from democratic politics. It was only after the Taff Vale judgment[17] of 1901, which effectively meant that unions could be held liable for business costs resulting from strike action, that the movement accepted the imprudence of confrontation at the point of production and the utility of having working-class political representation in Parliament. It was only at this point that the union movement recognised the importance of political representation at the highest structural level and threw in its lot with the Labour Party.

Socialism grew slowly among the working class, and even at its highest point it appears to have been something of a minority interest. The majority were not particularly interested in politics, and what interest they had tended to be shaped by entirely understandable instrumental concerns about income, work conditions and job security. Some topics grabbed the attention, but for many the details were unimportant.

The great twentieth-century successes of the Labour Party – and here we cannot look past the transformative Labour government of 1945 – were achieved on the back of the broad recognition among members of the working class that the party would seek to advance their interests. Unfortunately, it does not follow that a majority of working-class voters were committed to socialism. Labour won by a landslide in 1945 and responded with great vision and purpose to both the obvious economic injustices of the time and the devastation caused by six years of all-consuming war. However, even during this high point, the working class was more politically diverse than we tend to assume.

By 1950 the Labour Party had lost a huge amount of support. Its majority cut to only five seats, in 1951 the Labour government called a snap election with a view to securing a larger majority that would allow it to push through legislation with greater ease. Of course, it then lost the election to Winston Churchill's Conservative Party. It's a rather sobering thought that the most transformative government in British history was, in truth, restricted to only one term. In this short time the Labour government had rejected the absurd *laissez-faire* politics of the old order, followed Roosevelt in adopting Keynesian economic principles, and laid the foundations for the modern welfare state. In doing so it established many of the precepts that were to become integral to our understanding of a modern, healthy, integrative civil society. And yet it was not enough to secure the loyalty of a sizeable section of the modern working class.

We may initially assume that the British working class of the immediate post-war era was ungrateful, short-sighted and, as many liberal intellectuals tend to imply, irredeemably illiterate in matters of politics and economics. However, we must keep in mind that in the war's immediate aftermath poverty continued.

Food and good-quality housing remained scarce. Rationing continued well into the 1950s. The positive transformation we associate with the 1945 Labour government did not greatly improve the everyday lifestyles of working people during its term.

The relationship between the Labour Party and the working class held on with declining stability during the 1950s and 1960s, but it would never again be as politically relevant as it had been in 1945. A brief rekindling of old alliances swept Labour to power in 1997, after a full 17 years of equally transformative Tory government had set the charges for the demolition of the 1945 Labour government's greatest achievements. It was not to last. The Labour Party had adopted the most important facets of neoliberalised Tory Party policy and jettisoned many of its traditional values and commitments. It turned its sights away from the working class and towards the ranks of the professional middle class, where its focus has remained ever since.

Now, in 2021, the relationship between the working class and the Labour Party is one of, at best, ambivalence and, at worst, antagonism and antipathy. The party shows little interest in economic policies that can intervene and exert democratic control at the core of neoliberalism's global economic system, and little understanding of the problems that blight the lives of the UK's fragmented and anxious multi-ethnic working class. Before the 2019 election, those who bothered to vote among the British working class overwhelmingly supported the Conservative Party. Throughout 2021, roughly 45 per cent of the British working class intended to vote for the Conservatives at the next election. Labour was 17 points behind on 28 per cent.[18] We cannot think of a more profound about-turn in British political history.

A class against itself

Marxists often point to the principle that to be politically successful and exercise at least some control over its own destiny, the international working class must first become a class in itself and then a class for itself. Very basically, this means that, first, they must consciously identify themselves as a collective with shared interests, and then achieve the political power required to prioritise and further their interests.

As the first truly industrialised nation, it is reasonable to suggest that Britain has the world's oldest modern class system. As the nineteenth century progressed, class consciousness grew considerably. Amongst the new and expanding industrial working class, which at the time constituted the great majority of the population, social class became a key component of self-identity. This feeling of class belonging lingered long into the twentieth century. In some respects, it remains with us still, although in a rather diluted form.

As industrialism established specific sites of production, it ushered individuals from a variety of backgrounds into the new industrial workforce. There, the potential for many older cultural differences to be pushed into the background grew as work and new work-based settlements became the dominant features of everyday life. Industrial workers often recognised they had a great deal in common. Over time, specific class cultures took hold. Neighbourhoods became enclassed and class cultures began to be tentatively reproduced. Key values, beliefs, norms and practices – some obvious and some very subtle – were passed from one generation to the next. As they aged, each generation tended to independently encounter many of the same obstacles as their parents and – equipped with similar skills, attitudes and outlooks – achieved similar results.

There was, of course, an element of freedom. There were choices to be made. However, these choices took place within a context in which much was prescribed and inflexible. The dominance of waged industrial work, the absence or paucity of formal education for much of the nineteenth century, and a broad range of cultural factors – some internal and others external to the working class – curtailed opportunities for upward social mobility. Working-class men and women stayed working class, as did their children. It is certainly true that, during the early industrial era, young people did not experience the same degree of pressure to move up, acquire and display that is so crushingly prescriptive for young people today. People were generally happier to remain working class and, rather than seek to escape from it, some were willing to take on the work of furthering its diverse cultural, political and economic interests.

In the early industrial period, poverty – and in some cases extreme and absolute poverty – bore down unremittingly upon working-class experience. This hardship, and the material hardships of industrial labour, left an indelible mark on emerging cultures. Men and women found compensatory pleasures in working-class culture, and this became more apparent as the twentieth century unfolded and the terrible costs of extreme poverty receded. However, this should not distract us from the core experience that informed working-class politics. The men and women who crowded into the factories of the early industrial period were treated as units of production to be exploited to the maximum allowed within the law. The collective experience of coping with or resisting downward wage pressure fuelled an embryonic oppositional politics rooted in that commonality. For much of late modern history, the organised working class was the sole force capable of imposing anything more than palliative change upon the global capitalist system.

As we have been at pains to stress, this does not mean that the working class of the industrial era was entirely committed to socialism. It is, however, undeniable that the modern left initially created itself as a response to the experience of specific material injustices that took shape in the modern industrial age. However, capitalism never stays still, and it changes only in ways that allow its own development and reproduction.

As important sites of production moved from Western countries to the East, and into the developing world in the 1980s, class identity became less demanding and influential. For a variety of reasons that we have explored in detail elsewhere,[19] people began to feel less enclassed and more at liberty to adopt identities and lifestyles that appeared to be of their own choosing. Social welfare systems and cheap imported goods had allowed working people to keep their heads just far enough above absolute poverty and deep, chronic material insecurity. On that platform the collective identities that had fed the left in Britain and elsewhere for so long diminished enormously as neoliberalism's global project began to assert itself. In many cases traditional sources of collective identity were entirely recontextualised, to the extent that, instead of being a source of strength and a defence against harm and exploitation, they were seen as fetters upon individual freedom. Freedom had become the principal obsession. Obligation, solidarity, mutual support and self-sacrifice became harder to sustain.

After the initial process of neoliberal restructuring was complete, some social scientists suggested that we had seen the death of class.[20] They were right on the level of emotion and identity, insofar as younger generations tended to feel less enclassed. Young people drew from other influences – most notably mass media and consumer culture – to construct their self-images. They were less bound than were their parents to specific enclassed locales and regions. They were more likely to see their lives and their positions in the world as reflections of the choices they had made rather than the situations in which they had found themselves. They may have envied the rich – the constant publicising of affluent lifestyles and the voyeurism that accompanied 'celebrity culture' had an obvious ideological function – but very few were interested in entirely doing away with 'the rich' as a social category, or even pulling the top and the bottom significantly closer together. Rather, an increasing number wanted to join the ranks of the rich, and to do so they were happy to abandon political, social and cultural entanglements.

However, those social scientists who were to some extent right to proclaim the end of class as a psychological, cultural and political entity were wrong inasmuch as the economic and structural role of class remained very much a part of the neoliberal world. Indeed, the gap between rich and poor grew significantly during the neoliberal epoch. The drive to open up all regions of the globe to the predations of the market meant that impoverished workers in developing economies acted as the new hyper-exploited proletariat. Britain's working class was ushered into the low-grade services jobs that arose to compensate for the greatly reduced post-industrial manufacturing sector. These jobs were insecure and poorly paid, and often entirely free from the positive symbolism that allowed some workers in the old industrial economy to retain a degree of pride in their work and the skills needed to carry it out. They also tended to be non-unionised which, of course, reflected the increasingly individualised nature of neoliberalism's post-social world. Class continued to exist in the structural sense – although in a new, loosely stratified form – but it had been stripped of many of its positive cultural and political characteristics.

To paraphrase Baudrillard, who in the late 1970s began to address the death of civil society and the tranquillising effects of mass consumerism, *the factory walls could not be reinstated.*[21] The environments that seemed to cultivate and reproduce an awareness of collective interests and collective destiny were gone and could not return.

Baudrillard did not see this simply as a matter of class decomposition, and nor was he principally concerned with the profound effects of this process upon leftist politics. Rather, for him, all collective identities were breaking apart. All of modernity's integrative processes had reversed and the people were now being pulled in the opposite direction. How was it possible to talk of society in the absence of a sense of collective destiny and a broad faith in universal values? How was it possible to talk of a society when belief was personal and contingent, and when individuals had come to see themselves as equivalent to a miniaturised state: fully sovereign, with its own history, values and goals, and capable of constructing its own laws? How could happily distracted individualised consumers be persuaded again to confront the reality in which they lived? For Baudrillard, the answer was clear. The 'society' we encountered in our day-to-day lives was merely a facile, consumerised simulacrum, and there was no going back.

Baudrillard's dark prognostications were unusually prescient. The modern left had built its castle on what had appeared to be the firm ground of the people and their collective interests. As the neoliberal era began to reveal itself, this firm ground appeared to have turned to sand. There was little for the people to rally behind, and little to bond them together. As its castle crumbled, the left appeared to accept this regrettable situation. It would not seek to re-establish a firm foundation and neither would it seek to reinstate its walls. Rather, it walked away. Henceforth, it would embrace the cosmopolitanism of the open road. It would reinvent itself, and, somehow, it would be all things to all people. No longer would it preach of collective interests.

As the left meandered aimlessly into the neoliberal era, it seemed to be uprooted and swept along by liberalism's great, fragmentary tide. The myths of the past were to be left behind to drown as we were swept out into the open sea of our own mythical freedom. As this tide surged through every nook and cranny of collective life, the left's roots in universality were washed away. Our supposed destination was boundless freedom – a freedom from what we were told were the constraints of the past, a freedom in which we must all decide for ourselves. Of course, for Baudrillard and many other leftist intellectuals, this tide was not a creation of nature, and nor was it the mere outcome of a broad range of essentially neutral social processes. It had been whipped up by power, and the inevitable disempowerment of the people – as they relinquished their collective capacity to pull history in a different direction – was the principal goal rather than an unforeseen outcome.

Make America great again?

The United States of America's cultural landscape has never been particularly conducive to socialism. Socialism, at root, is about collectivism and submerging the interests of the self in a broader programme seeking mutual betterment. The American culture we see today grew in the shadow of Protestantism and the European Enlightenment. While we tend to associate Protestantism with freedom of conscience, and the Enlightenment with rationality and scientific discovery, it was the principle of freedom and antagonism towards institutionalised authority that became the ideological bedrock of political and social life. As the United States began to assert itself as a nation, it became clear that, across its broad culture – from its codified constitution to its much-vaunted legal system – the individual would be considered sacrosanct. All external authorities that might seek to compel, influence or judge the individual, or in any way restrict the individual's freedom, would be treated with suspicion and often outright hostility.

In this light, it is unsurprising that the American working class never became as cohesive as the British working class. The absence of class consciousness in the United States is one of the key reasons why the American left never really got off the ground. However, there are specific moments in the history of the United States that suggest it might have been possible for class to establish itself as a key feature of social identity. For a range of contingent reasons, these moments passed, and the American working class remained in a condition of shifting fragmentation seemingly without end.

It was not that American workers had avoided the forms of extreme exploitation exhibited in the British economy, and neither was it that an informed vanguard of committed socialists failed to emerge in the United States. Powerful trade unions developed to push back against exploitation, and the American left was blessed with more than enough committed intellectuals and compelling public speakers.

Diverse ethnic groups tentatively set aside cultural antagonisms to recognise their shared interests. These groups joined trade unions in the hope of relieving themselves of poverty, mistreatment and the corrosive insecurity that gnaws away at the lives of the poorest. And yet, the American working class was never minded to take the next step. Socialism remained the preserve of a small group of fringe radicals who were unable to establish themselves as a vanguard or an electoral force. Efforts were made to reach out to industrial workers and pass on to them the benefits of socialism, and there were some minor successes. However, for the most part, the American working class never really warmed to socialism. Its engagement with the trade union movement was for the most part instrumental and driven by the desire to secure a better deal within the system, rather than a desire to see the system deconstructed and replaced with something else.

Samuel Gompers' time at the head of the American Federation of Labor (AFL) is a useful case in point. Gompers dragged a range of craft unions together under the banner of the AFL, where they were better equipped to press their claims for higher wages and better conditions. Gompers was born in the East End of London. He received only a basic education and trained as a cigar maker. The Gompers – originally Gumpertz – family moved to New York in search of a better life. As a young man, Gompers became attracted to socialism. However, in time, and under the guidance of older men he admired, he decided to set such matters aside and focus his attention on the more practical world of trade unionism.

As his knowledge of the political left in the United States developed, he became increasingly irritated by its factionalism and the incessant machinations of its various component groups. Many committed socialists, he claimed, had been distracted by ceaseless party intrigues and vague ideas about future victories. They had consequently ignored their mandate to protect the interests of working men and women. Gompers was a pragmatist rather than an idealist, but again we should not assume that this pragmatism meant he set himself only trivial or short-term goals. Gompers focused on higher wages and better conditions for skilled union members without ever identifying himself as a leader or even a committed advocate for America's sprawling and diverse working class.

As war with Germany grew closer, the AFL threw its support behind the government and distanced itself from the pacifist left. It was both a sign of things to come and a reflection of the AFL's pragmatic and gently reformist leftism. The AFL was uninterested in future utopias. It accepted the capitalist system but also the mandate to fight to improve the situation of its members within it. As the horrors of Stalinism became more widely known, the AFL aligned itself very firmly with the interests of American industry and government. Key figures spoke out against communism and attempts were made to root out communist sympathisers. During the Second World War, the AFL refused to join the World Federation of Trade Unions, for which the TUC in Britain was the driving force, because it contained Soviet trade unions. Instead, it established a competitor group, the Free Trade Union Committee, which actively set out to disrupt Soviet attempts to bolster its power in post-war Europe.[22]

Gompers refused to be drawn into discussions about significant social change. Communism was abhorrent, and the interests of union members were harmed by any association with it. Gompers – and indeed the vast majority of trade union leaders – hoped to deliver to AFL-affiliated workers things that could improve their lives in the here and now. The pie-in-the-sky dreams of the radicals were at best a distraction, and at worst opened the door to the sort of totalitarianism that would inevitably curtail the freedoms fought for and enjoyed by working men and women. Gompers encouraged AFL members to vote for politicians who would advance their economic interests. He had little time for anything else.

Gompers kept his distance from organised democratic politics, and as the AFL grew in power it aligned with the Democrats rather than the socialists. The New Deal created a better environment for trade unionism and set the scene for the AFL's continued growth. As it grew, it maintained its commitment to anti-communism and the basic precepts of the American system.[23] In 1955 it amalgamated with the Congress of Industrial Organisations (CIO), forming the AFL-CIO, which continues to be the largest and most powerful collection of unions in the United States.

The CIO was more concerned with democratic politics, and some notable members had gone so far as to push for the formation of a new political party dedicated to advancing the interests of working men and women. A small number of key figures within the CIO, such as Walter Reuther, had once been members of the Socialist Party. However, as time passed it became clear that the conservatism of the AFL had tempered what remained of the tentative radicalism of the CIO.

Dealing with a less culturally divided and antagonistic population, British socialism was more coherent and influential. After a slow start, from the latter decades of the nineteenth century to the middle decades of the twentieth century, reformist socialist organisations built a useful political platform on which the British trade union movement could petition for significant interventions into the bedrock of industrial society. Fringe revolutionaries aside, trade unionists were often the most radical group on the left. However, the trade union movement in the United States approached the issue of expanding the rights and benefits of workers in a rather different way. American trade unions were far less likely to see themselves as the defenders of the entire American working class and far more likely to focus their energies on the interests of their individual members. Maintaining a reasonably civil dialogue with the representatives of American industry was often considered a necessity. And, of course, in the absence of any great ambition to transform society in the interests of workers, one of the most obvious precursors to better pay and conditions was high profits for business owners. The more profits went up, the better armed trade unions representatives would be in negotiations on pay levels.

As John Steinbeck is supposed to have once said, socialism never quite managed to establish itself in the United States because the poor tend to see themselves as temporarily embarrassed millionaires rather than an exploited proletariat. Whether or not Steinbeck ever expressed these sentiments is unimportant. What is important is that this commonplace, tongue-in-cheek observation contains a significant kernel of truth. Members of the American working class wanted to free themselves from job insecurity and exploitation. They wanted higher wages and better work conditions. And they joined trade unions in the hope of securing these benefits. But the vast majority of the American working class did not go much further than that. The American left was unable to build a political party that stood even an outside chance of securing a national mandate to govern.

Individualism remained sacrosanct. The thought of giving up or temporarily sacrificing one's freedoms, even where those freedoms are essentially notional and do not translate into tangible benefits for the individual, is anathema throughout large expanses of American cultural life. Every collective endeavour, from voting to declaring war, can be understood as the child of America's weird paradox of majoritarianism and free choice. This is the principal reason why political radicalism in the United States has always cleaved towards libertarianism rather than socialism or traditional conservatism.

The American liberal left has always been principally concerned with individual freedom. It has, since the 1960s especially, been fixated on freedom of expression and antagonistic to forms of cultural conservatism that might restrict the individual's ability to define his or her identity in any way he or she chooses. The American right, too, has always been concerned with freedom. For the most part, this has translated into an overarching antagonism towards the state and its various institutions. Any appeal for the state to intervene in American life always seems to be made with some degree of reluctance and regret. That both the radical left and the radical right in the United States express their dissatisfactions in this way tells us a great deal about the truncated and restrictive nature of American political culture.

However, some short-lived attempts at collective political organisation were made in the US. The Socialist Party of America was formed shortly after the British Labour Party in 1901. Like the Labour Party, it contained within it a diverse range of leftist thought. It also suffered a range of doctrinal disputes that hampered its development. The party grew at a reasonable pace during its first decade. It attracted some support from the trade union movement, but this support was always patchy and short-lived. Eugene Debs, one of the most important figures of the American left and a man of great commitment and considerable charisma, led the party for the first two decades of its life.

Debs was a man of the working class and grew up in Indiana. He was of French descent and started out as a fireman on the railways. His experiences of this industry inspired him to join the trade union movement, and he quickly became a local leader. After one particularly bruising industrial dispute, in which the army was called out to suppress a strike that threatened to interfere with the American postal system, Debs was sentenced to a short prison term. There, so the legend goes, he began to read widely and became a committed socialist. Aside from helping to found the Socialist Party of America, Debs also played a major role in establishing the Industrial Workers of the World – the Wobblies – probably the United States' most radical labour union.

Debs ran for president five times. The 1912 election was his best performance. He secured over 900 thousand votes. The winner of that election, the Democrat Woodrow Wilson, received over six million votes. The second-placed candidate, former president Theodore Roosevelt, received over four million votes, despite running under the banner of the short-lived Progressive Party. It was to be the last time anyone not representing either the Republican or Democratic parties came even within shouting distance of the US presidency.

Debs was a stirring orator and, like many in the early Labour Party, he often drew upon religious themes to get his point across. He was also a determined pacifist and outspoken critic of the United States' involvement in the First World War. His criticism of Woodrow Wilson's government and the war effort drew a charge of sedition, for which he was found guilty and sentenced to ten years in prison. Debs was released around two years later in 1921, partly because of his declining health. He lingered on only five more years but left a significant legacy for the American left.

Norman Thomas took over from Debs. He managed to make some headway during the 1930s. Thomas was the son of a Presbyterian pastor, and he appears not to have suffered the privations experienced by Debs and other working-class socialists. He followed his father into the Presbyterian Church and took on pastoral duties in East Harlem in New York. Thomas's interest in socialism grew stronger over time. He appears not to have been particularly drawn towards socialism as a young man, but his exposure to the material problems faced by ordinary people pushed him in that direction.

He was less radical, in terms of his aspirations for social and economic change, than many of his contemporaries, but there can be little doubt of his commitment to the cause. Thomas was, like Debs, a pacificist and had spoken out against the United States' involvement in the First World War. One of the most absurd injustices of the whole war, for both Debs and Thomas, was that members of the working class were expected to risk their lives for the nation, despite the fact that the nation offered them almost nothing in return. The American working classes lived lives of often quite significant hardship. Their wages were low, especially in non-unionised industries, work conditions were often very poor, and they had few legal protections against unscrupulous employers. Most were not able to consume beyond basic need and, in the absence of adequate state welfare provision, their lives were enshrouded by a heavy gloom of toxic anxiety. An illness, the loss of a job, in fact a crisis of virtually any kind, could plunge a family into destitution. And it was to the men of this class that the nation turned when its leaders chose to wage war on another continent.

The bands, pageantry and broad social approval that accompanied these men as they headed off for war would have quickly faded as the realities of armed combat became apparent, and that was especially true for those in the American Expeditionary Force, who joined the French on the Western Front as the conflict came to a close. Of course, the older European nations, who had been at war since 1914, suffered proportionally more than the Americans but, for Thomas, that was beside the point. As a pacifist, he thought war hideous. That so many wasted the gift of human life in order to press a claim about the ownership of land or some other resource was one of the great tragedies of human civilisation.

As a socialist, he noted that the burden of warfare fell mostly upon the working class, despite the fact that wars tend overwhelmingly to be precipitated by various constituencies within the ruling class. Members of the working class gave their lives for nations that treated them barely any better than cattle. As a socialist internationalist, he thought that the working classes of all nations had a great deal in common, and he could see no logical reason why they should wage war against one another for reasons that most did not fully comprehend. Their true enemy was the ruling class of their own nation, who remained totally committed to their own self-interest and blithely unconcerned by the hardships experienced by industrial workers and their families.

It is salutary to note that, in Britain, the Ministry of National Service Medical Boards' inspection of two and a half million men called up for service between 1917 and 1918 revealed quite staggering levels of physical ill-health. The extent of the problem encouraged Lloyd George, at the time prime minister, to comment:

> We have had a Ministry of National Service and carefully compiled statistics on the health of the people between the ages of 18 and 42 ... all I can tell you is that the results of these examinations are

startling, and I do not mind using the word appalling.
I hardly dare to tell you the results ... What does it
mean? It means that we have used the human material
in this country prodigally, foolishly, cruelly. I asked
the Minister of National Service how many more
men we could have put into the fighting ranks if
the health of the country had been properly looked
after. I staggered at the reply. It was a considered
reply, and it was 'at least one million'. If we had only
had that million this war would have been ended
triumphantly.[24]

The nature of the nation's ill-health, of course, reflected the
extent of poverty and inadequate diet among the industrial
working class. In the years leading up to the First World War,
a number of studies addressed the stature of schoolchildren.
Arthur Greenwood showed that 15-year-old children who
came from the professional classes were on average 18 pounds
heavier and two inches taller than the children of artisans.[25]
These inequalities were also reflected in the adult population.
The higher social classes literally looked down upon the
malnourished and exhausted working class. Winter, analysing
the quite extensive empirical evidence on public health and
social class produced during the early years of the twentieth
century, notes:

In rank order of height and weight, professional men
(5'7" and 10 st 9 lbs) were followed by shop-keepers
(5'6" and 10 st 1 lb). Just behind were engineers at
5'5" and 9 st 1 lb ... they were ahead of factory
workers, who averaged just 5'4" and 8 st 11 lbs.
Pulling up the rear were labourers, who were on
average 5'2" and 8 st 12 lbs.[26]

Such shocking statistics spurred calls for further social reform
and, in the inter-war years, considerable progress appears to have
been made. Even the Great Depression did not prompt a return
to entrenched deprivation and public ill-health associated with
the first decade of the twentieth century.[27]

The involvement of the United States in the First World War also revealed the ill-health of the American urban poor, although it did not impede the draft to any great extent. The Great Depression was of far more significance for the American left. While widespread social distress encouraged a greater proportion of the American public to become open to the prospect of significant social and economic change, the American left remained factionalised and unable to profit from widespread discontent. Many leftist intellectuals, keenly aware of the injustices of the American system, became briefly attracted during the 1920s by the promises of state communism. However, by the end of the 1930s, things were moving at speed in the opposite direction. Soviet show trials and Stalin's purges persuaded many intellectuals to denounce communism. Some notable American intellectuals went further and called for all communists to be excluded from the left's various institutions.

The American left's incrementally advancing hatred of communism was significant for a range of reasons, some of which will be explored in the next chapter. However, for the moment, suffice it to say that the proliferating defamation of communism removed the only truly comprehensible alternative to capitalism from the ideological map. Leftist politics would become generally negative in its orientation, inasmuch as it was forced only to identify those things it was against. Much energy was expended battling against the American system's excesses and trying to quell emergencies and crises that in some way negatively affected the lives of the people. However, it could not identify anything that it hoped to build which was truly positive and distinct from the existing order of things.

Ultimately, it was the centrist Democrats, in their new guise of interventionist social liberals, who stepped forward to address the unfolding social crisis that accompanied the Great Depression. In doing so, they secured popular support and a measure of voter loyalty. These loyalties were never quite as strong as those that existed in Britain, but they did nonetheless play a role in shaping elections and policies during the post-war era. Social democracy, embodied for Americans in the doctrine of the New Deal, was as far as the American left would go.

The New Deal – which, as we have seen, grew from a grudging acceptance of the efficacy of Keynesian economics – did not quite go far enough, but it did encourage many to form the view that the American system could become more equitable and just. If liberal democracy could deliver genuine social advances and boost the lifestyles of millions, many concluded that socialism was superfluous. The interests of America's expansive and already quite diverse working class could, it seemed, be advanced by voting for the Democrats.

The New Deal framework was maintained, at least after a fashion. Commitment to Keynes' model diminished over time, but nonetheless its position as an economic orthodoxy helped to bring about the prevailing sense of affluence and progress that followed the Second World War. Of course, not all were able to access the new age of affluence or bathe in its warm waters, and the grievances of excluded groups shaped the progress of the American left throughout the middle third of the twentieth century.

Here, of course, it is vital to address the experience of black people in America. The horrors of slavery had given way to the bigotry of segregation. Racism, especially in the South, was shockingly commonplace, and there can be no doubt that black people suffered enormously as warped cultural prejudices lingered on. It is not difficult to see how Garveyism began to draw the attention of many educated black Americans. Marcus Garvey's black nationalism pushed back strongly against the structure of Western civil societies, especially in the United States and Great Britain. He established the Universal Negro Improvement Association and African Communities League, which achieved a good degree of support in Jamaica, where Garvey was born, and in North America. The strength of his oratory and conviction, and the fear he appeared to cast into the heart of the American establishment, have encouraged some on the left to claim Garvey as one of their own. However, while he was an early advocate of the anti-imperialist cause, he was certainly not a socialist. Influenced by the writing of Booker T. Washington, Garvey remained a firm advocate of capitalism and saw greater involvement in the circuits of production and exchange as a means of achieving a degree of prosperity and liberty for black people. Garvey encouraged black men and women to establish their own businesses and to patronise, as much as they could, only businesses owned by their fellow black men and women.[28]

Garvey often spoke critically of W.E.B. DuBois, who had contributed to the establishment of the National Association for the Advancement of Colored People (NAACP) in 1909. Garvey's segregationism clashed with DuBois' integrationism. Garvey saw segregation as the only positive route forward for black people, whereas DuBois hoped to win for black Americans the full complement of rights given to citizens from other ethnic backgrounds. DuBois was a Harvard professor of considerable intellectual standing. His political work focused on the rights of black people and the injustices they faced in building communities and satisfying lives untainted by the racism of the white majority.

Booker T. Washington, at the time the most noted black intellectual and political leader in the United States, tacitly accepted white supremacy but asked that black people be given the opportunity to improve their own communities through engagement with business and the broad education system.[29] His goal was not to establish a new system in which black people could thrive, but rather to encourage the state to give black people the wherewithal to compete with white people within the system as it stood. DuBois' analysis was less accommodating but, like Washington, he saw access to education as the key to what he called 'black uplift'. DuBois did what he could to shatter myths about black people. He wrote about the creativity and untapped intellectual capacity that existed in black communities. As time passed, support for Washington's acceptance of segregation and white supremacy declined and support for DuBois' civil rights agenda grew.

A detailed evaluation of the American Civil Rights Movement is beyond the remit of this book, but it is vital that we acknowledge the peripheral presence of socialism within it. Socialism was not positioned centrally, but some notable civil rights leaders were committed to the cause. Bayard Rustin, for example, was attached to the Socialist Party in the early years of his political life and, while the principles of socialism took a backseat as the civil rights movement grew in strength, he appears to have remained firmly on the political left. Martin Luther King also spoke passionately against the predations of capitalism and the great corrosive harm caused by economic inequality. A firm advocate of trade unionism, throughout his work he displayed a deep commitment to equality of all kinds, and his anti-racism was rooted in an adapted Christian-socialist universalism. For King, the markers of identity should not matter. The colour of one's skin should not matter. All people are equal before God. King's goal was to secure formal rights for black people and do whatever could be done to dispense with the brutal and unthinking prejudice of racism in order to facilitate an age of equality, common interests and common destiny.[30] As we have seen, these positive social ambitions are entirely in keeping with the socialist universalism upon which the modern left was built.

It might reasonably be argued that the growth of black nationalism and the civil rights movement indicate the general weakness of the left in the United States during these years. Traditional socialism's core focus on equality in all its forms could have been put to work to address the diverse injustices suffered by black citizens. True socialism disregarded the ethnicity, religion, skin colour, gender and sexual orientation of those it sought to protect. In fact, traditional socialism went further than that. It attempted to convince its adherents and its audience that individual characteristics should be treated as an irrelevance. Every ethnic group within the working class was exploited but, if they recognised their shared interests and collective power, they could force change upon the system. Of course, some ethnic groups suffered far more than others, but traditional socialism recognised that only together could they change things. A sense of their own collective power and an abiding drive to rid the world of its most egregious injustices could see the entire working class and its political project attend to the specific needs of its component populations.

It was not to be. Racism was firmly rooted within the working class. At no point was traditional socialism strong enough to overcome it. The United States was not unusual in this respect, but one might reasonably argue that socialism struggled to get off the ground there because it was also forced to battle against the significant countervailing force of the nation's unique history of slavery and immigration. There also existed a high degree of instrumentalism. The underpinning cultural emphasis upon the individual encouraged white working-class men and women to think only of the personal risks of vocally joining the struggle for formal equality. The concrete benefits were off in the distance and difficult to accurately discern, and therefore many believed the sensible thing to do was to maintain the standard American focus upon their own material interests, while in a non-committal manner occasionally signalling their support for adjacent groups who might return the favour at some point. The terrible travails of working-class black Americans were thus commonly ignored. The gap between the social fragments could not be closed and eventually replaced with a sense of solidarity, mutual dependence and shared destiny. Despite a few heartening instances of solidarity and sacrifice, ethnic division remained throughout the United States' highly diverse working class.

How might the left's traditional focus on universality have changed things for black people in the first half of the twentieth century? The most obvious place to start is to acknowledge that many accounts of universality carry with them an unacknowledged exclusion. The call to 'include everyone' in some grand undertaking tends to be structured in relation to a hidden supplementary message: 'apart from those people, obviously'. It is certainly the case that black people in the United States during the first half of the twentieth century were excluded from the realm of true citizenship. We might speculate that the ethical route forward for traditional socialism was to build a new account of universality that actively included the hitherto excluded group. All true socialists should have aligned themselves immediately and unreservedly with the excluded community and reasserted socialism's traditional message of common cause.

However, at no stage did socialism in the United States have the strength to even conceive of such an undertaking. Individual socialists were, of course, moved to offer some assistance in the fight for formal rights, but there could be no new and truly inclusive account of socialist universalism.

Liberalism remained dominant, and so the gradual reduction of discrimination and exploitation, when it finally came, was filtered through its lens. Legal rights took precedence over entitlements and obligations, and individualism could not be replaced by a new account of the multi-ethnic commons. Rather than as a movement seeking to include all black people in its account of collective interests, individual socialists could do little other than simply lend support to the civil rights movement and a range of local causes that focused on specific instances of discrimination and abuse.

Eventually on the left, socialism simply merged with social liberalism and disappeared as a clearly defined political movement. Brief moments of political radicalism on the left tended only to drop in a few additional strands of libertinism rather than push the cause of solidarity and togetherness. Beyond the significant material advances and social stability associated with institutionalised social liberalism, in particular Roosevelt's New Deal, battling the cultural and legal conventions of American conservatism in order to embrace individuality and assert one's freedom was as far as things would ever go.

Dare to be different, middle-class left-liberals told their audience. Go your own way and do your own thing. Turn on, tune in and drop out. Such rhetoric did not challenge the system at all. Rather, it reflected and reasserted the primacy of individualism. Individualism could be endlessly commodified, and the radical individualism of the liberal left simply contributed to the reproduction of the system as it stood. The truly radical move would have been to confront this monolithic cultural and ideological impediment. Forget daring to be different; perhaps, momentarily, we should dare to be the same? Defer to collective decisions on investment and wealth-creation. Acknowledge those things of great value you share with your neighbour. Recognise that skin colour is unimportant. Accept that we must rely upon one another to progress. Embrace the beauty of obligation, responsibility and sacrifice to a higher cause. In America? Too much to ask. Far too much.

5

Changes

During much of the twentieth century, the left in the United States and Great Britain grew, evolved, splintered and shrank while being partly overshadowed by events in Russia. The Russian Revolution of 1917 was one of the most transformative events of the modern age. There could be no going back. The established movement of history was knocked off track and began to move in a radically different direction. World politics was transformed. For radical leftists, these events were initially invigorating and held huge promise. However, for the majority on the left, events in what was to become the Soviet Union tarnished their project terribly.

The revolution in Russia was followed by a painful civil war from which the Bolsheviks emerged as the strongest faction.[1] Lenin, the leader of the Bolsheviks, took charge of a country in chaos. He quickly took the country out of the First World War and set to work attempting to restore order. Occasionally, he responded sensibly and to good effect. His New Economic Policy (NEP) programme had a social democratic feel to it, which led many sympathetic observers in the West to form the view that, under Lenin's careful leadership, the new Soviet could strike a balance between market activity and state regulation that would see an end to the desperate poverty of the peasantry and the terrible conditions experienced by Russia's new and growing urban proletariat. With any luck, these sympathetic observers mused, the Russian Revolution could act as a model for the working class around the world.

For Lenin, however, the NEP was always just a short-term fix. He was a communist down to his marrow. He was entirely committed to the total transformation of Russia and the surrounding states, and he was sure that for the nation to move forward the profit motive had to be overcome. He was not a man for half measures, and he launched what was to become known as his Red Terror, which set out to eliminate the Bolsheviks' diverse political opponents.

It is inevitable and entirely proper that the activities of the Cheka, Lenin's new secret police service, strike us as repellent. However, it is vital to consider the context in which this repression occurred. At the start of the Red Terror, Lenin's Bolsheviks were locked in a ferocious civil war in which both sides committed atrocities. Assassinations became commonplace. Indeed, assassinations had been a feature of the Russian political scene for years, both in the build-up to the revolution and immediately afterwards. The value of human life had diminished considerably as poverty, hunger and political violence became normalised. The chaos of post-revolutionary Russia prompted a frantic scramble for survival and supremacy. Lenin himself almost died in an assassination attempt in 1918.

Certainly, many of those at the forefront of attempts to establish a new communist state had relinquished basic decency in the name of political expediency. Many of these men and women had then lived through the horrors of the Great War, and the terrors of the protracted civil war that followed. They had been surrounded by death for years, and some were, as the Red Terror got under way, still relatively young. The forces of the old order were to them not simply political opponents. The hatred was visceral, and for the most part mutually felt. They hoped not simply to defeat their enemies, but to wipe them out so completely they could never return.

Lenin died in 1924. During the long illness that preceded his death, others at the forefront of the party jostled to find a favourable position in what was a swirling byzantine atmosphere in which there were many fragile and instrumental alliances, many of which were entered into and sustained in a climate of perpetual anxiety and occasional jolts of deep, existential fear. All of the key players were perfectly aware that their fellow Bolsheviks were capable of murderous violence, and most appeared cognisant of the fact that even those who had sacrificed so much and remained totally committed to the cause would not be safe if they made the mistake of openly supporting the losing faction.

The two key personalities to emerge in the post-Lenin era were Stalin and Trotsky. Both had spent their adult lives devoted to the cause. Both were strategic, cunning and clever. While Lenin admired Stalin's commitment and ruthless efficiency, towards the end of his life he appears to have favoured Trotsky, who he believed was more likely to secure the success of the revolution in the long term. The common image of Stalin as a dim-witted bully is a total mischaracterisation, but Trotsky appears to have been the more intellectually precocious if less politically strategic of the two. He also appears to have had something of a flair for administration. It was Trotsky who rapidly upgraded and reorganised the Red Army to the extent that it was able to defeat its various opponents and establish the Bolsheviks at the head of a single-party state. And, just as it is wrong to see Stalin as a simple-minded brute, it is wrong to imagine that Trotsky was somehow able to emerge from the horrors of the revolution and the battles that followed with clean hands and a clear conscience.

Of course, Stalin outmanoeuvred Trotsky, who was expelled from the country in 1929 and eventually murdered in Mexico 11 years later. As the bodies piled up following Stalin's elevation, it was probably inevitable that many on the left in the West would attempt to rehabilitate Trotsky and speculate on what might have been if only Trotsky had managed to triumph over his great rival. Even to this day there remains on the left a small rump of support for Trotsky's particular brand of Marxism.

Many Western leftists looked on admiringly at events in Russia. The establishment of the Soviet Union represented a monumental break from the established order of things. Socialism was no longer simply a dream. A new egalitarian society was about to be built, proving – they hoped – that it was indeed possible for people to live in harmony, without the bitterness, competition and widespread poverty and desperation associated with the first century of industrial capitalism. These men and women did not have the benefit of hindsight, and nor were they equipped with the diverse forms of media that today grant us detailed and up-to-the-minute – if not entirely objective – information from around the world. Socialists in the American Midwest and the coalfields of South Wales could not immediately access a detailed account of the latest developments in Russia. It took time for optimism and hope to fade.

More pressing matters occupied the minds of many in the working class. It was among the left's intelligentsia that optimism and hope proved more resilient. In the immediate aftermath of the revolution, the great dream was that this crucial breakthrough might spark a series of further revolts across the West. Given that today we tend to see the capitalist model as basic common sense and an immovable feature of Western societies, we might be forgiven for thinking that this was pie-in-the-sky dreaming. However, in the years between the close of the First World War and the start of the Second World War, leftist uprisings were a distinct possibility. Even after the Second World War, Western states remained attuned to the 'communist threat', and it was only after the arrival of the relative affluence commonly associated with the 1960s that these concerns began to subside.

Support for the Soviet cause slowly declined as disturbing news from Russia began to leak into the Western press. The Kronstadt rebellion[2] persuaded many to form the view that the revolution had become corrupt. Those at the head of the new Soviet were clearly willing to suppress all opposition, even when it came from the left and was driven by the desire to ensure the revolution remained true to its principles. Other Western leftists persevered, first arguing that stories of brutality were exaggerated, and then that what was happening was no worse than the horrors unfolding closer to home. Some even went as far as to suggest that such actions were a regrettable necessity if a true communist state was to be constructed. The division grew wider between those on the left who believed it remained possible to establish a communist state, and those who treated capitalism as a *fait accompli* and believed communism was inherently authoritarian. This division effectively cleaved the Western left in two. As support for state communism withered, the left's general line of flight shifted permanently.

Even as the bulk of the left changed tack and moved towards social democracy, significant divisions remained. In a very general sense, the key divisions fell along the fissures, rifts and cracks we have already identified. Those at the forefront of the trade union movement in the United States were from the outset not predisposed to communism and quickly denounced the Soviets. As we have seen, the reality was that most involved in these key institutions were not socialists in the true sense. They were pragmatists concerned principally with the material interests of union members. They were also patriots, and by this time they were already very clear that supporting the United States meant supporting capitalism. Communism was unamerican. The injustices that existed in the American economy could be corrected by collective bargaining. The few remaining communists in the trade union movement were absurd idealists and should be rooted out without delay.

Similar sentiments were to be found in the British trade union movement, which, on the whole during these years, contained more radicalism than the American movement. However, radicalism and support for state communism were not necessarily the same thing. The syndicalism that was common on the British left towards the end of the nineteenth century had declined significantly, but political radicalism certainly lingered on in some quarters. Overall, however, key union leaders had become far more gradualist in their aspirations. There were now clear signs that the Labour Party could win office and seek to advance the interests of the working class. In the United States, the failure of the left to recruit the unions meant that it was that much harder to truly get a socialist political party off the ground. Many American socialists looked at the British Labour Party with admiration and a little envy.

Ernest Bevin is perhaps the trade union leader who most clearly encapsulates the movement's gradual shift in emphasis. Like so many Labour leaders on both the left and the right of the movement during these years, Bevin was born into the working class. He hailed from Somerset and began his working life as a labourer. He also took on other working-class jobs before getting involved in the labour movement in Bristol. Bevin was, for a time, a Baptist lay preacher,[3] and he is said to have possessed considerable oratorical powers. These powers, and his undoubted organisational ability, helped him climb to the commanding heights of the British labour movement, and then onwards to the pinnacle of British state power.

Bevin was the driving force behind the establishment of the Transport and General Workers' Union (TGWU) in 1922, which was quickly to become one of the most powerful unions in the country. He served as the union's general secretary between 1922 and 1940, and then moved into full-time politics as Minister for Labour and National Service in Churchill's wartime coalition government. Bevin's appointment was unusual to say the least. For a union leader who did not hold a parliamentary seat to be catapulted to the centre of government represented a significant break from the usual run of things. These were, of course, unusual times. Bevin was swiftly found a parliamentary seat in Wandsworth, London. The Conservatives did not run a candidate against him in an effort to speed matters along. He threw himself into the work. Churchill, of course, needed to have key figures in the Labour Party in his government. He was deeply unimpressed by many of them, but Bevin appears to have stood out. What endeared Bevin to Churchill appears to have been his staunch opposition to the pacifism that remained deeply embedded in some sections of the Labour Party. Despite disassociating himself from organised religion, he remained a godly man. However, the god he believed in was a god of battles rather than meek pacifism. Through his time in the coalition government, his stock quietly rose.

Bevin was in the main a socialist.[4] However, he was also a pragmatist who retained many of the conservative sensibilities that had been impressed upon him during his youth. His religious commitments and political beliefs were intertwined. Beneath his pragmatism lay a traditional Christian understanding of moral duty. Christianity was one of British socialism's principal building blocks, a cultural root and trunk it shares with British conservatism, even though the branches seek light in very different directions. Christianity subtly made its presence felt across the spectrum, at least until the advance of modern secularism and the rise of postmodernism made such beliefs largely irrelevant.

Bevin's socialism was really a product of a detailed understanding of the problems faced by the working class and a desire to improve their lot. People needed to be given a chance to grow, make progress and provide for their families. Bevin knew all too well that the poor were overwhelmingly willing to work and keen to support themselves. And there was not a trace of liberal relativism in Bevin's socialism. The lives of the working class would improve if they received a higher wage and better conditions. For Bevin, this was the key battleground of domestic politics.

He entered this battleground hoping to encourage employers to do the decent thing and give their workers the material they needed to build a good life for themselves and their families. If they were not willing to do so, they would find that the organised working class no pushover. If they did, both groups could continue to cooperate to their mutual advantage. Unlike his fellow union leaders on the other side of the Atlantic, Bevin appreciated that this cause could be advanced further and at greater speed if governments became involved in economic planning. He was, however, not given to the constant expansion of the left's mandate.

Bevin would go on to have an influential career in government. After Labour's historic landslide victory in 1945, he was almost appointed Chancellor of the Exchequer but was instead given the Foreign Office. He was also spoken of as a possible leader of the party, but it appears he was perfectly happy for Clement Attlee to remain in that role. The honour of managing the nation's finances was given first to Hugh Dalton, a key figure on the party's right wing. Dalton expended considerable energy attempting to control interest rates and resigned in 1947 after leaking budget news to a lucky journalist. Dalton was replaced by Stafford Cripps, another of the 'big five' Labour leaders of the immediate post-war era. Despite facing significant and growing economic problems, he continued to move forward with the Labour government's nationalisation agenda. Hugh Gaitskell then took on the Chancellorship. The inclement economic conditions faced by his Labour predecessors had hardly eased, but Gaitskell pressed on until the electorate dispensed with the Labour government in 1951. Labour went into that election promising to continue nationalising key industries, but by that time the great enthusiasm that greeted the end of the war and the election of the first real Labour government had fallen away. The change the people wanted could not be immediately conjured into reality.

As Foreign Secretary, Bevin played a significant role in establishing the peace in what remained a fraught post-war atmosphere in which the road ahead was far from clear. He was keen to draw closer to the United States and to Britain's continental allies. He was a committed advocate of Britain's entry into NATO, which was established in 1949. He also seems to have been happy to yield ground to nationalism and the calls for independence that were beginning to emerge throughout the British Empire. He played an important role in ceding independence to India in 1947. At around the same time negotiations were under way about the establishment of a new Jewish state in Palestine. Despite suggestions that he harboured prejudices against Jews, Bevin sided with the Americans and willingly withdrew British forces from the region in the prelude to the Arab–Israeli war in 1948.

Bevin is of principal interest to us here because he was, throughout his career, a deeply committed opponent of communism. While he was perfectly aware of the presence of communists in the TGWU during its early days, he did not seek direct confrontation. His goal as a union leader was to enrich his members, and he seems to have been generally of the belief that if he did his job well the attractions of communism would fade, and the union's small band of communist agitators would find themselves without a sympathetic audience.

Bevin did, however, speak out regularly against communism. He was certainly no shrinking violet, and he did not back away from conflict with the left of the Labour Party. Support for the Soviet Union lingered on in some quarters. As Stalin's repression became progressively harder to deny, support for communism and the USSR faded from view. Fewer on Labour's left were willing to speak openly and enthusiastically about the Soviet Union, but this did not mean that support had entirely disappeared. The battle lines shifted slightly. Key figures on the left of the party – for example Aneurin Bevan, Jenny Lee and the party's future leader Michael Foot – attempted to mobilise the soft power of pragmatism and spoke of the need to reach an accommodation with the Soviet Union. At this historical distance, such a strategy may seem perfectly sensible, but at the time this kind of approach seemed radically divergent because so many were moving in the opposite direction and openly endorsing the American cause.

While open support for the USSR continued to decline, many continued to press the case for a range of deeper interventions into the bedrock of British society. Nationalisation remained the core issue. Many on Labour's left were deeply committed to the process of expanding the sphere of public ownership. However, as the years rolled by, this traditional concern was replaced by others that seemed more suited to the changing times. Many in the unions were also deeply committed to the expansion of public ownership. From their perspective, it worked. The interventions made by the 1945 Labour Government already appeared to be paying off, and the lives of the working class were gradually improving. Incessant profit-seeking had been dispensed with and the public interest had come to the fore.

While foreign secretary, Bevin did what he could to advance what he saw as the Western cause of liberal democracy and combat the deadly threat of state communism. He had the support of many union leaders. The Cold War was, of course, not simply waged by the United States and the USSR. At the close of the Second World War, Britain was quick to launch its own anti-communist operations. The recent declassification of files from the 1940s and 1950s has revealed the existence of a covert unit in the Foreign Office, named the Information Research Department, which was devoted to anti-communist propaganda. The Information Research Department was Bevin's creation. For him, communism was a godless abomination that ran contrary to Christian principles, and he wanted the world to be rid of it.

The establishment of the Information Research Department was perhaps the first act in what has been retrospectively termed 'the Cultural Cold War'.[5] The Cultural Cold War centred upon the ideological battle between the Soviet Union and the Western powers. It was a battle for hearts and minds. For the Western intelligence agencies, capitalism had to win. Communism had to be so despoiled in the popular imagination that it could not extend its influence. An associated goal was, of course, to convince those who lived under communist regimes to withdraw their support and begin to push their nations towards the American system. Bevin was an economic interventionist and a cultural conservative, and hopeful that these two forces would shape the future. However, he seems to have been unaware that the powerful ideological apparatus he was establishing could eventually be deployed to help woo hearts and minds in an entirely different direction.

It has been claimed that the key Cold War ideological strategy of the Central Intelligence Agency (CIA) and other Western intelligence agencies was to coax the left in the West to curtail its radicalism,[6] but that is not strictly true. In fact, the West's intelligence agencies were happy for the left to be radical, as long as its radicalism did not threaten the continuity of the West's political and economic systems or risk the slide towards communism. Cultural radicalism was fine. Already, by this time, cultural radicalism seemed to involve little more than issuing perennial calls to dispense with existing conventions in order to facilitate further freedoms. Cultural radicalism, of course, did not run contrary to liberal democracy or to the liberal market system. Old dreams of socioeconomic transformation needed to be replaced with new dreams of cultural freedom.

The manipulation of leftist politics in the West was part of a wider strategy that talked up capitalism and democracy and talked down everything external to it. Freedom became the watchword of the time. The American system had it in abundance. Those who lived under communist regimes had none at all, and the communists themselves actively hated freedom and hoped to weed it out wherever it bloomed. Communism brought tyranny and desperation. Western capitalism would boost the living standards of all citizens in every nation that accepted its basic principles. And that the lifestyles of the American and British working classes advanced considerably during middle third of the twentieth century can't be denied.

Perhaps the most important weapon in this fight, at least from the Western point of view, was money. The power of the American dollar was enormous and would grow still further as the twentieth century progressed. Pumped up by its power,

Western popular culture seemed to exist in vivid technicolour. In the shadow of it, cultural life in the Soviet Bloc seemed grey and drab. America was a land of easy abundance. Car ownership was rising steadily. Already many were buying a house in the suburbs. Consumerism was growing rapidly. Labour-saving technological advances were quickly becoming a standard feature in every home. In the communist East, hardship and want seemed to be routinised and unavoidable.

If money was the most important weapon in this fight, those best placed to wield it were the democratic left. Of all the voices denouncing communism, it was the democratic left who were most persuasive. This was not simply because those in left-of-centre political parties already had the ear of the working classes. It was also because, especially after the New Deal in the USA and the Labour government of 1945, it had become clear to many that most of the left's desired goals really were achievable within the existing system. Why risk upsetting the apple cart? Sure, the existing capitalist system had its problems, but things were moving in the right direction. It was impossible to say the same about the Soviet Union.

A long list of intellectuals, artists and public figures were pressed into the service of Western democracy. Some were direct beneficiaries of American largesse, others profited from being strategically elevated into the public eye. Previously marginal intellectuals and artists were hoisted centre stage, and in every case what they had to say either subtly or openly supported liberal democracy and capitalism. One example of this broad and multifaceted strategy can be seen in the manipulation of George Orwell's work after his death. CIA operative Howard Hunt managed to arrange the acquisition of the film rights to Orwell's *Animal Farm* and pushed ahead with the production of the animated cartoon version of the story. The elaborate production was financed with CIA money and, of course, in the hands of the CIA's chosen production crew it became a direct critique of Soviet totalitarianism. The initial figure of oppression – the farmer, the personification of capitalism – is, in this early film version, largely absolved. Orwell's *Nineteen Eighty-Four* was used to similar effect. It is difficult to know what Orwell himself would have made of all this, but it seems important to note that towards the end of his life he assisted Bevin's Information Research Department to identify both authors who might assist the cause and pro-communist 'fellow travellers' worthy of investigation.[7]

Speaking out loudly in favour of democracy and offering virulent criticism of the Soviet Union wasn't a particularly taxing gig, and the Campaign for Cultural Freedom was not short of intellectuals willing to step onto the public stage to offer their own stirring rendition. Often this involved little more than the continued reaffirmation of basic principles. However, for the West it was vital that these principles appeared unchallengeable and ubiquitous. Vibrant intellectualism was curtailed by a firm horizon beyond which nothing of value was to be found. All agreed on the essential characteristics of freedom and democracy, and all were against totalitarianism and authoritarianism. Constructive criticism and nuanced analysis were contained within the field of Western liberal democracy, and if one's eyes strayed to the world beyond, the only appropriate response was immediate censure and suppression.

In many respects, the popular image of the public intellectual shifted and hardened during these years. Their stock-in-trade became a high-minded critique of existing social and cultural systems and a determined advocacy for freedom. If, to paraphrase Marx, the point was not simply to explain the world but to change it, then the focus for change had to be restricted to the vicissitudes and perceived injustices of 'culture'. Culture could be changed, but capitalism could only be critiqued with a view to prompting its piecemeal, gradualist evolution. To abandon it entirely was to invite tyranny.

The drive was, of course, to clarify and accentuate distinctions between the Western system and the communists in the East: freedom versus tyranny. Abundance versus poverty. Democratic political representation versus unyielding authoritarianism. The principal CIA-funded organ for these endeavours was the Campaign for Cultural Freedom which, from 1950 to 1967, was run by Michael Josselson. Josselson was a CIA agent, and deeply committed to the cause. His goal was to push the intelligentsia to ditch any lingering interest in communism and Marxism and commit to Western capitalism and liberal democracy. Once the intelligentsia had been recruited the message would cascade downward to the masses.

One of the key historians of the Cultural Cold War, Frances Stonor Saunders, notes that 'at its peak, the Congress for Cultural Freedom had offices in thirty-five countries, employed dozens of personnel, published over twenty prestige magazines, held art exhibitions, owned a news and features service, organised high-profile international conferences, and rewarded musicians and artists with prizes and public performances'.[8] This was not a project of only minor interest for Western leaders and key figures in the intelligence services. This was a major facet of their Cold War operations.

It was remarkably successful, although other factors clearly helped to secure the victory of Western capitalism and liberal democracy. Not least among these factors were the genuine horrors that had taken place in the USSR. When in 1956 Khrushchev publicly admitted the sheer scale of Stalin's repression, and the climate of fear it had generated, it was close to impossible for European intellectuals to continue to promote state communism as viable alternative to Western capitalism.

In the grander scheme of things, this grudging acceptance prompted a degree of melancholia among the left's small band of public intellectuals. All they could do, in the absence of their once idealised alternative, was to criticise the injustices of the capitalist system as it stood, in what seemed destined to be a constant project with no end in sight. While the intellectual left was to develop new interests on the field of culture that seemed to enliven debate, this sense of minimalism and melancholia lingered. Their discourse became essentially negativistic: they could wax lyrical about the horrors of capitalism and talk for hours about what they were against, but it became close to impossible for them to state openly and without qualification what they were for. There can be little doubt that many post-war Western intellectuals truly hated capitalism, but most found themselves in the ignominious position of having to grudgingly admit that it was better than all known alternatives to it.

Not all were melancholic. Many gladly accepted the mandate handed to them by the intelligence community and ran with it. In intellectual life generally, but especially in the social sciences and humanities, culture became a central field of vibrant political contestation. The drive to liberate individuals and specific cultural groups from the musty conventions of a supposedly conservative social order became standardised and rather routine. The key focus for these leftist intellectuals was how freedom was to be advanced. The standard leftist concern with class oppression and class conflict fell out of fashion and, as the 1950s gave way to the 1960s, many noted leftist intellectuals were happy to proclaim that the ongoing conflict between capitalists and workers was only one front in the great historical battle between the oppressors and the oppressed. New fronts were being opened up, and an abundance of intellectual energy spilled onto them to aid multiple struggles for justice.

Equality remained relevant, but it was slowly removed from its moorings in political economy. The inequalities that existed between men and women had been marginalised for generations and now needed to be moved centre stage. The inequalities that existed between ethnic groups also received incrementally more attention. Such social injustices tended not to be anchored in an analysis of economic forces as material inequality was shifted from structural cause to variegated cultural effect. Virtually every sphere of intellectual life veered sharply not to the left or the right but towards liberalism.

Many other traditional leftist themes atrophied. Individuals, it was argued, should be freed from the authoritarian diktats of an interventionist state, from traditional gender roles and norms, from the expectations of their parents, from heteronormativity, from popular condemnation and censure, from the myths of religion, from 'morality', from accepted knowledge and wisdom, and from established biographical patterns. The list grew ever longer as everything solid seemed to melt into air. So much that was previously categorised as known was removed from that category and put into question.

An accompanying critique was levelled at the institutions that seemed to be propping up the supposedly conservative social order: the criminal justice system; the welfare system; the education system; the tax system; religions; marriage; even the established conventions of electoral democracy itself. A huge amount of effort was poured into proving how the criminal justice system failed, how the welfare system failed, how the education system failed, and so on. Some of this material was of considerable worth. Institutions of this kind were rightly subjected to sustained intellectual critique. However, as the left liberalised, increasingly these institutions were portrayed as inherently and irredeemably oppressive, and in need of abolition rather than reform. Many radical liberal leftists became as unashamedly antagonistic to the state as their radical cousins on the liberal right.

In Britain, many on the left wing of the Labour Party had begun to suspect that the party's increasingly dominant right-wing was somehow in bed with various Western intelligence agencies. We now know for sure that they were right to be suspicious. CIA operations affected every facet of the post-war British left. There were ongoing attempts to weed out communists and other radicals from the trade union movement, and many of Britain's leftist intellectuals were happy to receive the backing of the Campaign for Cultural Freedom. It is also true that the CIA assisted Labour's right wing at the expense of the left. Hugh Gaitskell, who led the party from 1955 until his death in 1963, and other revisionists – like Denis Healey, who was Chancellor of the Exchequer from 1974 to 1979 – were the most notable beneficiaries. This group were called the revisionists because they hoped to 'modernise' the Labour Party. Of course, their project of modernisation was rooted in their shared desire to rid the party of its lingering attachment to socialism. The focus of their ire was the hated Clause 4 of the Labour Party's constitution, which articulated the party's commitment to common ownership of the means of production.

They were also as a group committed to the project of European integration and, in this fight, they received a good deal of assistance from the American intelligence community. European integration was, for a time, of great interest to the Americans. However, despite their attempts to boost interest in European integration – portraying it as the best means of quelling conflict and political radicalism while at the same time facilitating borderless trade and economic growth – a host of powerful forces lined up against them. In the 1960s, Labour's left wing was dedicated to defending national sovereignty and the ability of the nation's electorate to shape the nation's political economy through its elected representatives. That the Labour left of the contemporary period seem to be committed to European integration, or at least to membership of the European Union, and dismissive of concerns about the erosion of national sovereignty, represents a remarkable turnaround.

It would be easy to reach the conclusion that the British left was corrupted and dragged off course by the CIA and other intelligence services. There is now clear documentary evidence of the CIA's involvement in Britain and mainland Europe throughout the post-war period.[9] However, there is more to this story. Men like Ernest Bevin, Hugh Gaitskell and Denis Healey were not corrupted by American money and the prospect of power, or at least not in a direct and unmediated way. They did not take up the fight against the Labour left and the radicals in the trade union movement because the American intelligence community decreed it. And the same is true with regard to many leftist intellectuals who began to speak less about economic justice and more about cultural freedom. They did not throw their support behind the democratic system and begin to decry the horrors of state communism because they had been instructed to do so. Rather, the right wing of the British left fell neatly into step with the American intelligence community because their values and goals were in fact quite closely aligned. Many artists and intellectuals were already antagonistic to the state's involvement in the formal economy and committed to democracy and freedom. The general climate of the post-war age rendered the shrinking band of committed Marxist intellectuals simply beyond the pale. Rather than completely rework the content and framework of the left and appoint a new range of leaders, the intelligence services were able to subtly steer its direction, at least in part because that was where the left already appeared to be heading.

Bevin appears to have been a reasonably devout man, and from his earliest days in the trade union movement was avowedly anti-communist. Bevin's devotion appears to have wavered as he aged, and the force that prompted his reappraisal of his commitment to organised religion was the Church's apparent willingness to stand idly by while ordinary people suffered. However, he believed in God, socialism and democracy. He also believed the best way to serve his various constituencies was to win office and gradually reform what already existed. The horrors of communism were, he was sure, there for all to see, and in the historic fight between Soviet communism and Western capitalism there was never any question as to which side he would lend his considerable weight.

Gaitskell too was very keen for his party to throw off all previous associations with state communism and make it clear that the Labour Party was happy to work within the confines of the liberal democratic system. If the choice was between the American system, rooted as it was in representative government, and the state communism of the Soviet Union, where all political opponents had been silenced, usually fatally, then really there was no choice at all. One could either join the unworldly idealists on the left, who were willing to look past the horrors of actually existing communism and align themselves with an abstract idea that seemed ever more starkly at odds with the interests of ordinary people, or one could accept the framework of piecemeal reform and try to advance the interests of the underprivileged by winning office.

There is a further complication. We can imagine that many old-school Labour politicians from the working class were opposed to state communism on moral grounds, and because they were convinced that communism in reality would not improve the conditions of the working class. However, as time wore on, the socialists on the right wing of the Labour Party found themselves at first outnumbered and then completely swamped by a new class of right-wing Labourites: these incomers were essentially advocates of the free market, and they believed that the interests of Labour voters would advance if the state withdrew from the formal economy, stepped back from economic management and encouraged investment capital to drive innovation and create employment. Some were directly influenced by the work of Hayek, and keen to convince all who would listen that Keynesianism was over and that the Labour Party could succeed by developing a better understanding of the market.[10]

Others mistakenly saw themselves as pragmatists, disconnected entirely from ideological commitments, and willing to utilise whatever worked in the realm of ideas to drive economic development. They were, at least on their own terms, modernisers. The world they lived in was entirely disconnected from the world appraised by Labour's founding fathers. Comprehensive economic management had worked in 1945 because the world was recovering from war, productivity and market innovation had slowed to a crawl, technology had yet to draw disparate nations closer together and, of course, because the global market system was still in the early days of its development. The Labour Party needed to free itself from its fetishistic attachment to outmoded ideas if it was to advance the interests of 'working people'.

Labour's right wing had changed. Where once it was defined by its cultural conservatism, from the 1970s onwards, and perhaps even earlier than that, it would be defined by its faith in markets and its fear of 'big government'. Labour's left wing also changed. One might imagine that politicians from the working class tended to be the most radical because they had first-hand experience of the problems faced by ordinary people but, as we have seen, this certainly wasn't always the case. As more educated, middle-class men and women came into the party and filtered towards its left wing, they brought with them a significant quotient of idealism. This is not to say that working-class politicians tended not to be idealistic, but for the most part the experience of working-class life – then as now – tended to ground the individual firmly in reality and immediate needs.

One very clear example of these changes came along in the late 1950s and continued into the 1960s. Many of the trade unions allied to the Labour Party remained absolutely dedicated to further nationalisation. The vast majority of these trade unions remained dominated by the working class, both in terms of membership and leadership. Many trade union leaders of this era fitted neatly into the mould we have established previously: they were often but not always conservative on cultural issues, and quite radical in terms of economic policy and management. This economic radicalism was underpinned by an earthy pragmatism, but radicalism it was, nonetheless.

These men had seen the power of the trade union movement grow, and in many respects the movement reached the pinnacle of its power during this era. Even the Conservative Party had accepted the existence of a broad welfare state, many nationalised industries and significant state involvement in the economy. That the Conservative Party of this era also grudgingly accepted the state's responsibility to ensure full employment is, especially in relation to what followed, really quite remarkable. Both governments of blue and of red were keen to maintain cordial relationships with trade unions, and it is certainly true that unions in many industries were able to advance the interests of their members at greater speed than ever before.

It made sense for trade union leaders to push for further nationalisation. Low rates of pay and poor working conditions were still to be found throughout British industry. They were, however, far more common in the private sector. Trade union power had civilised many workplaces. Work in some core industries continued to be dangerous and physically demanding, but it also tended to be better paid and accompanied by much improved workplace conditions. Aside from these obvious and important practical benefits, nationalisation also tended to accord with the ideological commitments of many trade union leaders. Industrial capitalism – and the exploitation and desperate poverty associated with the first century of its rule – was, it appeared, being slowly replaced by democracy and common ownership.

Nationalised industries need not be doggedly orientated to realising a profit. These industries could be managed in the interests of workers and consumers and geared towards the maximisation of the industries' overall economic contribution. If judged to be in the public interest, industries could even run at a loss. The broad function of these industries within the overall economy could be explored, free from the remorseless drive to force down costs in order to force up profits. The nationalised rail network, for example, existed not just to produce profit through ticket sales. It employed a huge workforce. Those men and women could provide for their families. Their increased wages ensured that, after bills were paid, there was disposable income left over to spend as they saw fit. The money they spent flooded into a broad range of industries and, as a consequence, also acted to create and sustain employment. And onwards the cycle went.

Paying higher wages makes no sense to a private corporation, unless doing so somehow produces additional revenue and profit. For a nationalised industry – run by a government interested in the well-being of the entire economy – higher wages can produce a broad range of positive outcomes. Of course, especially in working-class occupations, higher wages tend to be spent immediately back into the economy, boosting aggregate demand, productive capacity and investment in multiple sectors. It also tends to mean that workers feel more secure. Feeling secure in one's work has a range of important outcomes, not least of which is a greater sense of happiness and fulfilment. Workers who feel valued also tend to work harder. They commit to the job and focus on the positives. A conductor on a train is more likely to smile and exchange pleasantries with travellers if she is paid well, believes herself to be valued, believes that the service she provides is appreciated, and is generally free from anxieties about how she will meet her various financial commitments.

While nationalisation produced many benefits for trade unions and workers, the continued expansion of the public sector did not receive universal support on the left. Questions remained about the benefits of nationalisation for consumers. In some cases, it was, of course, clear that consumers were beneficiaries. Core public utilities – water, gas, electricity, rail and so on – clearly offered stable prices and a comprehensive service while also benefiting other branches of the economy. Nationalised industries could, it seemed, deliver standardised services perfectly well. However, did it really make sense to nationalise other core features of the British economy? For many, technology- and design-driven industries such as car manufacturing were not suitable for central decision-making and the absence of competition, while the idea that large retail companies should be nationalised smacked of state communism and represented a step too far.

The stereotype of nationalised industries as leaden, union-controlled and dominated by restrictive bureaucracies had some truth to it, especially during these years. The private sector, by contrast, was presented as fleet of foot, freewheeling, innovative and committed to finding forms of market advantage that would, when taken as a whole, drive markets, design and technology forward. Did we really want to buy music, fashion, cars and holidays from state-owned and state-managed retailers?

And it was against this background that Clause 4 became a perennial sticking point for the modern Labour Party. The modernisers, who increasingly formed the party's right wing, were clear that nationalisation could go no further, and that the party would need to reimagine itself and its mandate if it was to move forward. The trade union movement and the party's left wing still favoured the interests of workers over the interests of consumers and continued to push for further nationalisation, but in doing so stumbled into a new adversary. This new adversary was not against nationalisation as such but tended to be more interested in democratising nationalised workplaces and loosening up the sclerotic bureaucracies associated with both state-owned industries and the other institutions of the post-war social democratic state.

This new adversary was the New Left. Many of its members retained an interest in the management of the formal economy, but their true focus was on the injustices of the cultural field. For many in the Labour Party and the trade union movement, the New Left was initially an irrelevance: a small band of intellectuals tied to the university sector who published their musings in obscure journals and failed to secure an audience in the working class. Members of the New Left were, however, proved not to be irrelevant at all. Their collective influence on the left was to be huge.

6

The New Left

Leftist politics changed at a fundamental level as the post-war era unfolded. In the previous chapter we explored some of the contextual factors that shaped these changes, but to develop a more detailed understanding of precisely how the left changed, we need to look more closely at the development of what became known as 'The New Left'. In this chapter, we look at its two major intellectual constituencies: the New Left in Britain, which grew from the Marxist humanist tradition; and the New Left in Germany and the United States, which established what became known as 'critical theory'.

Our analysis here moves away from the practical world of politics and economic planning to explore a range of intellectual matters. This is simply because it is in the realm of ideas that the roots of change are to be found. It would be a mistake to conclude that the intellectuals associated with the left during the post-war period had little or no influence upon the shape, content and approach of the left's trade unions and political parties. The influence of the left's intellectuals upon the practical world of politics is subtle, indirect and rather vague, but there can be little doubt that the intellectuals we discuss in this chapter and the next informed the left's post-war remodelling. By identifying new goals and concerns, and developing new forms of critique, they encouraged the gradual evolution of the left's political culture, which in turn prompted changes in the practical sphere of leftist politics.

The New Left in post-war Britain

The New Left in Britain had its roots in humanist Marxism. Humanist Marxists are generally committed to those aspects of Marx's work that focused upon the negative effects of capitalism upon the individual. The phrase also implies an idealistic faith in the inherent rationality and decency of the individual, despite the corruptive influence of capitalist enterprise.

In the early part of his career, Marx was more concerned with the inner life of workers. His writing had a romantic air that fell away quite sharply as he became more concerned with the 'economic shit' that was to preoccupy him as he endeavoured to bring *Capital* – his life's work – to a satisfactory conclusion.[1] Humanist Marxists tend to be much less concerned with this 'economic shit' than the despoilation of an idealised human subject crushed underneath the capitalist system's repressive boot.

The first generation of the New Left – E.P. Thompson, John Saville, Raphael Samuel, Christopher Hill, Peter Worsley and others – were historians who met at university. For the most part, the universities in question were Oxford and Cambridge, which gives some indication of the group's shared class background. The overwhelming majority of the group were either members of or closely associated with the British Communist Party.[2] As with so many others on the radical left, Khrushchev's 'Secret Speech' and the Soviet's suppression of dissent in Hungary and elsewhere pushed these young Marxists to disengage from the British Communist Party and withdraw their advocacy for state communism. Their long-held dream of deep social transformation changed in character, but it did not die.

The group had some notable working-class members. Raymond Williams, probably the most significant working-class intellectual to have emerged from the New Left, was born in the coal-mining town of Abergavenny in Wales. Richard Hoggart, another key figure, was raised in genuine poverty in Leeds. His most famous book, *The Uses of Literacy*,[3] draws on his childhood experience and the evolution of working-class culture, as commercialisation and early consumerism appeared to displace what were, to Hoggart, its long-standing organic features.

Hoggart and Williams were, however, outliers. It was not only their class background that set them apart. Intellectual differences also existed. Williams, for example, was always interested in the materialist underpinnings of culture, whereas the New Left, when taken as a whole, tended to push in the opposite direction. For them, cultures need not have a material basis. They could be reasonably organic creations, and they tended to flow from the uncorrupted tastes, attitudes and ideals of ordinary people. These scholars did not deny the obvious role of commercial enterprise in the cultural world of the mid-twentieth century, but they were quick to stress that the people had the resources to sidestep banal commercialisation and create cultures of their own.

E.P. Thompson's work, which we discussed briefly in the preceding chapters, offers a clear indication of the general orientation of this new intellectual and political collective. Thompson hoped to upend the engrained orthodoxies of academic history. Rather than writing history from the perspective of those individuals who appeared to play a defining role in events – kings, queens, high-profile politicians, and so on – historians needed to construct a 'history from below': a history about ordinary people, their experiences and their collective role in building cultures, economies, and multi-faceted political projects. Thompson's work was voluminous, serious, well researched and occasionally beautifully written. Many historians were keen to follow his lead, and the rather sedate discipline of academic history moved forward to better represent the great mass of ordinary people so often excluded from historical writing.

The installation of the first Labour government, a new and increasingly confident working-class movement, and the titanic battle between capitalism and communism seemed to reinforce the prevailing sense that old orthodoxies could be toppled. Thompson's project had caught the mood of the post-war British intelligentsia perfectly. His influence was felt well beyond the evolving parameters of academic history. In fact, the work of Thompson and other New Left scholars inspired the creation of an entirely new academic field. The rise of what was to be known as 'cultural studies' reflected the primacy of the cultural realm in British intellectual life from the late 1950s onwards.[4] Its popularity with undergraduate students has waned somewhat in the twenty-first century, but for a time 'cultural studies' was hugely attractive, drawing together a range of academic disciplines to form a vibrant space for critical analysis.

The work of Thompson and his peers in the first generation of the New Left also reflected the rise of what was to become known as 'cultural Marxism'. The phrase itself is perfectly accurate and should not fill us with fear. It was not, in its original usage, the creation of the far right, and nor was it intended to denigrate its proponents. In fact, the situation was rather the opposite. Traditional Marxism was understood by many to be dominated by economic analysis. Thompson wanted to shift Marxist analysis away from the dour world of economism and towards culture. The field of culture, in the immediate post-war period, seemed to be bursting into life. This was where the action was, and leftist intellectuals needed to create a new and penetrative account of a world that seemed to be changing at great pace.

The realm of popular culture seemed to be growing at an exponential rate, and the lives, interests and activities of ordinary people seemed to be changing rapidly as it did so. Some aspects of the new mass pop culture seemed to be democratising and reasonably open, despite the fact that the old class system cast at least some of it in shadow. To keep the work of Marx alive meant using his core concepts to capture the evolution of everyday life and the new forms of domination and injustice that were inevitably structuring its development.

Thompson's abiding intellectual preoccupation was with the agency of the working class.[5] 'Agency' here simply means the ability to act rationally, under one's own volition, and generally free from influences that might intrude upon the choices one makes about one's own actions. Thompson was sure that history displayed countless instances of the working class using its agency to resist unjust power. He bristled with indignation at the suggestion that the working class had been captured by capitalist ideology, and consequently laboured daily to ensure capitalism's reproduction and expansion.[6] The working class, Thompson was sure, was far smarter than the structural Marxists on the continent were willing to admit. They understood capitalism better than anybody and, for Thompson, to drive Marxist analysis forward it was necessary to listen to their experiences and learn from their insights.

Like all Marxists, Thompson was interested in power. While Marxists of various kinds offered detailed accounts of the power of the capitalist system and the ideologies that supported it, Thompson's account differed quite significantly. He offered what was essentially an interactive binary model of power: every instance of oppressive power inspired resistance. Capitalism did not simply impose its will upon an acquiescent civil society. The inherent power of civil society, and the working class especially, rose to meet the power of capitalism. History, after all, was shaped by an ongoing class *struggle*. And Thompson, who was far from impartial, wanted to talk up the ability of the oppressed to resist.

Thompson was able to find many instances in which the oppressed rose up against their oppressors. Of course, much was left to interpretation. As all good historical writers do, he built a context around his core narrative and, dropping in facts here and there, led the reader to his preferred conclusion. All facts needed to be interpreted and contextualised, and the central point that Thompson, as a committed Marxist with an unassailable faith in the agency of the working class, hoped to get across to his readership was that the plucky working class would always fight injustice, and often they would force the oppressor class to retreat.

Of the second generation of New Left scholars, Stuart Hall was by far the most influential. His work covered a huge variety of topics. From his rise to prominence in the mid-1960s until his death in 2014 he was arguably the Britain's most influential intellectual. His work – individually and as part of the academic community he led at Birmingham University, which became known as the 'Birmingham School' – was integral to the transformation of a whole host of academic disciplines across the humanities and social sciences.

Hall took on the editorship of the *New Left Review* (NLR) while still a very young man. The journal resulted from the merging of *The New Reasoner* and *Universities and Left Review*, both of which had been key organs for the first generation of the New Left. While he did not last long in the role, he brought considerable energy to British leftist intellectual life and did what he could to refocus leftist critique. Hall's first editorial for the journal gives a clear indication of the interests and concerns of the New Left. It is worth quoting at length:

> We are convinced that politics, too narrowly conceived, has been a main cause of the decline of socialism in this country, and one of the reasons for the disaffection from socialist ideas of young people in particular. The humanist strengths of socialism—which are the foundations for a genuinely popular socialist movement—must be developed in cultural and social terms, as well as in economic and political. What we need now is a language sufficiently close to life—all aspects of it—to declare our discontent with 'that same order'.
>
> The purpose of discussing the cinema or teen-age culture in NLR is not to show that, in some modish way, we are keeping up with the times. These are directly relevant to the imaginative resistances of people who have to live within capitalism—the growing points of social discontent, the projections of deeply-felt needs.[7]

Like Thompson, Hall was keen to push Marxism away from any lingering attachment to economism and towards the field of culture, upon which so much appeared to be happening and upon which the New Left felt able to identify great political promise. It is crucial to note that Hall believed the left had defined 'politics too narrowly'. Here, we might reasonably imagine that he was referring to the left's traditional preoccupation with electoral politics and the management of the economic sphere.

The common acceptance that Soviet communism had descended into barbarity meant that it had become impossible to push the British working class towards state communism. No one, bar the most radical elements of the intelligentsia, had any interest in moving in that direction. The state's involvement in the formal economy had made things undeniably better and, after a fashion, things continued slowly to improve. The Labour Party was far from perfect, but it had during its historic 1945–51 government set the tone for the modern political era. Even when the Conservatives were in office, the overall structure of industrial relations and welfare remained in place. The 1960s are often typified as a decade of general affluence, economic security and the blossoming of a host of new trends in popular culture. Clearly, things were far from perfect but, for the working class especially, they were better than they had ever been.

These features of the post-war landscape created something of a problem for the radicals of the New Left. They wanted to push much further. They refused to turn away from the injustices of the age. They refused to be bought off by relative affluence, or to be silenced by talk of 'never having it so good'.[8] Hall was a committed Marxist, and he hoped to move beyond capitalism entirely. He was morally opposed to the injustices he saw all around him. These injustices had evolved, certainly, but they remained. They bore down heavily on the poorest and those least able to protect themselves. Following the standard socialist strategy of attempting to attenuate capitalism's worst features was all well and good, but – given that further problems seemed to emerge like the sun with each new day – it was a ceaseless task that inevitably pushed the left towards dull reformism.

Given the New Left's abiding commitment to significant social transformation and the rapid and almost total dissipation of 'revolutionary consciousness' within the working class, it is easy to imagine how an air of melancholia might have set in. Capitalism was winning. Communism had become associated in the popular imagination with absolute evil. The benefits to be gleaned from trade union activism seemed to satisfy most within the working class. The Labour Party increasingly seemed to stand in for the entirety of the British left, and the party was now entirely committed to the continuity of capitalism. Meek reformism was as far as it – and the trade unions – seemed willing to go. All the evidence seemed to suggest prolonged defeat on the traditional field of politics.

The New Left, then, could identify nothing positive on the 'narrowly defined' political scene. There was no prospect that the left would make a significant intervention in the realm of political economy. Even if the Labour Party staged another landslide victory, there was no evidence that this would result in anything more than mildly progressive reform. However, while 'narrowly defined' politics seemed to have nothing to offer the radicals of the New Left, the field of culture seemed to be bursting with countercultural resistance. If the field of politics could be expanded to include the entire field of culture, defeat could be turned into victory. Here they could find what for them was the essence of true antagonistic politics: prevailing injustice met by irrepressible organic political resistance.

If all culture was 'political', then the New Left could break free from leftist melancholia and fill its time celebrating countless iconoclastic victories over entrenched power. On the field of culture, the young refused to be cowed into submission. They refused to be mindlessly interpellated into the prevailing order of things. This basic model structured the cultural analyses of the New Left. Revolution wasn't over. Revolution was happening every day as the young revolted against the staid conventions of the old, and as they refused to dress, talk, dream and think as they were told by the representatives of the ruling order. After all, every oppressive power produces resistance to it.

A huge amount of emphasis was placed on young people. Sociologists working at the Birmingham School for Cultural Studies devoted much of their time to detailing the inherent rebelliousness of young people who were quickly moving into the subcultures that had become such a key feature of the cultural landscape.[9] In their musical and clothing choices, these young people were kicking against the outdated cultural rules foisted on them by the parent class. They wanted to be free and build a life of their own choosing. They were capable of creating and living by their own norms and values. They also resisted the dull commercial conventions of the time. Even when out shopping at mass market retailers, young people were capable of stylistic innovation that poured mockery upon the leaden marketing strategies of the corporate world. They could creatively rework styles and symbols to poke fun at the stupid, uptight capitalist hypocrites and their absurd faux-religious 'morality'.

The intellectual gymnastics required to depict entirely corporatised and normative cultural trends as somehow resistant to the power of capitalism were often very impressive. How could clothing choices, musical styles and hanging out with one's friends be made to seem like a determined act to rid the world of capitalist authoritarianism?

New Left scholars dipped into aspects of abstract continental philosophy to make their case. Of particular importance was the field of semiotics – that is, the study of signs and symbols. New Left scholars were interested in how symbols could be used to shape meaning and interpretation, and it was the job of New Left semioticians to challenge the taken-for-granted meaning of subcultural style and dig deeper to identify what style really meant to those involved. The Skinheads, for example, with their shaved heads and in their standard dress of work boots, braces and so on, were expressing their desire to return to an authentic working-class cultural life that was denied to them. The Teddy Boys, with their drape coats and extravagant hairstyles, were attempting to appropriate and creatively adapt the exalted cultural capital associated with Edwardian-era dandies.

Even when these working-class youth groups became involved in crime, they were indicating their determination to fight against the injustices of the system. In committing acquisitive crime, members of the working class were fighting back against their exclusion from the legitimate sphere of high-end consumption. Violent crime expressed the anger many members of the working class felt about the injustices that framed their lives.

Misbehaviour in schools was also immediately suggestive of the agency of the working class. Schools were, after all, sites of oppression and enforced orthodoxy, where working-class kids were subtly pushed into exploitative working-class jobs.[10] They had to accept the tyranny of the clock and adopt an unquestioning, forelock-tugging submission to authority. It made sense for working-class kids to kick against a system that threatened to reduce their freedom, just as it made sense for them to be frustrated and angered by a system that was supposed to be democratic but refused to give them any legitimate chance to succeed.

It amounted to a huge body of work, but it was held together by an unwavering commitment to the agency of the working class and its ability to resist the injustices of the modern age. The scholars of the New Left busied themselves constructing detailed accounts of cultural life that were, in their view, redolent of a natural urge within the working class to resist. Every day young people were using their creativity, skill and insight to fight against social injustice. They didn't need to be taught or led or cajoled; their resistance to oppression was a naturally occurring phenomenon. The politicisation of the cultural field, and the New Left's dogged determination to interpret ordinary cultural activity as being motivated by an organic liberal drive to fight authoritarianism seemed to banish left melancholia by holding out the hope that someday soon a new day really could dawn.

Unfortunately, these tiny iconoclastic victories against what the New Left mistakenly thought was a dull-witted, ossified capitalist goliath never seemed to amount to much. The redefinition of politics to include the entire field of culture really didn't help to inspire change of any kind in terms of electoral politics or political economy. Somehow all of these rebellious teenagers grew up to become really quite conventional adults. The punks – so beloved by New Left scholars – came mostly from conventional, middle-class families. Their dalliances in fashion and music might have caused a mildly satisfying intake of breath among the most conservative elements of their parents' generation, but their brief walk on the wild side did not prevent most punks moving seamlessly back into conventional middle-class life when their rebellious, countercultural twenties came to an end. Most got married, had children, developed careers and took on mortgages, and their rebellious days were kept alive only by occasionally dipping into their corporately manufactured CD collection, now of course digitalised by giant global corporations such as Spotify.

Quite how the whole episode could be interpreted by New Left scholars to represent a cultural assault upon corporate capitalism and its supposedly conservative moral order is anyone's guess. The conventions these youth subcultures seemed to be pushing against were not fixed. Cultures evolved, certainly, because that is what cultures do. But there was no revolution. Capitalism continued.

The New Left's desire to creatively interpret entirely apolitical aspects of culture as their opposite immediately suggests an unquenchable idealism and a firm refusal to honestly appraise a reality that simply did not tally with their ideological commitments. Most young people simply wanted to have a good time, and their involvement in consumption had no political resonance at all. Capitalism was not challenged by youth culture. In fact, the opposite was the case. Capitalist markets evolved and grew as young people acquired more disposable income and commodities became increasingly central to processes of identity-building. It is impossible to resist capitalism at the point of consumption, and those who suggest otherwise really do not understand capitalism at all.

Another look at the excerpt from Stuart Hall's editorial, quoted earlier, will also reveal the identification of a new antagonist for the left. Borrowing liberally from the hippy counterculturalism of the time, and following the despoilation of the image of communism, the traditional enemy – capitalism – seemed to step quietly into the background. It was still considered by New Left scholars, but only very rarely did they offer a sustained analysis of its rapidly changing features. The new enemy was the authoritarian state.

The establishment of the modern welfare state had massively increased the state's mandate. The state had also stepped forward to take a crucial role in the management of the formal economy. With the growth of the state's mandate came a huge growth in state bureaucracy. The British left of the late nineteenth and early twentieth centuries had pushed for the state to intervene to protect the people from the predations of the market, and during the Second World War, and of course the crucial Labour government that followed, the state did precisely that. It pushed well beyond its usual territories, and it got involved in the lives of the people in ways that it had never done before.

The traditional debate about the relationship between the state and the individual evolved to fit the new conjuncture. It was inevitable that new concerns about the state's ability to limit the individual's intrinsic right to freedom would come to the fore. The modern left had for the most part understood this relationship in positive terms. The state was getting involved in the life of the individual in order to give her the tools she needed to become free. The state would equip the individual with an education, a job, a welfare safety net, and so on, and with these things she could build a life of her own. This was an account of a positive, social liberalism, and it clashed starkly with the negative account of freedom offered by the liberal right, which suggested the individual was most free when the state affected the life of the individual hardly at all. As the post-war era progressed, the left slowly began to decouple itself from its traditional account of the dialectics of freedom and state intervention. As the left – and especially the radical left – became increasingly libertarian in its general orientation, it began to dip into the right's standard account of negative freedom. The various institutions of the state were first judged to be flawed, and then irredeemably so.

Anarchism made something of a comeback, although very often it did so without being accurately identified and named. Criticism of the various ideologies that seemed to animate the state gradually morphed into criticism of the state as such. The concentrated power of the state was the problem. It was a dead weight that impeded the freedom of the people. Its supposedly positive features were massively outweighed by its diverse and ubiquitous negativities. Such beliefs seemed starkly at odds with many of the traditional goals of the left. While this hatred of the state and its institutions often seemed negativistic – inasmuch as it reflected the assumption that the state was irredeemable – it was underpinned by an unacknowledged and decidedly unworldly idealism.

The traditional left was worldly. Its cause and commitments were rooted in the immediate experience of everyday life, and its proposed solutions were underpinned by logical accounts of what was possible. During the 1960s, the left seemed to become increasingly unworldly. Its analyses drifted away from the real world and everyday experience. This trend continued and developed even more quickly after the advent of postmodernism. It focused on symbolism and abstract ideals, and much less upon the basic nuts and bolts of everyday life. The New Left's anti-statists were idealists because they assumed that once the state had been dispensed with, a new era of social harmony and human flourishing would dawn. This belief reflected a deeper faith that all humans are essentially good and – once the detritus of the state and the market had been cleared away – capable of working in concert with their neighbours to create a better world. That dismantling the state and its various institutions might usher in an era not of social harmony but of desperate chaos appears to have been generally unpalatable and was thus unceremoniously discounted. People were good and the state was bad.

The negativities that left-liberal anti-statists saw in the world were created and sustained by power and would disappear once that power had been dispensed with. The positive outcomes of state power – the rule of law, social order, the education system, the health system, the welfare state and so on – simply did not appear to enter their field of view. Power corrupted. A world without states and without hierarchies – even practical competence hierarchies that functioned merely to administer various features of social life – would inevitably be a better world.

Many on the left who could remember back to the pre-war years continued to see the expansion of the state's mandate as a good and necessary thing. However, as the New Left's influence grew, many younger leftists saw things quite differently. It would be an overstatement to suggest that the New Left was entirely anti-statist, but it is certainly the case that many radical anti-statists were drawn into the New Left's orbit. The New Left, after all, was producing novel and highly critical accounts of various features of state activity. For the New Left, these bureaucracies contained within them a broad range of biases, failures and injustices. Individually and collectively, the state's institutions aimed to enforce repressive uniformity. The unstated goal was not to assist the citizenry but to reproduce the prevailing order and its various injustices.

Lots of theory and research that came out of the Birmingham School became foundational to critical social science. Some of it is undoubtedly of great worth. However, the quality research that accurately reflected reality mixed with radical forms of critique that seemed totally divorced from it. The core intellectual concerns of the New Left filtered outwards to a whole range of academic disciplines and began the task of radically revising and altering all standard accounts of culture, identity, power and politics. Holding corruption and political bias to account when constructing explanations for various features of social life had for generations been part of social science and a range of disciplines in the humanities. However, the British New Left, drawing sustenance and approval from hippy counterculturalism, transformed the intellectual landscape on which this redoubtable task was performed.

The social sciences, in particular, adopted virtually every feature of the New Left's broad and multifaceted discourse. The state was identified as a perennial source of oppression, capitalism was only very rarely investigated in detail, and accounts of culture – and especially youth culture – became appreciative rather than objective. Everything that was old was conservative, and consequently strewn with bigotry and stupid, reductive myths. It is difficult to identify precisely when value neutrality in the social sciences began to decline in importance, but it seems reasonable to identify the 1960s as a turning point.

Agency, choice, freedom, oppression, stigma, labelling, resistance: a crude binary between unjust power and organic cultural resistance to it slowly became a fundamental point of engagement for every discipline in the social sciences. Many New Left scholars continued to revel in their status as intellectual insurgents shunted to the margins to protect the conservative status quo, but the reality was their discourse had moved right to the heart of their disciplines. They were now the titular leaders of British social science rather than its daring, countercultural antagonists. Even affluent Oxbridge dons began to sing their preferred tunes. Their influence was such that their discourse would be endlessly reproduced as normative, 'state of the art' social science to virtually every class of undergraduate students for decades to come.

We must recognise that this turn of the social sciences to the left was a turn to the liberal left specifically, rather than to the left in general. In the new social sciences, freedom was to be the principal moral end. It was an untrammelled good, therefore everyone should be given as much as possible. That freedom for the pike meant death for the minnow, as R.H. Tawney memorably put it, was scarcely considered.

Social scientists were enjoined to pick a side, and inevitably the overwhelming majority sided with the underdog. On the surface of things, underdog-ism wasn't particularly problematic. However, some significant negative consequences lurked beneath the surface. The answer to the underdog's travails were henceforth to be drawn overwhelmingly from the liberal rather than the socialist lexicon. Certainly, being on the left increasingly meant also being a liberal, and radical liberalism often masqueraded as socialism. Talk of capitalism, class and economic injustice gradually became rather passé.[11]

Over time, socialism and radical liberalism became synonymous. The joining together of these once distinct political ideologies contributed to the increasing homogeneity of British intellectual culture. Liberalism won the university. Old conservatives simply died out only to be replaced by young liberals of one type or another. Socialists had opened the door to the radical liberals, who then proceeded to appropriate much of socialism's traditional terrain. Students interested in socialism were taught a liberal version of it. Already discarded as a practice by leftist politicians, socialism would also be replaced as an idea by the left's new radicals. While radical liberal academics often considered the death of traditional socialism and conservatism no bad thing, the truth was that their deaths denied the liberal left an informed adversary with which it might productively lock horns. Left-liberal intellectualism rolled onwards, but it did not move forward dialectically.

The New Left's critique of the social democratic state and its various institutions revolved around the concept of authoritarianism. The liberal tradition had triumphed by redirecting leftist thought and politics away from political economy towards the field of culture. We might also suggest that, by constantly identifying the injustices of the bureaucratic state, the liberal left unwittingly aided the neoliberal right as it continued to push for the diminution of state power, the deracination of the organised working class and the introduction of the market into every sphere of human life. Certainly, by the 1960s, the cry to be free of the state's petty intrusions was as common on the political left as it was on the political right.

The New Left in Europe and the United States

British cultural Marxists formed only a part of the movement that we now call the New Left. The other major intellectual contribution to that movement was offered by the cultural Marxists of the Frankfurt School. The differences between these two transformative and reasonably contemporaneous intellectual groups were significant, but underneath these differences it is possible to identify numerous points of convergence.

The Institute for Social Research was established in Frankfurt in the 1920s by Felix Weil. Weil was a Marxist who wanted the institute to advance what he believed was the science of Marxism. The institute's first director was Carl Grünberg, another orthodox Marxist. However, it was under the directorship of Max Horkheimer in the 1930s that the institute – henceforth the Frankfurt School – began to achieve global renown. Horkheimer attracted a talented roster of intellectuals and together they dispensed with Grünberg's conventional Marxism and developed what became known as Critical Theory.[12]

The Frankfurt School's influence in Britain spread slowly and sporadically. Its scholars, greatly influenced by the fields of continental philosophy and psychoanalysis, displayed little interest in academic history. British intellectual culture has always been largely dismissive of the abstractions of continental thought, which is one of the reasons why Thompson's version of cultural Marxism caught on quickly in Britain, and the Frankfurt School's cultural Marxism did not. The Frankfurt School, however, made great strides in the United States.

It would be difficult to sustain the argument that the intellectual culture of the United States is more open to the kinds of abstraction one finds in the work of the Frankfurt School. The Frankfurt School's continued influence there might be better explained by the fact that a number of key Frankfurt School theorists fled from Nazi Germany to the United States and remained there until the 1950s. One might also argue that Frankfurt School Critical Theory contained an undercurrent of hybridised libertarianism and showed little interest in social class or the complexities of the rapidly evolving capitalist system. These features of Critical Theory fitted neatly with the United States' established characteristics of political radicalism.

That is not to say that the core texts of Critical Theory do not deal with capitalism, but it is to say that their critiques of the capitalist economic system are broad and generalised, whereas their critiques of capitalism's cultural effects are nuanced, multifaceted and, on the whole, unremittingly bleak. The liberal left in the United States tended to treat the capitalist system as a *fait accompli*, and only in the trade union movement did talk of class linger on into the post-war era. However, the Frankfurt School's intellectual assault upon Western culture drew a great deal of attention and seemed to give the liberal left in the United States a new lease of life.

The Frankfurt School's criticism of Western civilisation is undoubtedly incisive and occasionally convincing. These were, after all – especially Theodor Adorno and Walter Benjamin – intellectuals of genuinely historical significance. Their attack was unrelenting, and they certainly managed to land some effective blows. For the Frankfurt School, Western civilisation was brutal and strewn with manifold injustices. It had been built on tyranny and oppression and had stripped man of his humanity and freedom. It was not simply the working class that suffered. All groups from across the social hierarchy were invited to gaze into the Frankfurt School's deep well of cultural criticism to find resources that could be used to explain their diverse discontents.

In Wilhelm Reich's *The Mass Psychology of Fascism*[13] we can see quite clearly this shift away from standard Marxist class analysis. To simplify, the historical conflict between the proletariat and the bourgeoisie was reimagined as a conflict between reactionaries and revolutionaries. Reactionaries were committed to curtailing freedom and clinging on to outdated customs and rules, whereas revolutionaries were committed to dispensing with illiberality and creating an environment for human flourishing.

For Reich, in 1930s Germany the masses had turned to authoritarianism because they had been raised in a climate of sexual repression. The family, for Reich, was both a product of repression and a key institution that aided the reproduction of reactionary sensibilities. Religious life and the school system also contributed to a toxic atmosphere of pathological control. Nazism seized this surplus sexual energy and used it to drive its project forward. To fight fascism, Reich argued, liberal revolutionaries needed to topple the institutions and traditions that enforced sexual repression. Only then would the threat of tyranny fade.

Reich was neither the most gifted nor the most academically feted scholar to emerge from the Frankfurt School. Nonetheless, his early and rather crude account of the connections between sexual repression and the rise of fascism became the spearhead of the liberal left's countercultural politics. Rather than the foundation of a relatively harmonious social order, marriage and sexual fidelity were a fetter on the individual's freedom and produced a broad range of pathological effects. For Reich – and so many others on the New Left – the harms of sexual repression far outweighed those of sexual licence.

Such ideas had formed part of the radical left's intellectual firmament for generations. Even in the 1930s, there was on the left a long history of depicting the core institutions of Western social life as freedom-sapping tyrannies. Charles Fourier and Friedrich Engels, for example, both wrote with great verve about a future utopia in which people were free to pursue their sexual interests without restriction or condemnation.

As we've seen, the key focus of the traditional left was the material interests of the working class. Liberal socialists and cultural radicals had constantly pushed the left to widen its focus, but – until the rise of the counterculture – libertinism remained on the margins. It was usually the preserve of the affluent, mostly because such matters were only of interest to those who didn't have to worry about their material well-being. Most among the working class disregarded the left's tiny band of libertines. Many remained attached to the Church well into the twentieth century. Even when they no longer believed, many still subscribed to most aspects of the Church's moral system. The family continued to be considered a source of love and support rather than a tyrannical system that unfairly curtailed sexual desire, and the vast majority remained sure that it was the best environment to raise children.

It was not simply Christian and post-Christian members of the working class who felt this way. Similar messages abound in the other great religions. Not all families were a paragon of intimacy and care, but enough had experienced its wonders to ensure that commitment to the family form endured. All felt the pull of sexual adventure, and of course many submitted. However, the overwhelming majority felt that continuing to prioritise the interests of the family, and especially one's children, was the right thing to do. Even when they chose to follow their desires, many felt guilty for having done so, especially when it jeopardised crucial norms and existing relationships. The left's cultural libertines argued that such attitudes were rooted in mere prudery, and that a cultural revolution was needed to free the people from the illiberal attitudes of the time. The work of Reich and his colleagues added a degree of intellectual heft to this position, and the cultural libertines were, with the rise of the counterculture, able to command a greatly expanded audience.

Other Frankfurt School scholars also attempted to draw attention to the stark negativities that seemed to spring from sexual repression. *Eros and Civilisation*,[14] first published in the mid-1950s, was not Herbert Marcuse's first major work, but it is the book that established him as an internationally celebrated intellectual. In this work, he displays a more advanced understanding of Freudian psychoanalysis and a more comprehensive understanding of the broader philosophical landscape than Reich, but the overall thrust of his thesis is in some respects quite similar.

In *Eros and Civilisation*, Marcuse was interested in the repressive nature of 'industrial society'. While sexual repression had been tied to survival and the development of civilisation, its continuation into the industrial era suggested that it had become a tool used by elites to manipulate, control and harness the productive powers of the wider population. Domination had been rationalised. Eros, the realm of sensuality, love and bodily pleasure, had been subordinated to Logos, the realm of reason. The population were offered the pleasures of leisure and consumption, but these things could never yield true happiness. Marcuse suggested that, to move forward, the reality principle – put simply, the framework that regulates the pleasure principle and forces the individual to move away from base gratification – needed to yield ground so that the pleasure principle could take its rightful place in the individual's mental life. Eros should not be subordinated to Logos. Rather, these two fundamental realms should be fused together, to form a radical 'rationality of pleasure' capable of aiding the development of a new era of cooperation and the shared fulfilment of needs.

One-Dimensional Man[15] solidified Marcuse's place as the intellectual figurehead of the counterculture. His analysis is quite abstract and contains a good deal of jargon, but the book sold very well. In it, Marcuse extends his critique of industrial society and develops a more nuanced account of the growing importance of consumption within an evolving capitalist system. His account of 'false needs' usefully drew attention to the ways in which the population was encouraged to believe that happiness, satisfaction and a measure of individuality could be accessed in rapidly developing consumer markets. Consumers bought items they did not need in the belief that ownership of such items would make them happy. When they discovered that the pleasures of ownership quickly faded, they headed out to buy again. They also tended to work harder so that they would be able to buy more, and in doing so they drove the capitalist system forward and reinforced their own sense of 'unfreedom'.

For Marcuse, the affluence of the 1960s served to distract people from their subjugation. While many commentators continued to pitch the freedoms of the American system against the tyranny of Soviet-style communism, for Marcuse both systems were indicative of the pervasive authoritarianism of the modern age. America's much vaunted freedoms were illusory. As industrial society became more technologically advanced, its dominant ideology became ubiquitous and increasingly penetrative. Despite shallow indications to the contrary, the people were becoming more controlled and there were fewer opportunities for individual self-expression.

Marcuse's conclusion was that, given the prevailing conditions, the chances of securing positive social change continued to fade. The stifling climate of total control integrated, manipulated and marketised virtually every feature of human life. The working class had been politically neutralised by the establishment of consumerism's false needs. The left could look only to those who had not been fully integrated into the system – outsiders, radicals and minorities of various kinds – as the last potential wellspring of political resistance.

Erich Fromm also became a key intellectual figure for the countercultural left. Marcuse was often dismissive of Fromm's work, but their enmity was rooted in the narcissism of small differences. Their intellectual interests were in many ways quite similar. Like Marcuse, Fromm found great utility in Freudian psychoanalysis. Both were committed Marxists. However, the influence of Marx became harder to identify as Fromm's long career advanced. Fromm believed that freedom was the most important feature of human life and, as the influence of Marx faded, liberal individualism became the dominant force shaping his work. Put succinctly, one could embrace freedom, which Fromm believed was healthy and positive, or one could seek to escape it, which, he argued, tended to lead to a range of negative outcomes.

The advance of modern capitalism had, Fromm maintained, created a climate of cultural conformity. This conformity was indicative of the common desire to relinquish the burden of choice and escape freedom. Seeking to escape freedom could also drive the individual to destructiveness. The desire to disguise one's failure to embrace freedom could drive the individual to seek to destroy the freedom of others. Echoing Reich, Fromm also suggested that fleeing from the responsibilities of freedom could encourage the development of authoritarianism, which, of course, had become the great and perennial fear. For Fromm, Western civilisation had made human happiness appear unachievable, and it was in the shadow of this grim realisation that escape into authoritarianism had become a clearly observable historical trend. To live life as it was meant to be lived meant being brave enough to transgress established boundaries and take up the burdens of freedom. Only when we had truly set aside our loyalties to family, heritage, community and nation could we secure the fulfilment of our own inherent creative potential.[16]

We have chosen to briefly look at Reich, Marcuse and Fromm because their work had the greatest influence upon the intellectual life of the American left throughout the middle third of the twentieth century. Fromm's work was particularly popular, and he ascended to a level of intellectual celebrity of which today's professors can only dream. The United States had indeed become more affluent. The poverty of the Great Depression had been left behind. The New Deal had created a patchy safety net for the population, and mass production had led to full employment and incrementally improving lifestyles. Not all were included, but the general trend was clear. As the American economy grew and became more complex, the ranks of the middle class slowly increased. The nature of American cities changed as car ownership and suburban living became progressively more common.

A range of authors – perhaps the most notable of which are David Riesman, who wrote *The Lonely Crowd*, and C. Wright Mills, who wrote *White Collar* – addressed the growing sense of uniformity among the new American middle class. Surrounded by what would have once been considered abundance, they found themselves strangely unfulfilled. Something was missing, and growing numbers were keen to discover what that something was. Many were attracted to the liberal left's account of repressed freedom. Social rules, taught during socialisation and enforced by processes of stigmatisation, and outdated laws, enforced by a heavy-handed police state that refused to tolerate difference, were preventing individuals from living a life truly of their own design.

Post-war generations were, it seemed, not particularly inclined to accept the cultural conventions foisted upon them by their parents. While many among their parents' generation had endeavoured to become middle class in order to give their children what had been missing in the early part of their own lives, many children born into the new American middle class could not see anything particularly beguiling about it. They kicked against convention. They did not want to meekly accept their allotted biographical path. Get an education, get a job, get married, get a mortgage, have children: how could this be the 'land of the free' when so much emphasis was placed upon conforming to established identities and biographical patterns? The drive of the counterculture was, then, to fight against predestination and assert the right to free expression. They wanted to break free of the dull conventionality that seemed to await them. They wanted to choose for themselves. And it is against this background that the work of Marcuse and Fromm really caught on.

The rise of the counterculture during the 1960s is perhaps the clearest indicator of the gradual enculturation of leftist politics. The left had discovered new enemies and opened up new fronts in the war against tyranny and injustice. The old fight against economic injustice seemed either dull and unimportant or narrow and unsophisticated. As the absolute poverty of the nineteenth and early twentieth centuries faded from view, we may judge this to have been a reasonably natural development. A broad range of additional injustices had emerged that warranted the left's attention. However, it wasn't quite as simple as that.

The sustained decline of absolute poverty we associate with the middle third of the twentieth century resulted in part from the successes of the left and its ability to cultivate among the people an awareness of shared destiny and collective interests. The left's mandate was clear. In Britain, especially, the active involvement of men and women from the working class ensured that the left maintained its focus on the material interests of the majority. Now, the left seemed to be heading in the opposite direction.

The left's many liberal activists were far more likely to see it as a movement to address all forms of perceived injustice, and they wanted the left to stamp out these injustices wherever they cropped up. Throughout the left's long history, there had always been some who maintained that advancing the economic interests of the multi-ethnic working class should not be considered the left's focal concern. Innumerable injustices could be found on the field of culture, and these injustices harmed the lives of populations that deserved the support of the left. The left, they claimed, needed to broaden its focus. It needed to reposition itself as a broad activist movement that would draw attention to all injustices and constantly petitioned power to change reality so that it might better accord with their evolving humanitarian ethics.

As the post-war era unfolded, this aspect of leftist politics grew and became more insistent. It progressed at a quicker pace in the United States partly because there was little chance that socialists there would ever achieve governmental power. All the left could be in the United States was an activist movement. Many believed, however, that their position – external to democratic politics – came with a number of substantial benefits. If they played their cards right, they could prosper.

As an activist movement, the New Left would never have to worry about toning down its critique to satisfy popular opinion. Activists could be unflinchingly radical and move quickly from one cause to another. They could also offer moralistic critique that would, they hoped, push governments to institute changes on their behalf. They could reveal and draw attention to injustice and condemn all who stood in their way. In pursuing this course, the activist left could achieve genuine progress without ever being sullied by having to first win and then hold institutional power.

This component of the left also advanced quickly in Britain. Many on the British New Left were caught between pushing the Labour Party to be more radical and withdrawing their support entirely. Most concluded that the Labour Party had become submerged in the system and was now entirely incapable of addressing the injustices of the age. Some New Left activists began to move into the trade union movement in the hope of inspiring a new age of working-class cultural radicalism, but many more moved to support the broad range of cause-specific activist movements that seemed to emerge and disappear with a rapidity that seemed typical of the age.

The move away from serious class politics and towards diffuse cultural activism changed the left at a fundamental level. The deep structures that created and supported the Western way of life remained largely off-limits and poorly understood. Throughout its history, when the left had succeeded, it had done so by fostering solidarity and popularising an account of common interests. If the people stood together, recognised their collective interests and acknowledged those things that were shared, they had the capacity to push back against the system and secure meaningful advances to their lifestyles. Below the surface diversity of the cultural field lay forms of commonality that – if acknowledged and politicised – could produce tangible political gains and positive social outcomes.

However, as we moved into the middle third of the twentieth century, the left's traditional account of universality and common interests was flipped on its head. Commonality was disavowed while individualism was pushed to the forefront of leftist politics. Differences we were once enjoined to overlook were accentuated and positioned as fundamental and definitive. As the left moved further into the 1960s, it seemed as if the time had come for the cultural radicals who had always pushed the left to relinquish its attachment to the material realm. Freedom – always vaguely defined – mattered more than material well-being. People, they argued, should be given every chance to grow, develop and live a life of their own choosing, free from Western cultural authoritarianism.

Where the traditional left had been associated with the multi-ethnic working class, organised labour and the demand for decent pay and conditions, from the 1960s onwards the left was commonly associated with middle-class cultural radicals disinterested in work, dismissive of all rules and traditions, and concerned mostly with the tendency of the West's institutions to suppress freedom. Public opinion began slowly to change. The old image of the left was replaced with a range of new images. And the left itself was indeed changing. This much was inevitable. However, whether it was changing for the better was hotly disputed.

The student movements of the 1960s were populated mostly by young people from the expanding middle class. They saw themselves as radicals committed to fighting against various forms of tyranny. It would be wrong to suggest that there was no deep commitment in these movements, just as it would be wrong to suggest that their various foci were inconsequential. However, during these years there was also a sense that leftist protest had become more associated with the fleeting pleasures of transgression than the serious business of changing the capitalist world's fundamental economically grounded structures and processes.

Some even went so far as to suggest that the activist left of the counterculture descended into juvenilia. The left had become the preserve of a bunch of entitled middle-class teens and twentysomethings with virtually no experience of the world beyond the university campus. They spouted the radicalism of the university bar and remained childishly certain of their own righteousness. They were playing at politics and displayed forms of intellectual immaturity that tarnished the image of the left in the eyes of the silent majority.

Such an assessment seems to us a little harsh, but it is certainly true that the activist left that emerged during the 1960s was not predisposed to the hard work of building alliances, attracting committed support, and slowly building institutions capable of inspiring real change.

Many who joined student sit-ins and demonstrations were dismissive of the entire idea of institutionalised change and wary of the restrictive bureaucracies and hierarchies they imagined would inevitably follow. They felt a moral urge to do something, *anything*, to register their opposition in the here and now, and they hoped that doing so would spur those in power to give them what they wanted. And, of course, there was no programmatic account of what precisely should change, how it should be changed and what it should be changed into. At no stage did this kind of activism involve nuanced analysis. More often than not it was a call to radical and immediate action: something must be banned, scrapped or immediately conjured into reality. End hunger. Ban the bomb. End war. Stop racism.

While often the old left's political commentariat considered such claims simplistic and rather childish, occasionally such clear and unequivocal demands cut through the bullshit and went straight to the heart of the matter. 'Enough chit chat,' the countercultural left seemed to be saying, 'just get on and do it'. But who should get on and do it? A fundamental contradiction appeared at the beginning of the so-called 'cultural revolution' and is still with us now. The radicals who loved negative freedom and hated institutional authority constantly appealed to precisely that authority to enact the progressive changes they wanted. The activist left's principal strategy has always been to push institutionalised power to act on its behalf. Despite their ostensible radicalism, few activists were interested in investing the time and effort needed to take power in order to change things themselves.

Many old heads were not convinced that cause-based activism and sloganeering represented the best route forward for the left. The activist left's refusal to give weighty matters the intellectual attention they deserved inspired even Theodor Adorno – the Frankfurt School's most important intellectual figure – to rebuke the activist left for its 'actionism': the activists seemed compelled to do something immediately to register their passionate indignation, but there seemed to be no desire to put in the hard work needed to fully understand the problem. Neither did they appear to have thought through what might be realistically done to facilitate the desired end. For Adorno, the new activist left was full of righteous intensity but totally impotent and unable to drive real political change.

There was, many thought, a childish innocence to the new activism. There also seemed to be an associated petulance, as if these new radicals had it all worked out and anyone who disagreed, or even suggested a few tactical adjustments, was siding with the forces of oppression. They had little interest in history, and little thought was given to tactics and strategies that had worked in the past. They seemed sure that they had right on their side and convinced that all that was good in the world was encouraging them onwards.

Unfortunately, a new era of freedom did not materialise. The promised 'rainbow alliance' of cultural movements failed to coalesce into a coherent political force. However, the radical activist movements of the 1960s did, albeit indirectly, prompt the capitalist system to change. Many researchers now suggest we occupy the era of 'post-'68 capitalism'.[17] Put very simply, after the political tremors of the late 1960s, the capitalist system evolved by integrating and domesticating the discourse of its supposed antagonists. It learnt the lessons of 1968, ditched its residual conservatism and embraced cultural liberalism. Its markets expanded and diversified, actively catering for those who might criticise the capitalist system from any angle. In post-'68 capitalism, the heroes carrying us to a better future would be hippy billionaires and tech oligarchs who decried conservatism and the tyranny of the state, and endlessly talked up the raw democracy of the market. The old, uptight, pinstriped, steeply hierarchical image of capitalism had gone. The global free market would be open, multicultural and meritocratic. Global businesses rather than ossified state structures could help those who suffered in the developing world by integrating these populations as workers and consumers. Everyone was invited to identify and then exploit their own unique creative potential. The best ideas would triumph, and the entire global population would be the beneficiaries.

In this transformed environment, global corporations sought to endear themselves to consumers by attempting to reduce their carbon footprint or by actively promoting women within their structures. Capitalism would no longer be heartlessly profit-orientated. Corporations would join the fight for gender and ethnic equality and use their power to reverse climate change. Corporations would cater for consumers keen to do the right thing by offering them the opportunity to pay a little extra for locally sourced produce. One could patronise a high street coffee chain that promised it would assist the indigenous coffee growers of Guatemala. While states would always attempt to restrict the individual's freedom, markets would always help the individual to maximise it. Resistance to commodification was commodified. Strident criticism of the old capitalism had been appraised and acted upon. The new capitalism would be, on the surface of things, different. It would be meritocratic, climate conscious, global rather than Eurocentric, antagonistic to bigotry and all conventions that threatened to limit the individual's freedom. Capitalism would get behind the cause of social justice as long as the remit of that cause did not expand to include economic justice. Capitalism had evolved so that it might continue, and it drew its primary sustenance from the legacy of the cultural revolution.

Appraising the Frankfurt School

Frankfurt School Critical Theory developed in the shadow of Soviet tyranny. Like the New Left in Britain, an air of left melancholia seemed to hang over proceedings. Indeed, we might reasonably claim that the air of melancholia in Frankfurt was a good deal thicker because it did not inspire the optimism and idealism associated with the British New Left's brand of humanist Marxism. The critical theorists of the Frankfurt School could not construct a positive politics. Their thinly disguised hatred of Western civilisation produced only criticism. It was impossible for them to endorse state communism, and, in the absence of capitalism's last great adversary, they seemed unable to do anything more than commit to 'negative thinking'[18] and pick away endlessly at Western civilisation in the vague hope that their critique might at some stage inspire positive change. Precisely how was never really clear.

The Frankfurt School's collective assault upon many aspects of normal social experience established a style of critique that was adopted widely among the intellectual left. It is worth noting again that the poverty of the early industrial era had for the most part disappeared as the 1940s gave way to the 1950s, but for the critical scholars of the Frankfurt School this indicated only that the capitalist system had adapted its strategies to secure its continued supremacy. The freedoms of Western democracy were a mirage. Affluence was unfulfilling. True happiness was forever out of reach. Freedom had been commodified. The surface diversity of the consumer sphere hid banal homogenisation. Anything that might have been considered a positive feature of the West's shifting cultural life was deconstructed and subjected to sustained critique. Amid what was supposed to be an age of freedom, the people were more enslaved than they had ever been.

There were occasional flashes of brilliance in their critique of Western culture. However, it is difficult to avoid the conclusion that their collective work was at least partly motivated by a vague desire to strip away the West's redeeming features and present it as entirely bereft. Only when the people realised the true extent of their enslavement would they be motivated to topple prevailing orthodoxies and drive history forward. Taking Marx's metaphor of 'prehistory' – the idea that we have yet to embark on a truly human history – to its extreme, they could endorse nothing of the past or the present.

Their dense critiques of Christian hypocrisy, cold Enlightenment rationality and a capitalist market economy that commodified all organic cultures were noticeably absent of any attempt to identify a positive alternative. They battered away at their own mythologised version of Western civilisation and poured scorn on the West's religious and philosophical foundations. Their attack was unrelenting, and its sheer scale and diversity reflected the fact that these scholars, scornful of the past yet totally vague about the future, believed themselves to have nothing of consequence to defend. Nothing from the left's positive tradition could be trusted or redeemed.

The Frankfurt School's work was crucial for the counterculture because it set personal freedom and individuality against Western civilisation and established social expectations. It also poured scorn upon the working class, who seemed happily intoxicated by the inane tat churned out by the culture industries. Only vanishingly small aspects of high culture could be salvaged from the stinking remnants of Western civilisation. Their collective account of the ever more multifaceted suppression of freedom was pitched perfectly for a new generation of radicals who had little interest in advancing the traditional concerns of the left and the working class. The libertinism of Fromm, Marcuse and Reich reasserted freedom as the sole worthwhile political end, and – in the absence of any leftist account of higher causes or values – served only to equip the radicals of the counterculture with an ethical justification for their retreat to the cold ground of personal interest.

It is now quite common to connect the cultural Marxism of the Frankfurt School to contemporary identity politics. It is difficult to deny that an intellectual connection between the two fields can be made. However, this connection is not as straightforward as we tend to assume. Certainly, it would be wrong to suggest that Adorno and Horkheimer were themselves cultural libertines and committed to the goals of the counterculture. Even during the heady days of the 1960s, most Frankfurt School scholars worked hard to maintain a dignified distance from the field of practical politics. Marcuse, in fact, wrote in support of the student movements, but most remained aloof. They saw themselves as elite intellectuals, a secular priestly stratum, and only when they were pushed to articulate their politics would they repeat the standard line about how they hoped their intellectual work would somehow find its way to those most in need of it.

In many respects they were quite bourgeois in their cultural attitudes. Several Frankfurt School scholars appear to have been deeply attached to the very features of Western social life that inspired their swingeing intellectual critique. Certainly, the cultural Marxists of the Frankfurt School and the countercultural rebels who were so enamoured of their work made for strange bedfellows. Where Adorno was always meticulously turned out in a jacket and tie and spent his spare time listening to his favourite classical piano pieces, the rebels of the counterculture grew their hair long, smoked dope and listened to the kinds of corporately manufactured rock and roll that Adorno despised.

Much removed from the frontline of countercultural activism, some Frankfurt School scholars expressed misgivings about the new radical liberalism that seemed to have taken over left-wing politics. Key figures in the leftist counterculture, and especially the various student movements, seem to have assumed that they had the support of their favourite scholars, and on occasion looked to them for leadership. However, this assumption was flawed. The intellectuals of the Frankfurt School quietly worried about the left's line of flight and what the future might hold.

In private, Theodore Adorno was anxious that the left's new generation of cultural activists were drifting towards 'left-wing fascism'.[19] A movement that had initially seemed rooted in a naïve but peaceful libertinism had adopted a range of strangely illiberal attitudes. Their self-regard and certainty enabled them to strip all dissenters of the fundamental right to freedom of expression. Only their own views, they were sure, possessed any merit at all. All other views were delegitimised or reinterpreted as apologies for the brutal domination they saw all around them. Their passionate dismissal of institutions and bureaucracies merely served to disguise their own desire to establish new bureaucracies that reflected their own ideological preferences. Convinced of their own righteousness, they were also willing to mobilise conspiracy theories, dismiss rationality as a bourgeois conceit and push ever further towards an extremism that worried Adorno greatly.

The counterculture was taking on a darker hue. Leftist groups, especially in Europe, became involved in terrorism in the hope of awakening the silent majority to the diverse injustices of a post-war social democratic order that, while certainly not perfect, had in the West conquered absolute poverty, made a patchy but worthwhile commitment to full employment, and equipped the multi-ethnic working class with incrementally improving lifestyles. Despite their deeply felt indignation, and despite the fact that these rebels refused to accept the tyrannies of the cultural order, Adorno could not bring himself to offer even muted support.

Adorno's reticence led some radicals to target him directly.[20] When student radicals occupied the Institute and disrupted his lectures, rather than kowtowing to their shouty self-righteousness, he phoned the police. This act, for the student radicals, revealed Adorno's hypocrisy. Female students bared their breasts at him in the hope of proving that he was a prudish cultural conservative all along. Adorno tried to speak calmly and logically to the protestors. He wanted them not to disengage from politics entirely but to refine their critique, improve their strategies and express themselves in ways likely to convince and inspire. Adorno was left shaken by events and died shortly afterwards.

It seems unlikely that Adorno ever saw a connection between his own critique of Western culture and that offered by the countercultural rebels who were rapidly altering the left's political direction and popular image. It is more likely that he saw the counterculture as a collection of student rebels more interested in briefly experiencing the pleasures of transgression than overcoming the West's systemic injustices.

Adorno was wrong on the first count, and only partially correct on the second. There are connections between the cultural Marxism of the Frankfurt School and the liberal radicalism of the counterculture, just as there are connections between the Frankfurt School and the field of identity politics that dominates the intellectual left today. These connections are rather loose and ephemeral, but their existence should not be denied. The Frankfurt School pushed the left away from materialism and political economy and towards the field of culture. It destabilised the left's traditional account of universality and collectivism and encouraged it to place much greater emphasis on individualism, freedom and identity.

Adorno was right to see the countercultural left as being generally more interested in the pleasures of performing radical politics than in the hard work of inspiring positive change, and many of his anxieties about the New Left's irrationalism and creeping authoritarianism seem, at this historical distance, to have been rather prescient. However, what Adorno could not have predicted was that the activists would be so successful in effectively rebuilding the political left in their own image.

7

Postmodernism, neoliberalism and the left

As the 1970s progressed, the economic liberalism of Milton Friedman and his colleagues in the Chicago School moved closer to overcoming the Keynesian orthodoxy. Many notable figures in the left's mainstream political parties were happy to see the back of what they had come to believe was an economic model that created coddling dependencies and curtailed the dynamism and creativity of the entrepreneurial class.[1] And as neoliberalism rose to the heights of government and transformed itself into a new economic and political orthodoxy, the dominant cultural wing of the left continued its flight into abstraction.

Intellectual life took what became known as its 'cultural turn'. All eyes seemed to turn to the cultural field. The intellectual frameworks of the past were believed to be unsuited for a world that seemed to be becoming ever more complex and changeable. The foundations of Western thought appeared to be rooted in assumptions that no longer reflected the lives of a population that had freed itself from the myths that weighted so heavily upon the lives of their parents and grandparents. Older generations, it was claimed, had led rather predictable, static lives, but the same would not be true for those growing up in the neoliberal era. The lives of the young would be creative, unpredictable and hypermobile. The young were more likely to switch nations, social classes, political allegiances, homes, identities, jobs, and so on. They had also freed themselves from the collective identities of the past. They would be autonomous individuals rather than members of sprawling social groups.

The intimacies of personal life were also changing. Romantic relationships had become brittle and were increasingly liable to break apart under the slightest strain.[2] Friendships would also be constantly appraised for their utility, and enduring personal connections would be a much less significant feature of the lives of young people.[3] Perhaps more important was the supposed shift in ethics. The young would appraise their own lives and judge the lives of others differently. They would be more calculative and ends-driven than their parents and grandparents. They would seek out their own best interests in a more brazen and unadorned manner, and they would do so because the institutions that once condemned blatant self-interest were falling into irrelevance. All were expected to fight hard to secure personal benefits. Certainly, this was the message constantly repeated by the neoliberals who had established themselves at the very core of the system. The common good – and the old virtues of duty, altruism, sacrifice and humility – seemed to disappear from popular and political discourse.

Social scientists often responded to such analyses by claiming that they were overly pessimistic and much that was positive in the lives of earlier generations remained operative in younger generations. There was some truth in this response. Virtue had not simply fallen out of the world, and not all people had heeded the neoliberal call to prioritise material self-interest. However, pessimistic accounts of social change were often rooted in the identification of trends that, if left unchecked, would continue to erode the expectations of modernism and establish self-interested individualism as a regrettable social norm.

Looking back, it is difficult to deny that society did indeed change in the predicted ways. As traditional forms of security fell away, individualism seemed to displace all remaining collectivist impulses. That is not to say that everyone became aggressively instrumental and entirely devoid of human kindness, but it seems to us perfectly clear that traditional virtues seem in abeyance, and self-interest has become an obvious, and unremarkable, feature of personal and collective life.

As we have seen, throughout the middle third of the twentieth century many notable leftist intellectuals called for this kind of cultural revolution. The old institutions and structures that seemed to pattern modern lives were presented as freedom-sapping tyrannies, and the social democratic state's bureaucracies were said to be key sites of oppression that perpetuated bigotry and social injustice. In some respects, the people were indeed freed from the institutions of the old order. Certainly, there did seem to be more opportunities for personal choice and self-expression. However, as the state retreated, the result was not freedom in either its negative or positive guises. The entire terrain of civil society was yielded to the market. There seemed more opportunities to choose, but most of the choices on offer were determined by the market. As Adorno and Horkheimer[4] once noted, the diner had to be satisfied with the menu. The individual could choose, but only between predetermined options over which he or she had no control. This was not freedom but a new set of rules by which the individual must play the game.

Old conceptions of the good life withered and died. In the neoliberal era, a good life became a life in which the individual had consumed to excess, a life defined by diverse and occasionally extreme experiences, a life in which the individual had denied herself nothing. And, of course, money was the key to securing this consumerised good life. While great emphasis was placed upon the expansion of possibilities, in important respects life's possibilities became more constrained.

The radicals of the New Left played a significant role in driving forward the cultural turn. They created and pushed hard to popularise new forms of cultural analysis, and, by constantly calling for the West to establish freedom as its principal goal, they had done all that the markets and the Western intelligence services could have asked of them. Much of the left appeared to have lost interest in either regulating or moving beyond capitalism. Acting as an advocate for the cultural freedoms of individuals and minority groups now seemed its principal focus.

Many leftist academics in the humanities and social scientists were beginning to declare the modern era dead and buried. A postmodern era – an era in which the core features of modernity were absent – was opening up, and it promised to be freer and more in keeping with the interests of its increasingly mobile populations. As the 1970s advanced, interest in postmodernism slowly gathered pace. Architects, artists and writers were increasingly willing to move beyond the orderliness of modernism and experiment with form.[5]

Similar moves were afoot in philosophy. Optimists suggested that we had entered a post-ideological age. The ideologies of the past would increasingly be judged irrelevant. Free-thinking individuals would no longer be constrained by dogmatism. Intellectual and political life would become a smorgasbord of boundless choice. A new generation of post-ideological politicians would take ideas from across the political spectrum and, using the best available evidence, craft policies with much improved chances of success.

Of course, what these authors were really talking about was not the end of ideology but the end of ideological contestation. Liberalism had defeated its various antagonists. Conservatism and socialism were dead. Communism was dead. The end of history had been reached. Liberalism's success was such that its was able to establish its own ideological features as 'common sense'. Talk of pragmatism was really yet more talk of endlessly applying the basic features of liberal discourse.

Post-ideology was but one of a whole host of 'post-' discourses. Post-feminism, post-communism, post-structuralism, post-coloniality, post-Marxism, post-industrialism, post-nationalism – the list seemed endless. The fundamental claim of all 'post-' discourses was that something had ended and something new was beginning to open up. A tipping point had been reached and things were changing. The old frameworks were too restrictive. New ideas were coming to the fore.

The most important of these discourses was postmodernism. In many respects, it was the catch-all repository for all other 'post-' discourses. For the ex-Marxist philosopher Jean-François Lyotard, postmodernism was best understood as a growing 'incredulity towards metanarratives'.[6] Lyotard claimed that, as Western society moved into the final third of the twentieth century, the grand explanatory systems developed in earlier epochs inspired only incredulity. The people no longer believed. They had lost faith in all dominant explanatory systems.

All of the great philosophers had offered grand systems. These systems attempted to capture the structures and processes that shape social life, history, thought, action, politics, consciousness, morality, and much else besides. They are quite literally 'big stories': elaborate, multidimensional accounts of what we are, what we do and why. However, for Lyotard these metanarratives were inherently restrictive. They inevitably failed to capture the diversity of human experience. People were, for Lyotard, diverse and changeable. Human lives resisted categorisation. The postmodern era would be defined instead by a profusion of 'micronarratives'. Everyone was unique. No two lives were the same. Everyone was capable of interpretating the world. Basic intellectual touchstones – for example truth, progress, objectivity – should be interrogated, deconstructed and their utility reconsidered in relation to the fluidity and diversity of the postmodern age. The reader could be as creative as the author. Human knowledge was moving beyond the rigidity of the modern age.

The concept of morality is a useful place to start. Morality, postmodernists claimed, had no material basis and no foundation in truth. Its structure tended to reflect the lessons of the great religions, which were themselves grand narratives rooted in myth. Salvation, life after death, rules delivered on tablets of stone: it was all mystical nonsense that curtailed freedom and forced people to live in fear. People should be encouraged to subscribe to or disengage from moral systems as they saw fit. Morality forced people to live by rules. The rules themselves were reductive, immobile, blind to context and created without popular consent. Why should the free individual be compelled to abide by myth-based rules enforced by some overarching institutionalised power?

The exalted status of science and scientific method was also earmarked for deconstruction and reappraisal. Science had garnered a reputation for impartiality, but it was polluted by hierarchies and normative practices that shaped the results of supposedly objective experiments. Scientific objectivity was a myth, and scientific knowledge a mere social construct manipulated by elites.

Many critics of postmodernism's gradual rise to prominence presented it as a form of idealism, and it is true that there is a significant quotient of idealism in postmodernism's core texts.

However, if it was a form of idealism, it contained within it an often-unacknowledged negativistic aspect. Postmodernism threw into question the entire idea of incrementally advancing knowledge. What we had thought known was not known. What we had thought true could no longer be considered truthful. Whatever beliefs we had managed to gather together must first be 'problematised' and then disbelieved.

Postmodernism went well beyond healthy scepticism. It was driven by the desire to disabuse civil society of its illusions. Every idea and every established truth were presented as mere texts to be deconstructed. Nothing could be generalised. No claim was irrefutable. Everything once considered reliable was now untrustworthy. Those who accepted the logic of postmodern critique were, apparently, able to free themselves from myths, accept their own freedom and recreate themselves as they saw fit.

Postmodernism was thus an intellectual terminus of sorts. Read in the context of the great contributions to philosophy, it seemed depressingly unambitious. Its tone was ironic and self-satisfied. It did not seek to construct anything. Rather it sought to deconstruct everything. The collective hope of the postmodernists was to break apart every edifice, even though all seemed sure that nothing of value would ever be found at the core.

Many of postmodernism's key protagonists were leftists, but they had little or nothing to say about the traditional concerns of the left. The past could not be used as a guide to the present or the future. Nothing that constrained the individual could be considered legitimate. Despite the fact that it was often presented as a leftist movement, postmodernism was in fact built upon the *negative* conception of liberty we commonly associate with the neoliberal right.

As we've seen, the reforms pursued by traditional socialism, and those put into practice by social democratic governments during the first half of the twentieth century, reflected a commitment to *positive* social liberty. These interventions were driven by the desire to give the individual the wherewithal to become free on a stable socioeconomic platform that combined collective contributions with personal liberties. However, over and above minimal welfare provision, postmodernists saw nothing in modern social democracy worthy of commendation or preservation. Social democratic interventions produced, they argued, freedom-sapping bureaucracies geared towards the reproduction of cultural uniformity and the status quo.

In Britain, the United States and France, social democratic governments had truncated inequality, taxed wealth at a high level, and equipped the working class with a degree of security and much improved living standards. However, the postmodernists saw only creeping authoritarianism in social democracy. The progress of the age was a mirage. The traditional concerns of the left – poverty, inequality, insecurity and so on – were rarely considered. On the rare occasions that they were, they tended to be seen not as fundamental problems. Rather, they were understood in relation to their capacity to reduce freedom. The left's new intelligentsia – in their rolling critique of institutions, collectives and bureaucracies, and in their advocacy for a vague, substanceless freedom – were moving at speed away from socialism and towards the solipsistic individualism advocated by the neoliberal right.

Much of the postmodernist literature is impenetrable. Often it seems deliberately so. Unfortunately, this is where leftist thought took us as we moved into the 1970s and 1980s. Rather than discuss this material in detail, we will focus on the work of Michel Foucault, who can be considered the post-'68 period's archetypal postmodern libertarian. Foucault became the left's most feted intellectual during the 1980s, and he remains one of the most cited social theorists in the world today. His work tells us a great deal about the intellectual evolution of the left. However, before we begin our analysis, we want to draw readers' attention to the increasingly abstract nature of leftist philosophising.

This is not to suggest that the great intellectual figures of the early left did not engage in abstract thought or write in an annoyingly abstract style. However, it is to suggest that their philosophising always remained tied to reality. They hoped to reveal the hidden structure of reality and the forces that determined its shape, content and dynamics. Often, these figures hoped that their work might in some way lead to the mitigation of reality's manifold negative features, and some hoped that their work might assist in the task of transforming reality so that it better served the interests of the people. However, the ties that bound leftist philosophers to reality withered as the twentieth century progressed. More often than not, from the 1960s onwards, abstract philosophising was orientated not to the real world and its problems but to abstract ideals that seemed increasingly divorced from it.

Neither the *Nouveaux Philosophes* nor the left's postmodernists were interested in the people, their problems or their needs. Many seemed more interested in their own self-image as all-knowing philosopher kings. To justify their lofty status, they produced abstruse accounts of texts, language, discourse, interpretation and meaning. Reality was, for them, simply a text to be read, interpreted, deconstructed and reimagined: a field onto which their fragmented abstract idealism might be applied, rather than a field with objective forces, processes and outcomes they might seek to understand or illuminate for others. The gradual drift of the intellectual left away from reality is important and revealing.

Despite being commonly understood as radicals, many postmodernists gave up entirely on the traditional goal of changing the world. This was not simply a reaction to Soviet atrocities, and neither was it a consequence of the threatening return of leftist political violence in 1968. It reflected their deepest intellectual commitments. Radical political change had become passé. Socialism was, they argued, a product of the nineteenth century and simply wasn't equipped to address the problems of the postmodern age. Socialist politics inevitably cleaved towards the creation of monolithic institutions and bureaucracies and encouraged forms of state control that reduced the individual's freedom. Socialism always sought to govern too much. For postmodernists, the principal political focus was to encourage the state to govern less.

Rather than change the world, for the postmodernists the really radical thing to do was to change the self. To change the self was not easy, but disengaging from normal, everyday life enabled the individual to move towards true freedom. The ties that bound the individual to conventionality could be severed, and when she had freed herself from all prior constraints, a boundless process of experimental self-creation could begin.

Foucault's freedom

Foucault was at the very epicentre of the Parisian intellectual scene.[7] He was on the left, but he was certainly not a socialist. Neither was he a communist or a social democrat. There was, of course, a diversity of leftist groups in France at the time. Some were committed to traditional socialist goals, but many more were essentially libertarian groups concerned with securing new freedoms for specific subsets of the population. For them, the authoritarian state was the true enemy of the people, and the goal was to free the individual from all forms of condemnation and control. The socialist left was shrinking and retreating, and the libertarians were in the ascendency.

Foucault was an intellectual provocateur who had constantly struggled against the norms of civil society. Despite his professional success, he appears to have felt at various points in his life marginalised, constrained, out of place and negatively judged. His experiences at the margins prompted in him a commitment to diversity and to lifestyle experimentation, and a drive to redirect critique towards what for him was the stifling nature of conventionality.

His first book, *Madness and Civilisation*, was an immediate hit and established Foucault as an important intellectual figure in France. The book displays many of the core characteristics of Foucault's oeuvre. Perhaps the most important of these characteristics was a commitment to challenging what for him was the myth of Western progress. The people were not becoming freer, wiser or more civilised. Western institutions were not becoming more democratic, tolerant or humane. The control system constantly refined its tactics, and its ability to mould the experiences, attitudes and beliefs of the people was, in the final third of the twentieth century, more advanced than it had ever been.

Foucault claimed that, throughout the history of Western societies, madness had been dealt with in a number of distinct ways. Where once the mad were considered to possess wisdom and were treated with care, the post-Enlightenment period brought segregation and confinement, and the modern era an intrusive attempt to cure what by this stage was categorised as 'mental illness'. The general structure of this argument is quite similar to his later work, *Discipline and Punish*, which looked at the evolution of the French criminal justice system. The state had subtly moved from attempting to subjugate bodies – through torture, segregation, and so on – to attempting to control and discipline the mind. The criminal justice system, just like the mental healthcare system, seemed increasingly humanitarian in its mission, but its humanitarianism produced in the individual the very characteristics and features it sought to control.

Madness and Civilisation's dominant message was that madness was socially constructed. The mad were not necessarily dangerous or threatening or ill: they were simply different. They were less constrained by social convention. The application of negative labels enabled power to deny the mad a voice and exclude them entirely from the social body. It was also possible to discern another core message. Foucault wanted his readership to tarry with the notion that madness could be considered a positive thing. Hadn't madmen freed themselves from the constraints of the social order? They were different, certainly, but shouldn't a tolerant and free society be able to profit from difference? Throughout his work, Foucault sought to redirect critique away from marginalised groups – in this case, those categorised as 'mad' – and towards the repressive state and civil society, which were happy to judge, condemn and oppress all those who did not conform. Perhaps normality itself was pathological? Perhaps society would be healthier if it accepted radically divergent forms of identity and behaviour?

It was certainly an interesting central thesis. The book was treated as a major intellectual intervention and stirred much debate. Why should society seek to fix those judged mad? Why should it push them to become 'normal'? What was so great about normality, and who got to decide upon the boundaries of acceptable thought and action? Foucault's thesis seemed radical because it sought to redirect the standard analytical focus. In his drive to rehabilitate madness, Foucault seemed keen to encourage in his readership the uncomfortable feeling that their own conventional attitudes might well be illogical and oppressive. The problem wasn't madness or the mad.

The fundamental problem was popular attitudes to those who seemed in some way different.

Of course, anyone who has encountered genuine mental illness might tend to challenge the general principles of Foucault's thesis. Mental illness cannot be reduced to the status of a mere 'social construct'. It is connected to material changes in the brain. Schizophrenia, for example, is a terrible, traumatising condition, best addressed not simply by the removal of stigmatising social symbolism but by the best available antipsychotic medicines and psychiatric treatment. To present it as a form of otherness to be accepted – celebrated, even – is wrong. Those suffering from this condition are not battling to be free from oppressive normality; they yearn to be 'normal'. They long to be free of disturbing, intrusive thoughts of which they are not the author, and which can relentlessly accost the individual with terrifying delusions of external threats. Of course, the real-world effects of mental illness, and the pain and sadness that tend to go along with it, were of little interest to Foucault and the radical libertarians of the Parisian intellectual scene.

Foucault's later works, *Discipline and Punish* and the multi-volume *History of Sexuality*, established his reputation among fashionable liberals as one of the greatest thinkers of his time. Rather than recap the basic features of these famous books, it seems to us more important to explore Foucault's attraction to what, at the time, was the increasingly dominant economic and political orthodoxy of neoliberalism. Foucault sensibly stopped short of fully endorsing neoliberalism, but he was very keen to explore the possibilities that neoliberalism opened up.

Foucault had taken up a visiting professorship at the University of California in 1980. He threw himself into the gay scene and experimented with sadomasochism (S&M) and other extreme sexual practices. His interest in S&M seemed to blur the intellectual and sexual aspects of his personality. Foucault was, of course, interested in power, submission and control. S&M, he claimed, offered new opportunities for personal pleasure. The interplay of power and submission, and the ability to consciously choose to occupy one specific role, or indeed move between roles, was not just liberating; it opened up a space in which the individual might recreate and reimagine himself and his relation to others. He also experimented with hallucinogenic drugs, and again found that they presented him with the ability to redefine himself and see the world from a radically new perspective.

Foucault had long been an advocate for what we might reasonably consider extreme forms of sexual activity. His work on the history of sexuality explored from multiple angles the interplay between sex and power, the control of sex and sexual pleasure, and the social construction of ostensibly normal sexual appetites and activities.

In the 1970s, Foucault also joined many other leftist intellectuals – including Jacques Derrida, André Glucksman, Roland Barthes, Jean-Paul Sartre, Gilles Deleuze and Simone De Beauvoir – in signing two letters, published in *Le Monde*, that petitioned the French government to lower the age of sexual consent. The letters were a response to the imprisonment of three men in their mid-forties convicted of having sexual intercourse with boys and girls aged 13 and 14.

The leftist French intelligentsia seemed to be firmly of the opinion that it was possible for a 13-year-old child to consensually engage in sexual activity with a middle-aged man. They also seemed to have believed that the state, in punishing these men, was being grossly regressive and controlling. The state had no business in the nation's bedrooms. The state's laws and policy programmes should, they demanded, be radically updated to reflect changing social attitudes. The convicted men had simply responded to irrepressible desires. And furthermore, why should the state assume coercion, when there seemed to be growing evidence that children become interested in sex long before the onset of puberty? Why was the state unwilling to countenance the possibility that these young people had freely engaged in sexual activity, and that the blossoming of these sexual relationships might be considered a positive feature of their lives? Clumsy attempts to repress sexual desire, the intellectuals seemed sure, were far more damaging than its free expression.

Elements of the British left also began to advocate for the rights of paedophiles. Paedophiles were, of course, a stigmatised minority, and so some on the New Left felt immediately inclined to rally to their defence. The boundaries of acceptable sexual conduct were repressive. Why should the sexual interests of some be considered legitimate and the sexual interests of others illegitimate? On what basis was that decision made? As Foucault had claimed, attitudes to minority sexual interests were in the past far more liberal. That our attitudes to sex had become more prescriptive was absurd. Sexuality was boundlessly diverse. Children began to develop an interest in sex long before their sixteenth birthday. Why should the state disallow children from the realm of sexual pleasure? Why should a child be denied the opportunity to enter into a positive, consensual sexual relationship with an adult male if he or she chose to do so? The law was static and blind to the fact that age was no barrier to physical and psychological attraction. Life-affirming intimate relationships could develop between children and adults.

The Paedophile Information Exchange (PIE) was a British advocacy group and a support network for paedophiles. It was set up in the mid-1970s and disbanded a decade later. The group published magazines and pamphlets, trying wherever it could to win institutional support for its cause. In practical terms, PIE petitioned for the decriminalisation of incest and the lowering of the age of consent. They also hoped to encourage civil society to adopt a more enlightened understanding of human sexuality. If this could be achieved, the stigma that accompanied their predilections would begin to fade and the world would be a better and more tolerant place.

PIE was accepted as an affiliate group by the hugely influential National Council for Civil Liberties (NCCL), which today is called Liberty. The NCCL was effectively an organ of the liberal left and functioned as a clearing house of sorts for prospective Labour Party politicians. In academic life, too, there were growing calls to destigmatise paedophilia. Professor Ken Plummer,[8] a sociologist from Essex University, is perhaps the most noted expert on this topic, but many others sought to redirect critical attention away from paedophiles and towards civil society and its illiberal attitudes. Paedophilia had inspired, apparently, a long running 'moral panic'. The scale of the panic and its diverse negative effects far outweighed the forms of harm directly associated with paedophilia itself. Powerful groups, we were told, were keen to enforce conventionality and maintain the status quo by whipping up public anxieties about paedophilia. Their goal was to encourage the majority to bear down upon a minority in an effort to reassert the power of the system and the timelessness of its moral foundations. Paedophilia was, they argued, nothing to worry about. Instead of worrying about the private activities of a sexual minority, what the public should have been worrying about were the authoritarianism of the state and the moral conservatism of the social mainstream. The problem wasn't paedophilia. The problem was the willingness of many to condemn what they didn't understand, and the ability of the powerful to manipulate popular sentiments for their own malign interests.

Many liberal academics and leftist politicians were sensible enough to withhold vocal support. However, such arguments were immediately considered rigorous and appropriate and failed to cause much of a stir. It was, after all, an age of radical libertarianism. Or at least it was in academia and in some small subsets of the broader population. Many from the social mainstream found such arguments baffling. Weren't these arguments simply elaborate justifications for the terrible abuse and exploitation of children by predatory adults? Weren't those who made such arguments paedophiles themselves, and weren't they, either consciously or unconsciously, seeking to remove popular condemnation of their predilections so they could be openly and unashamedly practised?

This episode was a clear insight into just how wide the chasm between the libertarian elements of the left and the working class had become. That so many on the liberal left refused to acknowledge the huge physical and psychological damage that often results from the sexual exploitation of children might strike us as shocking, but in fact their response was quite predictable. Factions within the liberal left instead chose to adopt what by then had become its standard strategy: they simply denied a reality that did not accord with their ideals. Anyone who spoke honestly of this reality was dismissed as a bigot or told to be silent lest their honesty inspire a reactionary response. Rather than face reality, some on the liberal left preferred instead to promulgate a distorted idealistic account of sexually precocious prepubescent children having their rights to sexual pleasure unfairly restricted by an authoritarian state.

Eventually, the tabloid press began to look closely at PIE and its various activities. Popular opinion was most certainly not on the side of the paedophiles and, in the wake of news stories, key figures in the NCCL rushed to distance themselves from the group. A series of police investigations led to the arrest and conviction of many of PIE's leading figures, including Tom O'Carroll, the author of *Paedophilia: The Radical Case* and perhaps Britain's most noted advocate for the rights for paedophiles.

For O'Carroll, the membership of PIE, and the radicals of Parisian intellectual scene, it must have for a time seemed that their cause was gaining traction. PIE even appears to have won some government grants to support its activities,[9] and, in France, Giscard d'Estaing's government had surprised many by indicating its willingness to consider reform. Growing numbers were beginning to speak out against the rigidity of sexual orthodoxies and the necessity for change. However, the advance of their agenda occurred only in particular institutions and forums. The moral majority were certainly not inclined to accept the validity of their claims.

This is not to suggest that the social mainstream's attitudes towards sex were, during the 1970s and 1980s, fixed in stone. In fact, popular attitudes towards sex had changed a great deal in a relatively short period of time. The social mainstream was much more liberal in its views in the 1970s than it was in the 1950s, and elements of the left certainly contributed to the process of liberalisation. And it was not simply heterosexuals who had been 'liberated'. Homosexuality, while certainly not fully accepted, no longer inspired the popular distaste and legal repression it had done in previous decades. Homosexuals slowly began to find their way into mainstream popular culture without having to deny their sexual preferences. Popular attitudes were changing, but the general public were not ready for the warp-speed change the left's libertarians demanded.

Foucault was sure that any institution that had the capacity to judge or constrain the individual's conduct was illegitimate. For the left to move forward, it needed, once and for all, to dispense with socialism and focus instead on freeing the individual from the disciplinary state. Many of the state's core institutions could be dispensed with entirely, and those that could not needed to be radically reformed with a view to ensuring that the sovereign individual was impeded hardly at all. Foucault's firmly established anti-statism chimed immediately with the anti-statism of the neoliberals who continued to batter away at an already spent Keynesianism with a view to establishing neoliberalism more firmly as a political and economic orthodoxy.

For many leftist intellectuals, the neoliberalism of Thatcher, Reagan and Mitterrand was immediately preferable to the social democracy of Attlee, Truman and de Gaulle simply because neoliberalism proposed to govern less. The children of Protestantism and the Enlightenment, convinced that no authority beyond the suitably educated individual conscience is necessary, embraced the neoliberal project that promised to roll back the frontiers of the state and give back the freedoms taken during the post-war social democratic age. Foucault and so many others saw in neoliberalism not a regressive move back to the pre-war years, which had been characterised by extreme inequality and the dominance of the market of huge expanses of everyday life, but the opening up of a new vista free from the state's constant attempts to control and discipline the population. If the state could be made to retreat entirely from the private realm, and especially from the field of sexuality, space would begin to open up in which the enlightened individual could take creative control of her own life.

Both Foucault and the neoliberals hoped to rid society of the interventionist state. It is true that they did not hold exactly the same reasons for seeking this goal, but it is also true that their bespoke reasons did not clash to any great extent. For Foucault, the state restricted personal liberties and its drive to discipline the population distorted identities, lifestyles and practices. For the neoliberals, the state restricted the activities of the business class, hampered corporate profitability, and unfairly taxed wealth and income at high rates. The enemies of the enemy became tentative friends, and the unwritten alliance was struck.

We may initially conclude that the views of liberal academics during the middle third of the twentieth century were entirely divorced from the world of practical politics. However, the views of these academics certainly did filter through to popular culture and the political mainstream. Their influence was subtle but significant. Their ideas filtered throughout the left's political culture, and as one generation exited the stage of mainstream politics, the next brought with them the ideas and general orientations they had absorbed during their political socialisation. We are not suggesting that Foucault's work encouraged the left to suddenly lurch towards a liberal account of the minimal state. As we hope you can now see, the left had been heading in this direction for some time. What is really telling is that the neoliberal right and the cultural left had, by the late 1970s, found themselves largely in accord. Socialism and social democracy were no longer part of the picture.

8

Identity politics

In Chapter 7, we noted that postmodernism accelerated existing processes that were already liberalising the left and moving it further away from its traditional values, policies and sources of support. In advocating a creative individualism free from the intrusions of the state and the judgements of the social order, it also paved the way for contemporary identity politics. However, the truth of the matter is that post-structuralism played a more active role in determining the shape and content of twenty-first-century identity politics. Postmodernism and post-structuralism are often conflated, but to shed light on the intellectual foundations of identity politics, we need to briefly disentangle these two terms.

Post-structuralism denied the existence of the underlying binary linguistic structures that had been the basis of structuralism. The structuralist Saussure had argued that the relationship between the external 'referent' – the thing being observed and represented – and the sign we construct to represent it is arbitrary, and therefore susceptible to the structures of social convention. Post-structuralists went one step further to claim that the relationship between the sign and the 'signified' – our personal mental representation of the sign itself – is also arbitrary. What we had thought of as structured meaning tied to the referent's properties and qualities was actually fluid, open and ambiguous, and able to be constantly deconstructed with no apparent end in sight. Therefore, social convention and the rigid divisions between its binary categories – man/woman, true/false and so on – could be constantly questioned and disrupted.

If there was no end in sight, there was a means in sight. Derrida, the left's most noted post-structuralist, suggested that a 'democracy to come' would end Western domination and carry on forever in a fluid, open-ended discussion as we abandon modernity along with our binary social structures and selves to explore the great diversity of 'otherness' that flickers in an endless process of becoming.[1] Unsurprisingly, the modernist binary category bourgeois/proletarian was one of the first to be chucked into post-structuralism's mincing machine.

Postmodernism was, in effect, a quasi-religious movement, a secular polytheism. As we saw in Chapter 7, it replaced traditional deities with graven images based on the self and its pleasures. Iconic postmodern figures – Bowie, Madonna and others – rose to prominence in part because of their willingness to playfully transcend traditional binary categories while encouraging their audience to focus on the boundless possibilities of self-creation.

Identity politics in its current form grew out of the traditional struggle for civil rights by women and ethnic and sexual minorities. But what is identity politics? Put simply, it is a high stakes game in which distinct self-identified groups compete for advantage, but these identities today are no longer restricted to the traditional groups that participated in earlier struggles for civil rights. While identity politics drew from both postmodernism and post-structuralism as it expanded, it would be wrong to imply forward movement. Rather, identity politics signalled simultaneous moves back to pre-modern tribalism and forward to a greater variety of 'identified' positions. It took from postmodernism a new fragmentary logic which, when intersectionality was added to the mix, broke apart larger traditional tribes in a process of seemingly endless proliferation. Post-structuralism provided intellectual support for those keen to free themselves from established structures of conventional meaning. However, despite the modish jargon, its regressive aspect is hard to deny.

The advantages to be won in the game of identity politics are bestowed by various forms of institutionalised power, and there is also a supplementary competition to secure popular consent for allocated advantages. Success rests upon the presentation of compelling arguments about comparative victimhood and, of course, discrediting the claims made by other victim groups is very much part of the competition's rough and tumble.

'Intersectionality', a term coined by the American legal scholar Kimberlé Crenshaw,[2] is basically a schema for organising identitarian categories on intersecting scales of power, disadvantage and discrimination. One assumes that the more identitarian positions the post-structuralist current throws up, the more complex the intersectional schema has to become, although it does seem that the more traditional categories of race, gender and sexuality remain prominent. The term is now central to the politics of the American liberal left. However, despite the common belief that 'identity politics' is exclusive to the left, the tribal identitarianism that seems so common today has throughout history been more typically associated with the political right. It has, for the most part, been the right that stressed the exclusive nature of communal identities and singled out their comparative advantages and competitors. Defending the community from external competitors while incrementally advancing its interests is a traditional theme in the discourse of the nationalist right. The left, now completely devoid of any genuine attachment to solidarity and common cause, has come to accept the inevitability of proliferating postmodern tribal conflict and competition.

As we will see, the left's acceptance of this new tribalism occurred in a climate affected by the competitive individualism we associate with postmodernism, and the economic insecurity we associate with neoliberalism. However, in the act of adopting the right's competitive tribalism as a mechanism of cultural progress, the left had finally abandoned the solidarity project altogether. The founding principles of the left are now entirely absent. Clearly, solidarity no longer animates the left. Not in the true sense. There are moments of coming together, certainly, but in such instances 'solidarity' is instrumentalised, and so loses its fundamental character. It is performed rather than felt. There can be no true solidarity among multiple competing interests seeking advantage or compensation.

The absence of its founding principles gives the contemporary left a strange, ahistorical air, as if it is simply conjuring up policies and goals in a random, ad hoc manner. There also seems to be very little detailed knowledge of the route the left has taken to this strange destination, and very little acknowledgement that the traditional left once had principles that often seem diametrically opposed to the contemporary left's new focal concerns. An obvious example can be seen when the leftist defenders of identity politics claim that the entire field of politics is rooted in identitarian struggles. For them, politics always involves a competition between opposing identity groups. That so many contemporary leftists make this argument is revealing. Those who make it appear to tacitly accept competition as an inevitable and not wholly negative feature of contemporary society. Their ambitions seem to extend no further than simply making the competition fair. They also seem to assume that traditional leftists who still advocate a politics of collective progress are bad faith actors keen to dismiss the unique forms of oppression suffered by various minorities. Equally revealing is their dismissal of socialism as just another form of identity politics. Blind to the complexities of the socioeconomic realm, for the liberal left the working class is an identity and nothing more.

Ignorant of economics and scornful of any pretence towards shared interests and commonality, all they leave us with is a Schmittian kaleidoscope,[3] a resolutely bleak vision of a world scarred by eternal enmity. All cultural groups must play the competitive game of identity politics to the best of their ability if they are to stand any chance of prospering. The weapons to be deployed in this remorseless competition are claims about injustice and victimisation. Within this context of unrelenting competition, the prosperity of the identity group rests upon its ability to persuade political and corporate elites that it has been subject to processes of victimisation. If the claim is accepted as valid it justifies the redistribution of power and resources from the centre to the specific points in the margins. But never to the working class as a whole.

To understand this fundamental transformation of cultural and political engagement, and why identity politics has taken root on the left, we need to explore in more detail the ties that bind the neoliberal right and the liberal left. The intellectual commitments of both groups have structured the development of this system of identitarian conflict. We are not suggesting that these two distinct groups have surreptitiously conspired and worked in concert to kill socialism and disempower the multi-ethnic working class. Rather, our point is that the fundamental commitments of these groups have brought us, in a relatively organic manner, progressively closer to this end.

Talk of difference and diversity is everywhere these days. However, 'diversity' seems to refer solely to rather basic, surface characteristics. When corporations announce they hope to 'diversify' their workforces, they mean that they are keen for their employees to come from a range of ethnic and religious backgrounds, possess a variety of minority sexualities, and include those who define themselves as trans. Many employers are now actively engaged in the attempt to make their workforces as 'diverse' as possible. However, quite often surface diversity disguises a deeper homogeneity, and this is especially true in workplace settings that require a college degree.

These corporations may employ people from every ethnic group on earth. Every knowable sexuality may be present within the workforce. But if every member of that workforce subscribes to the same ideologies, comes from the same socioeconomic background, lives in the same neighbourhoods, votes for the same political parties, sends their children to the same schools, and utilises the same forms of media, then 'diversity' becomes a subterfuge. 'Diversity' in the true sense is absent. It has been supplanted by a shallow, two-dimensional representation.

'Diversity' is usually tied to the rhetoric of inclusion but, again, those to be included must first signal their willingness to accept the established logic of progressive cultural liberalism. When we encounter institutions that proclaim themselves to be committed to 'inclusion', we must ask, 'that's great, but who is secretly excluded?'. Of course, 'inclusion' is really concerned only with the inclusion of approved groups. Just as liberal 'tolerance' excludes those deemed intolerant, liberal 'inclusion' excludes those who have failed to clearly demonstrate their unwavering commitment to the exclusive form of 'inclusion' liberalism wants. Digging just a little beneath the surface positivity of 'inclusion' reveals the institution's hidden ideological commitments, and points towards the cultural uniformity that underpins 'diversity' and 'inclusivity'.

Spending a prolonged period in institutions or workplaces that champion 'diversity' and 'inclusion' often reveals them to be rather uniform and depthless places. Everyday life offers a far more accurate and honest glimpse of diversity. As we go about our day, we may encounter an incredibly broad range of people, all of whom possess unique personal stories, all with their own attitudes and views. We may encounter people with a different skin colour from ours, men and women who worship a different god, people from a different social class, and a broad range of everyday people who have lived a life seemingly quite different from our own. We may encounter friends, strangers and enemies. We may encounter depoliticised men and women, just as we may encounter individuals committed to any political position imaginable. However, as we experience the diversity of everyday life, we will often be struck by the rather obvious fact that amid all this diversity lies a range of experiences, feelings, views and hopes that have the potential to bond us together.

Perhaps, paradoxically, the ideological category of 'diversity' functions to facilitate its opposite? Perhaps, rather than encouraging true diversity, the discourse of 'diversity' actually promotes ideological conformity and cultural homogeneity? Certainly, the emphasis postmodernists placed upon individualism seemed to function in this way. Clearly, if everyone feels compelled to be different, and dips into the consumer sphere for the tools to fashion their unique individuality, then beneath difference lies an unacknowledged sameness. Mightn't we reasonably speculate that – in reducing people to their surface characteristics in order to facilitate cultural categorisation and justify institutional claims to 'diversity' – we are stripping people of their own uniqueness?

This brings us to the fundamental paradox at the heart of identity politics. Identity politics draws from a range of intellectual currents that stress individuality and individual freedom, and often those who play the game of identity politics stress the importance of accepting boundless individuality and moving beyond out-of-date conventions that shape our appraisal of others. However, identity politics simultaneously pushes its subjects in the opposite direction. Often, individuality is denied in order to stress the homogeneity of ethnic or religious groups, or those who have the same sexual interests. Spokespeople for these various groups often negate individuality in order to stress the cohesion and uniformity of their particular identity group. They might suggest, for example, that all group members have experienced the same things and hold the same views, attitudes and aspirations. The emphasis placed upon the homogeneity of the identity group becomes more problematic when individual members publicly disagree with what its leaders have defined as the group's fundamental beliefs. For example, black conservatives are not simply marginalised but often stripped of their ethnic identity by those who grant themselves the authority to speak for the group as a whole. Rather than tarry with the suggestion that black people possess a range of political beliefs, very often the impetus of vocal identitarian activists is to strip black conservatives of their blackness in order to reassert the political homogeneity of the identity group.

As identity politics advanced, new forms of demonisation began to emerge. Throughout history, processes of demonisation have tended to emerge on the political right, and those demonised tended to be positioned at the margins of civil society. However, while condemnation of minorities remained present across the political landscape, postmodernism also seemed to open up the possibility of reversing standard processes of demonisation. Demonisation of the state, traditional culture and mainstream civil society became increasingly common. Some features of these new forms of demonisation were, in time, depoliticised. In some settings, what might be considered myths or gross exaggerations were repositioned as unchallengeable truths. Contestation and antagonism seemed to have been irrevocably moved from the economic field to the cultural field.

The emphasis identity politics places upon the redistribution of power and privileges reflects this broader point. Amid the cut and thrust of competition, the inherently unstable neoliberal market system is treated as a *fait accompli*. Of course, traditional leftist politics was principally concerned with achieving true political power and using it to manage investment, production, participation and distribution with a view to ensuring the economic inclusion of all citizens. However, identity politics has no interest in establishing a fairer socioeconomic system. Rather, it is solely concerned with the reallocation of resources produced by a demonstrably unfair socioeconomic system.

And there is a further complication. There is no guarantee that reallocated resources will be divided equally within the identity group itself. In fact, any honest appraisal of today's politicised identity groups will reveal often steep hierarchies in which highly educated individuals from minority cultural backgrounds are able to secure personal privileges while poorer and less educated members of the same identity group continue to languish in the lower echelons of the old class system. Successful individuals become emblematic representatives of the group, despite the fact that, beyond the most basic characteristics, they are not reflective of the group as a whole.

Identity politics establishes a new system for the designation of elite status. Rather than moving forward as a distinct and cohesive entity, the group becomes highly stratified as successful figureheads secure redistributed advantages while the majority benefit hardly at all. This returns us to a perennial theme. While the logic of identity politics divides the working class along the lines of ethnicity, religion, sexuality and gender, bespoke groups supposed to be bonded closely together by cultural interests continue to be divided along class lines. Hierarchies with widening socioeconomic divisions are an obvious feature of all identity groups, despite the fact that the preferred public image is of common cause.

Once this system became an established feature of our political and cultural life, all were forced to play the game. Martin Luther King had once looked forward hopefully to a day when people would not be judged by the colour of their skin but by the content of their character. However, postmodern identity politics seemed dedicated to the task of ensuring such a day will never come. The cultural field fragmented into defensive identity groups, all of which seemed dedicated to the task of refusing to acknowledge the obvious forms of commonality that continued to exist between them. Many of those who were positioned as leaders or spokespeople for these groups all seemed to come from a similar educated and liberal background. This simply repeated a standard process – seen throughout the history of the left – that disempowered and marginalised the working class and prioritised the interests of the liberal middle class. While identity politics further fractured the modern social order, in each fragment the steep hierarchies of neoliberalism were reproduced.

This is the landscape in which populist reaction grew. The leadership of various identity groups levelled a range of allegations at white majorities, most of which centred upon historical oppression and white cultural supremacism. Many of these allegations were factually correct but deprived of crucial contextual detail. While it was argued that intersectionality was an important tool in contemporary political analysis, it was judged irrelevant when it came to addressing the horrors committed by the 'white race'. The aristocracy, the bourgeoisie, the professional class and the working class were unimportant distinctions that obfuscated the supremacy of white people generally. All white people, regardless of their class background or their unique personal characteristics, remained dedicated to securing the continued supremacy of the 'white race'. To many white people, this seemed overblown, inaccurate and unfair. They simply could not see themselves as beneficiaries of imperial brutality and the ideology of white supremacy. The lives of many were typified by toil and hardship, and in no way did they feel superior to anyone. Why should they be held responsible for the crimes committed by men long since dead just because they happened to have been born with the same skin colour?

The common response to this question was that earlier generations of the 'white race' had committed awful crimes, and then bequeathed the benefits to the next generation. These privileges had then tumbled down through the generations, ensuring the continued supremacy of the 'white race' in every social, cultural and economic arena. Again, this argument seemed to possess a vague logic, but many felt that, upon closer inspection, it lacked nuance and seemed to be driven not by historical evidence but by anger, frustration and a deep fear that the injustices of the past could resurface in the present.

Weren't the material benefits of colonialism hoovered up by the aristocracy and the business class? The working class of the industrial age was treated terribly, and often lived in the shadow of absolute poverty and destitution. What sense did it make to suggest that the working class of the industrial age had been a direct beneficiary? What sense did it make to suggest that the desperately poor members of the working class were able to conjure up great privileges to bequeath to their children, or that the aristocracy or the business class had become suddenly benevolent enough to share the spoils of conquest with the vulgar units of production that populated their factories? Most could accept that the imperial age was indeed typified by terrible deeds. Most were happy to acknowledge that the transatlantic slave trade was an abomination. However, most were not ready to accept that they were the beneficiaries of such horrors.

The rise of identity politics deepened divisions within the white population just as it sought to erase them completely. Many members of the educated middle classes were persuaded by the logic of identity politics and aligned themselves with historically oppressed minorities. Some felt guilty for having the same skin colour as oppressive historical figures. In some settings, members of the white middle class tried to unload some of this guilt by instrumentally adopting the language and identity of a marginalised subset of the white population. Some were so traumatised by their unchosen connection to a historically oppressive group that they disavowed their ethnicity and adopted – often surreptitiously – the signs of a minority identity.[4] Others, trapped in institutional settings committed to identity politics, felt it best to simply keep quiet and go along. A sense of fear and trepidation rippled through the white middle class. To be judged – either fairly or unfairly – a racist or a sexist, or to be found to be in any way antagonistic towards a minority, would mean being immediately stripped of the benefits that came with membership of the professional middle class. Even if one was not persuaded by the left's increasingly *de rigueur* stereotypes, it was best never to admit to such views.

Clearly, many white people in the working class did not see themselves as beneficiaries of 'white supremacy'. Deindustrialisation had stripped them of the last vestiges of economic security, and huge numbers had, since the dawning of the neoliberal age, resigned themselves to simply 'getting by'.[5] Their engagement with the white middle class in institutional settings exacerbated divisions. Many assumed that middle-class professions looked down their noses at the white working class. Very often these assumptions were quite grounded and entirely understandable. The increasingly common assumption among the white middle class was that many members of the white working class were bigoted, uneducated and uncouth.[6]

Many members of the white working class formed the view that the white middle class was driving identity politics forward. It seemed to grow from a range of cultural and political tropes that had become commonly associated with the metropolitan middle-class left. Despite the obvious emphasis identity politics placed on minority identities, in institutional settings it was often members of the white middle class who were in the driving seat. By this time, white members of the working class already associated the white middle class with 'the left' and believed the left to be now principally concerned with cosmopolitanism, open borders, multiculturalism and political correctness, and opposed to forms of fundamental economic change that would benefit the multi-ethnic working class.[7] Often, identity politics was judged to be simply a vehicle for the liberal middle class to secure its dominance in all key social and political institutions.

The rise of identity politics prompted a profoundly important shift in the nature of white racism. Throughout the modern age, white racism had been rooted in the myth of racial and cultural superiority. This sense of superiority had been actively cultivated during the age of Empire to justify the acquisitive ambitions of the elites that dominated the politics of European nations. However, as the postmodern era established itself, white racism was flipped on its head. A prevailing sense of inferiority among the white working class was used to justify developing forms of racism and anti-immigrant sentiment. Some among the white working class felt that they were at the back of every queue. While ethnic minorities and recently arrived immigrants had vocal political representation, no one spoke up for the white working class. Ethnic minorities benefited from the support of the white middle class, but the opposite was true for the white working class. Talk of jobs quotas, 'minority only' hiring drives and immigrants taking limited public housing stock became ubiquitous.[8]

When placed against this background, it becomes clear why the populism that emerged in the wake of the global financial crisis had a predominantly right-wing feel to it. Identity politics was believed to be the latest incarnation of leftist radicalism. The mainstream left had abandoned the working class and remained fetishistically attached to the economic policies of the neoliberal right. Poverty and insecurity were on the rise while cultural divisions seemed to deepen by the day. Any political opportunity to bloody the nose of their opponent – white elites with significant political and institutional power – had to be taken.

Cancelled

What became known as 'cancel culture' was born of the increasingly zealous, high-octane world of leftist activism. To be accepted, it was no longer good enough to be committed to justice, fairness and equality. Even subscribing to the basic tenets of leftist identity politics wasn't enough. One had to be a constant vocal representative for the liberal left's increasingly hard-edged cultural project.

Social media offered the perfect environment for the exclusions and punishments that are the fundamental objective of cancel culture. As more leftists felt the pressure to constantly articulate and lend support to the left's pugnacious cultural radicalism, social media platforms began to resemble medieval courtyards in which dissidents could be punished with the full force of public shame and humiliation.

Smearing and destroying the individual's reputation and career is an ancient practice that throughout history often led to devastating feuds. However, smearing tended to be a rather elitist pursuit, practised by public figures more than capable of defending themselves and returning fire in political campaigns and other power struggles. It was commonly believed that allowing it to diffuse throughout the social body would lead to chaotic violence. Throughout the history of all known cultures, formalised religious and legal systems always placed limits on the practices of smearing and accusing individuals of being guilty of some sin or crime. The fundamental objective was to take the entitlements to establish guilt and punish perpetrators out of the victim's hands in order to prevent informal cycles of revenge that would plunge societies into violent disorder.

The sociologist Max Weber traced the historical evolution of Western law, describing four principal developmental phases – (1) formal irrationality, based on the prophetic revelation of supernatural judgments; (2) substantive irrationality, based on conscience and the emotional evaluation of individuals believed to possess a high level of moral probity; (3) substantive rationality, based on the moral structure of religious texts; and (4) today's formal rationality, based on tangible evidence, precedence set by concrete cases, systems of universal abstract categories and, most importantly, due process carried out in an institution independent from all cultural and political groups. In all of these systems, the dispute between alleged victim and alleged perpetrator is handed over to a third party to prevent a potentially endless, violent dispute between the victim, the perpetrator and their families or supporters.

Such regrettable practices have throughout history returned when law has temporarily broken down. The informal summary justice of cancel culture, a modern variant of the substantive irrationality outlined above, inevitably cultivates a desire for the renewal of formal justice, and we are already beginning to see a fightback from those who remain committed to free speech, public decorum and due process. How this battle plays out in the medium term remains to be seen. However, we can already see that the cultural leftists, having rejected the working class as the agent of history and the democratic state as the organ of economic management, are incapable of leading a new solidarity project.

New divisions and simmering antagonisms proliferate, and soon there will be no coherent cultural left to which new recruits must swear allegiance. It seems likely that the more successful individuals from identitarian groups and their middle-class supporters will abandon the field of radical dissent and leave behind followers unable to find success.

Cultural leftists who have found their way into key roles in key institutions will constitute tomorrow's social management class operating on behalf of a reconfiguring global capitalism. What we are witnessing now is not commitment to oppressed groups or fundamental socioeconomic transformation but the reconstruction of the sub-dominant elite – those who manage social life on behalf the global capitalist economic elite.

The emergence of the new sub-dominant elite is not restricted to public institutions. As we have seen, the active integration of minority groups has become a key feature of the contemporary corporate world. When feminist writer Nancy Fraser[9] handed the cultural left a warning that identity politics was in danger of being appropriated by the capitalist elite to sow further division and prevent the re-emergence of traditional class politics, she was roundly dismissed. That Fraser's prediction came true was no surprise to those who were aware of the roots shared by neoliberalism and identity politics.

As well as ignoring Fraser at the turn of the millennium, the left also ignored earlier and quite fundamental shifts in corporate strategies and consumer culture.[10] What had been conservative, authoritarian corporations first began to change their image in the early 1960s, in response to the emergence of rebellious young people with disposable incomes. The 'hip turn' of the corporate sector boosted the attractiveness of products in the eyes of young generations weaned on the ethos of individual freedom. It was an advertiser's dream, and the industry exploded into a galaxy of seductive images. Woke corporatism is simply a continuation of this earlier hip turn that has now risen up the ranks to the management stratum to capture employees as well as customers. It keeps up with cultural trends and applies all the advanced strategies hip capitalism developed over 60 years to incorporate and neutralise youth rebellion and identitarian struggles in a few simple moves – censor real oppositional politics, feign care about identitarian struggles, institutionalise acceptance of the new rules and make acceptance part of employment practice. The final move is crucial, because it adds a sharp, dangerous and fearsome material edge to the process of social cancellation, an edge that scares the whole working-age population. Renounce anything associated with socialism, think twice about joining a union and promise to work flexibly or you don't get a job. Brutal, simple and effective, but very easily dressed up as ethical and progressive.

Endgame

The cultural left has dragged us into a genuinely Schmittian[11] world, in which politics is conducted as proliferating, divisive cultural wars instigated by the recognition of friends and enemies. The left's failure to arrest this fragmentation is rooted in its failure to understand the three broad developmental phases in the intellectual context that underpinned the rise of identity politics. First, postmodernism and post-structuralism acted as a broad-spectrum corrosive eating away traditional conservatism, socialism and the organic institutions on which they were dependent for their moral energy, cultural values and normative social cohesion – family, work, church, unions, masculinity, femininity, and so on. Second, the left's activist class ditched serious class politics and veered sharply away from established conventions to alienate the left's traditional support. This class came to dominate popular perceptions of the left, and the abandonment of any pretence to authoritative leadership eroded the credibility of the democratic state as an economic manager.

Third, the endgame's final destination: key sections of the left accepted and eventually championed 'progressive neoliberalism': a mixture of hardcore neoliberal economics, 'rainbow capitalism', identity politics and punitively moralistic cultural progressivism. Notionally left-wing cultural activists can now draw upon the support of the corporate sector and find their way into influential positions within its structure. In return, neoliberals have received a willing new partner that can be trusted to foster division, steer popular discussion away from economic matters, seek the cancellation of opponents and generally do all that can be done to prevent the return of serious class politics.

9

The politics of nostalgia

Many left liberals in academia,[1] politics[2] and the mass media[3] are certain that the populist revival among the working class in the post-crash era has been driven by a regressive nostalgia for a time when they were wealthier, more secure, more valued and more firmly established in the social hierarchy. Some of these commentators have even gone as far as to claim that members of the white working class who have lent their support to populist movements are nostalgic for a time in which they were accorded higher status than individuals from ethnic minority backgrounds.[4] In such analyses, the continued march of progressive multiculturalism has stripped white working-class voters of their unearned racial privileges, so these voters have abandoned the left and voted for a nationalist right that promises to restore them.

The 2016 Brexit vote is a useful case in point. While for most contemporary leftists the result of the referendum came as a shock, those sections of the left that remain in regular contact with working-class voters beyond the larger cities understood that it was entirely predictable.[5] Some academics immediately denied the existence of clear evidence indicating that the majority of the working-class voters preferred to leave the EU.[6] Others were happy to simply decry Leave voters as hateful xenophobes.[7] Without further thought, many on the liberal left cut the Gordian knot, split the working class along ethnic lines and portrayed anyone amongst the white working class reluctant to immediately offer unequivocal support for all progressive cultural causes as the embodiment of absolute evil.

These responses were simplistic, hurtful and divisive. However, they should have come as no surprise.

White working-class Leave voters were, apparently, nostalgic for Empire.[8] This narrative continues to be the most popular academic explanation for the British people's majority decision to leave the EU. It tends to be promulgated by academics who believe themselves to be socialists, and who look favourably upon the neoliberal EU as if it were a bastion of progressive politics, the source of all positive social protections, and our sole defence against a slide into destitution and right-wing authoritarianism.

Yet this narrative is a horrible distortion of reality. Anyone with first-hand experience of life in working-class communities in the run-up to the Brexit vote knows that people hardly ever discussed or even thought about the age of Empire. To suggest that voters hoped to leave the EU because they wanted to restore the privileges associated with an Empire none had ever experienced – and some had never heard of – is absurd. The real reasons why so many among the white working class voted for Brexit were much less grandiose and tended to reflect their immediate experience of the world around them.

The dominance of this narrative suggests that many on the left have little or no experience of the lives, attitudes and beliefs of ordinary people, yet somehow feel qualified to explain those lives, attitudes and beliefs. Clearly, many leftist academics and journalists in Britain feel absolutely sure that the best route forward for the working class is to adopt the beliefs and political concerns of a thoroughly liberalised and largely middle-class left that neither understands nor cares about them. It is hardly surprising that so many aren't persuaded.

The claim that the working class voted to leave the EU because of a nostalgia for Empire tells us much more about those making it than it does about the people and behaviours it attempts to explain. Here were middle-class socialists decrying the majority of the working class as incorrigible bigots while totally ignoring the economic context that underpinned the vote. They could not see that the EU enforced compulsory neoliberalism across its member states. While it is true that anxiety played a significant role in voter decisions, for the most part these anxieties were not about what might happen should the present status quo be disturbed. Rather, many working-class Leave voters were anxious about what would happen should the status quo remain unchanged.

Clearly, many voted Leave because they hoped to arrest decline. Working-class Leave voters had been falling throughout the neoliberal age, and they wanted to take any opportunity that might arise to rid the nation of the conventions that had established themselves over the past 40 years. Of course, many of their frustrations were quite separate from the EU and its effects, but the referendum functioned as a proxy issue that suggested an opportunity had arisen to change direction. Immigration certainly formed part of this picture. Many could see with their own eyes that mass immigration increased competition and made getting and keeping a job harder. Many believed that continued high levels of immigration threatened the continuity of their cultures. But to suggest that anxieties about these things are unjustifiable and rooted in racism is at best an unhelpful simplification and at worst a hateful slur.

The common leftist suggestion that working-class voters opted for Leave because they hoped to bolster imperilled privileges tacitly endorses the ceaseless social and economic competition of the neoliberal age. Here we have professed socialists claiming that members of the white working class should be stripped of their unearned privilege so that the ostensibly 'fair' competition of a minimally regulated market system can continue. They are not against the competition inherent to the market but merely want to see that all groups are fairly lined up when the starting pistol is fired.

Privileges and success, it seems, are fine as long as they are 'earned' in the present, and according to the rules of open market competition. They appear sanguine about the hyper-exploitation of cheap, insecure and non-unionised immigrant labour. Rather, they want all to be given a fair opportunity to be hyper-exploited. They dismiss out of hand the fears of the white and older multi-ethnic working class. Disintegrating neighbourhoods, disappearing cultures and traditions, impoverished and insecure labour markets, declining job opportunities, drug markets, crime, anti-social behaviour, disappearing services, boarded-up shops and pubs, the paucity of affordable housing of a reasonable standard, and a sense that things will be harder still for the next generation, are, apparently, of little consequence. Instead, they project the worst possible motivations onto communities they have clearly never visited and know nothing about.

In the contemporary liberal imagination, nostalgia is always regressive. It indicates a perverse attachment to times past. It often involves the mythologisation of those times: we deny their reality, preferring instead to cover it up with positive imagery. We tend not to be nostalgic for negative experiences or times when things were tough, unless we can rehabilitate difficult memories by, for example, recalling the strength of character we displayed in overcoming a challenge, or the selfless assistance of others when things went wrong. We may look back fondly on our childhood, schooldays, family holidays, and so on. We may lapse into reveries about the communities that shaped our development and sense of self. Sounds, tastes and images might set off a chain of memories that connects us momentarily to a past we value deeply.

Often, recalling positive memories encourages us to regret the departure of those times. We might regret decisions that took our lives in a different direction. We might mourn a lost love. We might regret a career choice or losing touch with old friends. We might long to hear the beautiful resonant sound of a choir singing in a great church, savour the smell of our mother's baking, or again experience the side-splitting laughter we once enjoyed with childhood friends. This kind of nostalgia is very common, and it tends to be associated with those who have said goodbye to youth. The young may pour scorn on nostalgia, but it will inevitably ambush them at some point as they grow older.

However, for many on the liberal left, such memories do not represent the substance of our past or our nostalgia for it. Feminists, for example, are often quick to point out that, throughout the modern era, women tended to be financially dependent upon men, were paid at a lower rate and were often unable to follow their preferred career paths. They were expected to take on the majority of housework and childcare and were also subject to high rates of domestic abuse. For the most part, they are right. However, an entirely critical account of modern community life is just as flawed as an entirely positive one. There is truth in this account, but it is also true that many women lived reasonably happy and worthwhile lives in which their husband was not an oppressor but a source of support and love. The reality is that modern community life was diverse and complex, despite its supposed homogeneity, and the same is true for the individuals who lived their lives within such communities.

Other activists also point out that modern communities, especially in the industrial working class, were inherently exclusionary. They enforced conformity with regard to gender and sexuality, refused to accept outsiders, and used stigma and sometimes abuse and violence to enforce their unwritten cultural rules. Again, there is truth here, but this is certainly not the only story one can tell about modern industrial communities. Remembering industrial communities fondly tends to deny what is a far more mixed reality, but then the same is true for those who tend towards unrelenting criticism.

Nostalgia is complex, inconsistent and subjective, and our positive recollections of times past need to be understood as such. Nostalgia at root offers the individual the opportunity and material he or she needs to engage in forms of self-narration and meaning construction. Memory is crucial for grasping who we are and what matters in our lives. One of the many reasons why Alzheimer's disease is such a terrible affliction is that it erases our memory of where we have been and what we have achieved and experienced, along with memories of our attachments to others who gave our lives colour, depth and purpose. We tend to undervalue memory, and nostalgia is a particular kind of memory, a way of remembering that serves an important but undervalued function. Memorable snippets from our lives, some of which we may return to quite regularly, help us to grasp a compelling but also changeable sense of who we are, how we relate to others, and what in our life truly counted and nourished us, as well as a sense of where we are going that relates to where we have been.

For the left's radical liberals, of course, nostalgia also seems to suggest a dissatisfaction with the present. It is often claimed we *retreat* into nostalgia, and in doing so we turn away from the present and choose myth over reality and distortion over truth. Nostalgia for a time of settled and relatively homogenous community life is interpreted as distaste for the healthy cultural diversity and fluidity we tend to see around us today. Nostalgia for a time in which the left sought to advance the interests of the working class is interpreted as a rejection of the current left's focus on problems faced by women, ethnic minorities and the LGBTQ+ community. For most left-liberals, nostalgia among the white working class is inherently and irredeemably sexist, heteronormative and racist.

Class differences are important. Middle-class leftists are less likely to see decline in their own lives, and so they are less likely to look back fondly to a time when things were easier. They may feel nostalgic for positive periods, perhaps during their youth, and they may use nostalgic memories as a form of reassuring self-narration, but their nostalgia is less likely to be based on a memory of lost security.

Nostalgia can, of course, take many forms but, in most cases, we are nostalgic for a time redolent of emotional comfort, a time in which we felt at ease with others, with our identity and with our place in the world. And, again, we tend not to be nostalgic for a time of great turbulence, unless it can be transformed into a positive story about ourselves or our relationships to others. Those who have personal experience of great financial hardship tend not to be nostalgic for times in which financial insecurity overshadowed their lives, unless those memories can be rehabilitated. Beneath nostalgia is a desire to experience the comforts of security.

For many middle-class leftists, the fluidity of contemporary culture and the instability of our economy and labour markets tend not to inspire feelings of insecurity. Fluctuations in everyday reality are often a source of pleasure, understood to represent incremental improvement rather than decline. The mixing of cultures, they argue, allows them to come into contact with others they would otherwise never know or understand. Economic globalisation has increased the diversity of goods that can be bought cheaply. Change is inspiring and propels us further away from the grotesque injustices of the past.

We should note that, while championing diversity, most middle-class liberal leftists live in middle-class neighbourhoods.

They often send their children to private schools. We are not suggesting that there is anything inherently wrong in this. What we are suggesting is that only rarely do these middle-class leftists engage with diversity in the true sense. They may meet and interact with members of minority ethnic groups, but the vast majority of these 'others' are fully integrated into middle-class professional culture in their occupational and leisure lives. The engagement of middle-class leftists with 'diversity' also tends to be framed by consumerism. They may eat the food, go to the festivals or decorate their houses with the symbols of other cultures, but for the most part that is as far as it goes. They inevitably engage with a shallow, two-dimensional facsimile of cultural diversity, and feel progressive while doing so.

This issue becomes salient when liberal commentators criticise the white and older multi-ethnic working class for wanting to hold on to their own traditional regional and national cultures. Middle-class liberals may advocate multiculturalism, but in important respects their experience continues to be monocultural. They may become friends with middle-class liberals who hail from minority ethnic backgrounds, but they share a great deal in terms of politics, tastes and attitudes, and many of these individuals might reasonably assume that the process of integration is as easy as abandoning the last vestiges of racial prejudice.

However, in areas of economic decline, no matter how much the white working class abandons prejudice, there is little incentive for incomers to integrate. For middle-class liberals, the situation is quite different. Many migrants – and many among the white working class – hope to join the ranks of the professional middle class, and they are reasonably content to change their very being, from their beliefs to their physical appearance, in order to do so. However, in locales of economic decline, complex and messy antagonisms grow in the cultural fault lines that traverse neighbourhoods and separate ethnic groups. Occasionally, there is a positive coming together, usually rooted in the recognition of shared interests. However, the inability of middle-class liberals to see the world from any angle other than their own tends to mean that they continue on with their remarkably narrow account of growing cultural antagonism.

Middle-class liberals have no direct experience of these fault lines. They have, thankfully, very little first-hand experience of poverty, crime, violence and abuse, and tend not to face the plethora of challenges and dangers faced by the multi-ethnic working class, especially in the larger cities. Because they can't see anything to worry about in the present, apart from the terrifying monster of authoritarian nationalism that stalks their worst nightmares, they assume that nostalgia for a more stable past is unjustified. Rather than express a measured dissatisfaction with contemporary life and a desire for something better, they demonise nostalgia as a regressive reaction of the ungrateful who cannot see the benefits of the progress won by decades of resolutely applying liberal values to everyday culture.

A British Election Study in 2016 found a strong correlation between voting Leave and a sense of national decline.[9] Almost 80 per cent of Leave voters strongly agreed with the statement 'things in Britain were better in the past'. The study also found that Leave voters possessed less 'social capital' and felt a general absence of control in their everyday lives. Of course, these views are, for the liberal left, nothing more than products of the reactionary nostalgia that blights the white working class. Working-class Leave voters wrongly believe things were better in the past; the liberal left is sure that they were not. And why can't these nostalgic reactionaries recognise the triumphs of cultural progress? Why can't they see that things have improved enormously since the old days of closed community life?

For some on the liberal left, the answer is perfectly straightforward. Members of the white working class see decline because they have been forced to compete with recently arrived immigrants. And they have lost. They see decline because their unearned privileges are being crushed by brighter, hard-working immigrants. They refuse to recognise the huge advances made on the field of culture because they are bigoted and believe their skin colour should ensure their status as a privileged cultural group.

It clearly doesn't occur to some left-liberals that many aspects of everyday life have actually declined, and not just for the white working class. If, for a moment, they were to take an honest look at reality, they would see that decline has affected the entire multi-ethnic working class, and less occupationally secure sections of the middle class. Work is far more unstable and often very poorly paid. Getting and keeping a job is more difficult. Finding affordable housing of a reasonable quality is now a daunting prospect. Work – especially working-class work – is often alienating, demanding, demeaning, and certainly far less satisfying than many traditional forms of industrial labour that contributed to palpable, finished products. And, as we have seen, the working class has been deserted by its traditional representatives. It has few articulate and resolute advocates to oppose its many critics. The welfare system is more brutal. The quality of schooling has indeed declined. Its neighbourhoods really are in decay. Its fears for the next generation are realistic and well founded.

Perhaps, rather than assume that the prejudices of the working class distort reality, we should turn the tables and explore the possibility that the prejudices of the middle-class left distort both reality and working-class prejudice? After all, copious evidence suggests that those with high social and educational capital tend to support 'economic globalisation',[10] despite the fact that it has stripped the multi-ethnic working class of traditional forms of labour; disempowered organised labour; concentrated huge wealth in the hands of a tiny super-elite; prompted the opening up of remarkably exploitative sweatshops throughout the developing world; contributed enormously to the climate crisis by spurring the development of global supply chains of dizzying size and complexity; facilitated the fast-paced commodification and dumbing down of all aspects of all culture, and much else besides. Their support for all forms of globalisation is predicated on the obvious fact that they have not been too badly affected by these powerful forces, and in the absence of any real negative experiences they can look favourably upon those things they understand as the advantages.

Many also deny globalisation's diverse harms and instead carry the belief that its victims bring it all upon themselves. In their determination to portray the white working class as beset by fear and fetishistically tied to an unjust past, middle-class liberals fail to acknowledge that their own politics is also structured by dark fears. Of course, the fears of middle-class liberals – protectionism, nationalism, authoritarianism, cultural homogeneity, an absence of choice and 'illiberalism' generally – are always judged to be grounded and fair, whereas the fears of the working class are judged to be illogical, uncharitable, prejudicial and regressive.

Those with higher social capital also tend to favour high levels of immigration,[11] but, we have to ask, how do they engage with and understand the real processes and consequences of immigration? We have already suggested that many on the middle-class left encounter diversity through the prism of consumerism, dipping in and out of immigrant communities before heading back to the leafy suburbs. We have also claimed that the liberal left tends to strip immigrant groups of their authenticity, preferring instead to present them in ways that suit the standard left-liberal narrative. The affinity that many feel with immigrants, despite never having engaged in an honest encounter with immigrants who are not also members of the liberal middle class, is yet another indication of their desire to leave the real world behind to dwell in a sanitised ideological representation of it. In this representation, all immigrants are victims, and deeply committed to the goal of multicultural toleration and acceptance.

However, immigrant groups are extremely diverse in their heritage and outlook. Some are desperately poor while others are incredibly rich. Many are quite conservative in their attitudes, while some are indeed liberals. Some are open, altruistic and dedicated to all that is good in life. Others are rapists, murderers and terrorists. Some prefer integration, others separatism. All human communities display this kind of diversity. But to suggest such a thing clashes headlong with left-liberals' rose-tinted view of multicultural diversity and their account of the sources of prejudice and social conflict.

To present a particular ethnic community in an entirely positive light, whether it is composed of immigrants or not, strips this community of its authenticity. The community is rendered simply a blank screen onto which its supposed advocates – who often are not members of that community and have only limited experience and knowledge of it – can project their preferred images, symbols and representations. This act of stripping immigrant communities of their authenticity is invasive and domineering, even if it is done with the best intentions. The positive aspect of multiculturalism is about accepting all cultural groups *as they are*, rather than allowing elites to take up the task of representing minority groups in ways that suit their own ideological and political preferences. Perhaps we should follow this line of thinking through to the end and suggest that some sections of the liberal left now display a *pan racism* that reduces, distorts, misrepresents and – even when they attempt to be positive and helpful – ultimately harms the groups of which they claim knowledge and understanding?

The responsibility to remember

The symbolism of place and community is passed like a Maussian gift[12] from one generation to the next. These gifts are not to be consumed but retained, protected and passed on to the next generation. By bequeathing powerful shared memories down through the generations a community ensures its continued life, and this is one of the reasons why it is entirely normal to treat such memories with a degree of solemnity. Each generation effectively carries the expectation of all preceding generations to sustain the symbolic life of the community. This is a weighty burden by any stretch of the imagination, and it is little wonder that communities can become quite animated if they sense that the existing generation will fail in this sacred task.

Acknowledging the gravity of this bequest and the responsibilities that come with it helps us to understand the common fear that we will fail to sustain the culture for the next generation, and that all that was passed on to us will evaporate, and the trials and tribulations of our ancestors will count for nothing. To dismiss this process as meaningless and riven with regressive nostalgia ruthlessly imposes on all communities a horizon of banal, soulless and ahistorical universal liberalism. True differences are stripped away as all are compelled to reject their past and rhapsodise about the freedoms of the present. We are all free to define and redefine ourselves as we see fit, and we are free to draw upon any aspect of commodified global culture to do so. We are told we should not be held back by a weighty sense of obligation to our ancestors. We should no longer feel ourselves constrained by their laws, rules and protocols. The obdurate sense of obligation that many still carry is, in reality, an inverted and distorted fear of the diverse freedoms now available to us. And, as we have noted, many feel that left-liberalism's current campaign to discard attachments to the past is far from universally applied, which, of course, raises suspicions, hardens attitudes and deepens the class and cultural fault lines currently pulling society apart.

All we can see of the present so far is a hall of mirrors: a multitude of distorted images from all points on the political and social spectrum, the inevitable destination of 50 years of fragmentary postmodernism. All these images share is their unreliability. Things of great value have been rendered inaccessible for a significant portion of the population. This profound sense of loss is fuelling a desire to re-establish some coherent symbolism that might allow traditional groups destabilised by decades of neoliberalism to re-establish shared identities and political projects free from the gnawing cultural and economic insecurity that is so pervasive today. Before we can see a way forward, the first step out of the hall of mirrors must be backwards, out of the door through which we came in. Is it truly regressive for each group to establish a firm foundation for itself as it is propelled by forces currently beyond political control into a murky, uncertain future?

Postmodernism transformed our relationship with history. In some respects, our sense of the historical continuity of time was disturbed. Our relationship with our shared past shifted. For huge expanses of human history, our ancestors acted as a symbolic audience who sat in judgement of our lives and deeds.[13] Whether their causes were right, wrong or forged in error-strewn ambivalence, our desire to measure up to their mythologised heroism fashioned our identities, ethics and politics. However, the neoliberal era seemed to throw this timeless relation of ethical judgement into reverse. Over the past 40 years or so, we in Western liberal democracies have, generally speaking, stopped seeking the approval of our ancestors. Instead, we now place ourselves in the position of judgement, and rarely do we show mercy in our assessments.

Whole generations, long since gone, are now regularly impugned and symbolically sentenced for their prejudices, parochialism and generally deplorable attitudes. This profound shift in the standard mode of intergenerational judgement is especially noticeable on the liberal left. Understanding of the past, appreciation of its labyrinthine complexities, and the essential balance of apology and celebration have been displaced by the tantrums of the infantile narcissist who has just discovered his parents were anything but perfect.

The liberal left's condemnation of our illiberal history – in many ways as true as it is false – is, of course, a pointless exercise. It may momentarily help to assuage the vicarious shame left-liberals have chosen to internalise, but it is otherwise entirely useless. Where the imagined judgements of our ancestors can shape our behaviour, our judgements cannot shape theirs. But, again, the past, present and future coincide here, because we must assume that the true goal of condemning the past is to affect the present and the future in some way.

In truth, this is far deeper than mere virtue signalling, although that is often a superficial part of the process as left-liberals seek to avoid shame and exclusion by expelling any possible doubt that they are worthy members of the group. The practice of spectacular condemnation rather establishes a series of cautionary tales that further reinforces our commitment to compulsory liberalism. Of course, events and epochs in the past are condemned precisely to serve the core moral command that we must fight against all forms of illiberalism to prevent the horrors of the past from resurfacing in the present and the future.

This is not to say that it is always unequivocally wrong to condemn the past. Rather, it is to say that we should explore the past honestly and in as much detail as possible – even where the details are inconvenient to our ideological position – and use universal morality set in a context of free and open debate to structure our evaluations. Ideological condemnation is not necessarily wrong in and of itself. However, it is crucial that we do not confuse ideological condemnation for moral condemnation, or present one particular ideology – liberalism – as if it and universal morality are ultimately one and the same thing.

The novelist L.P. Hartley once presciently noted that 'the past is a foreign land; they do things differently there'. The lesson is that, if we hope to understand and explain past events, they must be contextualised. We cannot use the ethics, assumptions and beliefs of today to evaluate a past quite different from our own time without historicising them, or understanding that they are themselves products of history. To truly understand, we must travel from the present to the foreign land of the past in order to grasp the forces that shaped past events. Elements of universal morality have existed across history, usually in a struggle with the brutality into which we frequently descended as we faced misunderstood circumstances and the intended and unintended consequences of our error-strewn actions, but as we have already suggested, universal morality no longer casts the shadow it once did. Today, we are far more likely to use our own narrow ethical vision to appraise the lives and deeds of those who can no longer defend themselves.

Impugning our illiberal past, then, provides a useful function for postmodern cultural politics. Academic history is now a battlefield for playing out the political conflicts of the present. Objective empirical historians mindful of context are now forced to fight for an audience against those who seek to project their ideologically customised moral judgements onto a world they have never known. In this postmodern time warp, Caribbean pirates can be reimagined as social justice activists committed to equality, diversity and inclusion. The fall of Rome and the descent into the violent struggles of the Dark Ages can be redefined as a time of devolutionary progress, freedom and growing cosmopolitanism rather than civilisational collapse. The principal force behind the fall of Soviet communism can be posited as an upsurge in urban graffiti.[14]

Postmodern revisionist scholars are firm in their belief that contemporary liberal ethics are in fact a timeless judge of humanity rather than particular to the present, and not necessarily guaranteed to continue forever. The unconscious goal of such accounts seems to be to compel all non-partisan readers to rally to cultural liberalism's cause in order to ensure that the horrors of the past do not return. In waging war against standard accounts of specific epochs and events, authors are actually writing a highly selective story about where we are now and how we got here, and what we need to do to improve upon what already exists. In doing so they truncate and impoverish our understanding, making the construction of political solutions to our present gathering crises a good deal harder to identify.

However, such trends have not severed lingering attachments to a past in which most people felt a greater degree of security. Nostalgia suggests we imbue particular times and places with the characteristics of home. Our fundamental sense of security is tied to the deep comfort we feel among those who accept and value us exactly as we are, warts and all. When we return to our figurative home we can be truly at ease, and many of the simmering anxieties that intrude on our everyday experience dissipate. And they will dissipate because we are home.

Our attachment to a time and place does not necessarily mean we turn away from the problems of the present and choose instead to live in the dreamworld of an idealised past. Rather, our acknowledgement of the benefits of our beloved time and place can act as the impetus to create or rediscover in the present those things we love about our past. The great power we give to these good things means that they have a greater capacity to triumph over the bad as we endeavour to build a new home with the best materials.

If our experience in general terms has been a good one, our love of our particular past equips us with the hope that it is still possible to transform the present, that our lives do not need to be defined by the gradual erosion of security, that the happiness and emotional and existential repose we have felt before – all of us, somewhere in time and space – can again return to elevate our experience. Others, too, can benefit from the wonders we have known, just as we can benefit from the wonders they have known. This desire to bestow particular goods upon the world can act as a powerful integrative force but, of course, for the left to appreciate and utilise this force would require a major shift in direction. Often it appears that the activist left does not want the good things we can offer, and often it seems that it does not want us to set up a new home. Its deep commitment to its own ethical and cultural universe means that anything external to it tends to be dismissed or defamed.

Many among the working class feel set apart from the new liberal mainstream. They cannot see a place where they might belong in either the neoliberal economy or liberal-postmodern culture. Their skills are redundant; their history judged meaningless and irrelevant, their tastes crass and passé. With every passing year the gap seems to get wider. It has been made clear to them that, if they remain as they are, their admission to the future will be denied. The only choice for these men and women is, it seems, to accept the liberal injunction to dismantle and discard their identities, forget their past, and join everyone else in the endless struggle for some fleeting sense of significance in the consumer mainstream. To remain attached to their identities and histories is to accept irrelevance. To aid this process of transformation, the liberal left is at hand to encourage them to replace their positive memories with shameful regrets and apologies. Isn't it inevitable that many will use the morsel of power still available to them – namely, the right to vote – to register their dissent?

The truth of the matter is that hope for the future finds a platform in recollections of a more positive past. In looking back, we are paradoxically redirected to a future of which we once dreamed. Things will inevitably be different, but we can at least try to make them as good as we once thought they might be. This is not to say that all nostalgia is inherently positive; very often disappearing into memory has no political resonance whatsoever. However, it seems to us important to understand that the past is always alive and awaiting interpretation. We can seek to change the future by attempting to bring the more optimistic promises of the past to fruition. The benefit of hindsight honestly evaluated will help us to avoid mistakes as we construct means to our ends.

With regard to the politics of the contemporary left, to set ourselves the task of recreating in contemporary reality the conditions that gave rise to our favoured mythologised past would be to step into the future rather than regressing into history. Would it really be so bad if the organised left sought to recreate – in modified and updated forms – the conditions and effects of its undoubted high point, the modern social democratic age? Don't many of us need what the social democratic state once made freely available? Mightn't, say, the return of full employment, incrementally improving lifestyles, and health and education systems we can be proud of represent a step towards a more positive future?

To suggest, as liberals are often wont to do, that the return of such things will inevitably mean the return of other things we don't like about the social democratic age is to miss the point. Of course, the social democracy of the 1950s and 1960s reflected a specific historical context that cannot be recreated. Instead, we might ask, how could we build an equivalent – and cautiously idealised – system today? How can we secure full employment, and how can we guarantee that work will pay enough to enable all citizens to live a good life? How can we build expansive welfare states, comprehensive public education programmes and secure world-class healthcare for all? Can we adopt strategies from the past, like the public ownership of key industries, higher levels of state spending, state involvement in the market, tariffs and the recreation of national and regional supply chains that will fit with the current energy transition and partial deglobalisation that await us just around the corner? Our goal should not be to recreate the past in the present, but to identify the positive aspects of the past and to think seriously about how they might be reimagined in the present, not as final destinations but routes to a better future. For us, the fundamental drive should be to facilitate the return of security and a degree of satisfaction to all people. Only when we are secure in the economic, cultural and psychological realms can we truly begin to reap the benefits of freedom.

10

A return to economics

The return of populism after the 2008 global financial crisis was, given the left's abandonment of interventionist economic policy and alienation of its traditional voters, inevitable. However, as we have been at pains to stress, the dominant narratives that accompanied the return of populism were remarkably one-sided and tended to ignore the long history of Western populist responses to technocratic arrogance and economic injustice. The American economist Michael Hudson has drawn upon a substantial body of anthropological work that reveals remarkably different attitudes to populism. In eras stretching from Ancient Rome to post-bellum America, populists were regarded as heroic representatives of the populace, a body of people living in a specific territory they regarded as home. Populism was the principal source of solidarity and political energy in struggles against extractive landholding elites in the Ancient World across the Middle East and the Mediterranean. Large-scale economies became increasingly based on credit, which allowed accelerated expansion because labour and materials could be bought before sales. Defying laws and norms clearly laid down by Judaic and Pagan religions, powerful landholders used their substantial assets to become major creditors, irresponsibly indebting farmers and eventually acquiring more assets as the debt burden became impossible to pay. Drawing upon the stabilising activities of the initial palace economies, state authorities offered an alternative source of currency issue as credit which could be bound by powerful laws and decrees that ensured indebtedness would not bankrupt too many families. Most effective were periodic jubilees, which would wipe slates clean, relieve debt, reverse foreclosures, restore property and reboot economic activity.[1]

The fundamental political struggle in the Ancient World was rooted in economics and property ownership. Put simply, state authorities functioned to prevent landholding creditors using private loans to become oligarchs. Small subsistence farmers were actually pledging their livelihoods as collateral and therefore risked the permanent loss of everything they had worked for and on which their lives depended. Private landholding families who acted as creditors wanted to abandon restrictive laws and debt jubilees to make the forfeiture of property as payment for debt permanent. They struggled against state authorities who wanted to stabilise economies in order to retain satisfactory production levels and produce individuals loyal and healthy enough for military service. Neither side was motivated by pristine values and life was hard, but on balance the majority were significantly better off under the authority of the state. Populism was simply popular support for *tyrants* – at that time a word with positive, noble connotations because it denoted rulers who would overthrow oligarchs and redistribute land – who would command states and legislate in the interests of the majority.

The 'decadence' that Gibbon[2] placed centrally in the fall of Rome was the triumph of the landholding, moneylending families against the populist tyrants, who, like Caesar and the Gracchi brothers, were often murdered by oligarchs. The decline in production and health – compounded by the constant use of fraud, coercion, foreclosure and political assassinations, all looked upon helplessly by weak, corrupt emperors – dispirited and impoverished the population. As Hudson[3] reminds us, the barbarians had always been at the gates, but the progressive internal deterioration of morality and political life in Rome was the main factor in its demise.

Other ancient cities had fallen for the same reason. When Christian eschatology relocated the debt jubilee in the afterlife, Western history became a deinstitutionalised struggle to establish the rights of creditors to retain assets paid to service debts above the rights of debtors to have debts cleared and property restored. The debtor must always take the risk, the lender must always be paid. After a very long wait, this was interrupted to some extent by the establishment of the limited company in the nineteenth century, but the creditor could still asset-strip, while the bankrupt debtor would still lose all property associated with his or her business.

The great ideological reversal of reality was to portray the creditors as the noble elite, and the indebted, wage-dependent people as the dangerous mob. This narrative is central in a lot of liberal literature[4] and retains a significant presence in both academic life and popular culture. The fear of crowds present in the analyses of Le Bon[5] and Canetti[6] derives from an assumption that the mob is always replete with bigotry, in essence a nativist, exclusionary and hostile sub-democracy with no rational leadership, plan or moral purpose.

The liberal elite have always feared that the common people will be put on a pedestal and given the sort of strong leadership they crave, the inevitable result of which would be brutal authoritarianism. However, more penetrative analyses[7] have shown how populist sentiment can be led by democratic means – the people's art, literature and theatre is often adept at expressing popular experiences and concerns, feeding into education and politics to press for the economic reforms on which substantive social reforms depend. What in history was the ordinary people's demand for economic reforms is now understood by some liberal commentators as an ugly concatenation of ignorance, tribalism, envy, surly discontent and mob violence.

Populism has been framed as intrinsically bad, so we don't see it as a legitimate political reaction to the failures of the liberal elite. But what was it when it had some political shape? In the United States during the nineteenth century, Bryan's Populist Party was actually a labour party, lining up producers against emerging oligarchs, corporations, banks, trusts and other elite economic institutions involved with credit, foreclosure, asset-stripping and the extraction of surplus value at the point of production. Populists demanded that the government issue fiat currency, nationalise railways, seize land owned by speculators and asset-strippers, and relocate national banks into post offices. In the 1930s, Roosevelt put similar ideas into practice in an effort to combat the Great Depression and offer the American people a New Deal. He also abandoned the gold standard, strapped regulations around bankers and creditors, made speculation more difficult, supported unions, expanded public sector employment and established a welfare system. After yet another economic failure of the liberal elite and the implementation of policies that worked, Roosevelt was roundly denounced as a populist.

The great transhistorical ideological move is to deter the people from demanding the sort of politically controlled, democratically agreed economic reform that is fair, feasible and effective. Because Soviet communism's unworkable central command economy was a palpable disaster, it is ambitious, feasible, effective and popular social democratic reform that the liberal elite fear most. Hudson proposes 'progressive tax policy, limitations on inherited wealth, debt write-offs or a replacement of debt with equity as means of preventing or reversing the concentration of wealth in the absence of an external crisis'.[8] But, given the scale of the present crisis and the problems that lie ahead, is this ambitious enough? Neoliberalism's chaotic demise and potential alternatives have been discussed, but the current mainstream left across the West has quite systematically marginalised those discussions. In such a climate of repression and silence, less rational and organised forms of populism were inevitable.

Neoliberalism's murky past

In its attempt to build on traditional communal values, forge democratic institutions and repurpose the sovereign nation-state to work on behalf of working people, what was the traditional left up against? Of course, most of the left's informed analysts know that the initial answer to that question is 'neoliberalism'. It's not a difficult concept – a political doctrine that prefers the minimally regulated global free-market to be the principal system of economic organisation. This system continues to govern the lives of a large proportion of the world's population. It is against true democracy, against organised labour and against the state, unless the role of the state is restricted to protecting free markets.

What brought this thing upon us? Contrary to popular opinion, it wasn't the work of Thatcher and Reagan in the 1980s, or even that of the neoliberal think-tanks that began to spring up and influence the mass media and politicians after the Second World War. It began life during the final years of the Habsburg Empire, which had been a free-trade playground for a powerful banking and investment elite, based mostly in the opulent streets of Vienna. Here the Austrian school of economics was founded, which in the 1920s received funding from the Ford Foundation, a US think-tank always alert to possible ways of spreading free-market doctrine, with which, incidentally, Henry Ford himself did not entirely agree. The Austrian economists hatched one of history's most audacious economic plans. Even though the principal strain that eventually collapsed the Habsburg Empire was the mounting dissatisfaction felt by individual regions over an uneven distribution of wealth and power, these doctrinaire economists, supported by the investment elite, were convinced that if the world's nations could be persuaded to roll out the free market worldwide, this time it would work.

The British Empire model was influential but, with its commitments to nation-building, administrative institutions and subsidised infrastructure development, too rigid, cumbersome and costly. At first the Austrian thinkers saw a positive role for nation-states as subservient hands-on economic managers. However, in the 1930s leading neoliberal intellectual Friedrich Hayek, reflecting on the difficulties experienced by the Habsburg and British Empires and observing the even greater difficulties encountered by the fledgling Soviet command economy, was persuaded of the impossibility of economic management on such a scale. Here we see the beginning of the risky move to trust the forces of the unregulated market to 'correct' problems and restore equilibria over an unspecified period of time, even though life might be tough for those waiting for the correction to happen. Somehow, nations and their politicians needed to be persuaded that this was the way forward.

Hayek and his growing band of supporters, including the increasingly influential Ludwig von Mises, had also witnessed the rise of the German and Italian national socialist and fascist states. Whilst taking little notice of the deep social problems that after the Wall Street Crash had set the context for the rise of these monstrosities, the fledgling neoliberals decided they were – along with Soviet communism – the inevitable political forms a firm nexus between the working class and a powerful state would take. The risk that a permanent and overwhelming relationship of power between the two might be established was great, especially if democratic states could learn to cooperate and trade fairly across the globe. The nexus must be broken.

But, for Hayek and his followers, worse was to come. As we have seen, with popular approval Roosevelt had implemented state-centred Keynesian economic management policies in the 1930s as a response to the Great Depression, first in 1933 and with renewed vigour during his second term after 1937. Criminal activity was significantly reduced, and the high American homicide rate dropped by almost a half as a growing number of people found legitimate livelihoods, some directly provided by the government.[9] Whereas the monstrosities of Nazism, fascism and Stalinism were easy to discredit and demonise, the early and very popular successes of Keynesian economics and social democracy were not. Alerted by this political threat, the neoliberal vanguard first met in Paris in 1938, at the Walter Lippmann Colloquium.

Lippmann was, of course, a high-profile American journalist, so from the start links were established with the mass media. In the midst of complex discussions of burning issues such as freedom, individualism, free markets, finance and wealth creation, the principal enemy was identified – the organised working class and the democratic state together taking up the reins of Keynesian economic management. According to an economist who spoke up at the colloquium, the organised working class must be 'eliminated'.[10]

The principal ideological tactic was to persuade as many people as possible that social democracy was really a wolf in sheep's clothing, the first step on 'the road to serfdom'[11] and totalitarian brutality. It was an effective tactic, because individual freedom was Western liberalism's foundational value, and the totalitarian states of the post-war era were indeed palpably monstrous. However, social democracy pressed on to become a reasonably popular orthodoxy. Neoliberals were forced to work hard in the background, refining their tactics while waiting for an opportune moment to advance. Think-tanks were set up, businesspeople and academics recruited, and slowly some advances made in the major political parties.

Their big opportunity came during the stagflation crisis in the 1970s. The logic of neoclassical economics, enshrined in the Phillips curve, instructed us that inflation and unemployment tend to work in opposite directions – if unemployment falls too far beneath its 'naturally occurring rate', inflation will kick in. This was grist for neoliberalism's ideological mill because they now had a mathematically proven excuse to blame the organised working class for the inflation that would allegedly increase prices, eat away savings and perhaps turn into the hyper-inflation that paved the way for Nazism. This is, of course, utter hokum, all of it. High inflation is usually caused by price rises rather than wage rises. Hyper-inflation is very rare. When it does occur, it is usually caused by supply-side shortages or owing large debts payable only in foreign countries. Weimar Germany – which after the First World War had suffered from both – had in fact conquered its hyper-inflation by 1924. The Nazis secured less than 3 per cent of the vote in 1928 and won a narrow victory in 1933 after four years of the mass unemployment, insecurity and poverty that followed the 1929 Wall Street crash.

The true tragedy for the left is that stagflation could have been solved in the 1970s without moving even one step closer to a dreaded totalitarian state. Once again, the liberal centre and the left faltered and failed to grasp the opportunity. Partly to blame were the internal failings of the Keynesian theoretical model, which still saw money as a private asset rather than credit issued by central authorities to use as investment and a medium of exchange. At the time, most Keynesians – with the notable exception of Joan Robinson,[12] who knew it was about price control – agreed with the neoclassical monetary position that inflation can be controlled if new money is pumped into the economy up to full employment. However, if employment falls, money creation must be reduced accordingly and interest rates must be increased, which hampers business development, causes more unemployment and punishes borrowers whilst making neoliberalism popular with money hoarders, creditors and older people reliant on savings.

The kernel of the great myth is that inflation is an internal, logical monetary phenomenon explained by the Phillips curve. The mythical logic of austerity was once again ideologically reaffirmed in political thinking. However, both neoliberals and Keynesians failed to consider the oil shock, which was an external factor. In the 1970s, when the OPEC countries kept raising their oil prices year on year, energy costs in Western production systems became more expensive. Had Western states created more money to maintain production and profitability, inflation would have increased at a manageable level roughly in accordance with the oil prices rises before eventually settling down. However, in the grip of neoclassical mythology, central banks reduced the money supply by raising interest rates and therefore deterring borrowing and spending, which in turn reduced demand, slowed down growth, reduced production output, made goods more expensive and actually exacerbated inflation. The result was stagflation – unemployment and inflation rising together.

Stagflation seemed to defy the logic of the Phillips curve. Numerous possibilities for easing our way out of stagflation presented themselves – subsidising the production system's energy costs, encouraging savings, tightening consumer credit controls on peripheral goods, introducing judicious price and income controls, and many others. However, because Keynesian economic modelling had been infiltrated by neoliberal ideologues after his death, and the same group of people had infiltrated the education, media and political systems, the money supply was presented as the sole cause. Contemporary monetarism was born.

In the midst of the crisis, these same neoliberal ideologues struck with a penetrating ideological campaign. They infiltrated, and began to take over, conservative and centre-left social democratic parties in the West, making moves to end the Keynesian orthodoxy, dismantle the organised working class and capture the state to reduce its role to that of an emergency market-fixer operating mainly through independent central banks. They worked hard to make Keynesian economics, left-wing governance and the unionised working class as unpopular as possible by blaming them for the instability, inflation and unemployment caused by the oil shock. In Britain they organised a huge press campaign – blaming strikes and wage demands rather than price rises – which was neatly condensed in the effective Conservative slogan before the 1979 election: 'Labour isn't working'.

Tabloid media exerting pressure on the populace, rather than neoliberal ideologues infiltrating the political elite and controlling major institutions, continues to be the left's knee-jerk excuse for losing. But what did the established British left do? Labour Prime Minister James Callaghan, already an advocate of the notion that wages rather than prices were the main cause of inflation, ignored all other possibilities as he accepted recession, unemployment and wage restraint which, of course, paved the way for Thatcherism. In the United States, President Carter abandoned his New Deal principles and caved in, replacing the incumbent chair of the Federal reserve with arch-monetarist Paul Volcker in 1979.

Towards the end of the 1970s the powerful United States and British economies were about to become fully marketised. Neoliberalism's path had been cleared because the orthodox Keynesian left had been murdered while the mainstream social democratic left had committed suicide. Meanwhile, the Western system of values and norms was experiencing its own exogenous shock as the cultural left waged its parallel war against morality and all established social conventions. Even if we admit that a few regressive traditional norms needed to be discarded, a period of chronic economic instability was not the ideal time to do it.

Economic education is of vital importance to future democracy, but genuine heterodox economic perspectives are still marginalised in schools, universities and governments, while Keynesianism is regarded as only of historical interest and often taught as a cautionary tale. Post-Keynesian economists who predicted the global financial crisis are still ignored and marginalised in governmental and academic circles.[13] The global financiers seem to have disappeared from the mainstream left's critical radar, dismissed as a mythical bogeyman invented by racists on the far left and far right. This is a protective exercise.

What is to be protected is the belief that only the private banking technocrats can make sensible investment decisions, while states and everyday people must be permanently discredited. This is now the bedrock of the ideology, which over the millennia has mutated from oligarchic narcissism to an exclusive technocratic claim to competence.

Politics' new economic landscape

If this ideological grip can be loosened and a new democratically grounded politics forged, those who operate in various spheres of influence must listen to ordinary people about their basic life experiences, clear their vision and sharpen their focus on the fundamental structures, processes and hubs of concentrated power in political economy that shape the lives of all. We have reached a point in economic history where there is no time and no room for nostalgic or futuristic metaphysical doctrines of either the structural or post-structural variety. We're all in this together whether we like it or not.

The COVID-19 panic alerted both the United States and the EU to the forgotten fact that the retention of at least some degree of manufacturing capacity in essential industries – particularly healthcare, energy, transport and defence – is a national security issue. Both have declared China to be not just a tough competitor but an economic and existential threat. This sort of reactionary knee jerk will become more common whether the neoliberal globalist project hits the rocks and disintegrates or begins to rebuild itself in a modified form. The disruption, austerity and insecurity likely in either scenario will inflict economic and cultural harm on many people.

On Friday, 4 February 2022 President Joe Biden signed the COMPETES Act, just two months after he boycotted the Chinese Winter Olympics, citing human rights abuses. He announced that the Americans are building a $10 billion semiconductor factory, which will increase national security, create thousands of jobs and inflict damage on the Chinese export economy. At approximately the same time, American bondholders also froze $9 billion worth of Afghan central bank assets, which will cause poverty and social upheaval, and make the Afghans think twice about doing mineral deals with China. In other words, the Biden government is laying the foundation stones for precisely the sort of aggressive economic nationalism that Steve Bannon lobbied for and President Trump tried to implement. To the chagrin of both liberal rationalists and post-liberal moralists, it will be justified by the logic and ethics of the Green New Deal – shorter supply chains and modernised production processes hopefully powered by cleaner energy sources will mean less pollution, while new jobs will score a major hit with the working class.

Of course, when in office Trump and Bannon were labelled sexist, racist, nativist, fascist and so on. Underneath that was the real threat of economic nationalism combined with a greater degree of isolationism and political independence. Yet Biden and the Democrats, steering the United States down a similar path but with less independence and still under the close control of global corporations and financiers, are portrayed as progressive liberals caring for minorities. The neoliberal media machine accused Trump of having a corrupt relationship with the existential threat of Russia. Along with Afghanistan, Iran, China or any other competitor with their own independent political system, Russia can be justifiably criticised in front of Western populations force-fed on identity politics as imperialistic, racist, sexist, homophobic, human rights abusers and so on. Consequently, they can be legitimately targeted for economic sanctions or military pressure without too much protest. They may well be culturally regressive in some ways, but it's the sense of immobility and incorrigibility that neoliberals stress. They will always be like that, we are told, unless they adopt our way of life, beginning with the first compulsory step of agreeing to play the roles allocated to them – usually as reliable raw energy and mineral suppliers or sweatshop production hubs – by neoliberalism's supranational economic management system.

Alongside escalating geopolitical tension, there are basic economic reasons why we can't sit around waiting for a new politics to fall from the sky. Time is short. In the wake of falling profitability, the global financial crisis and the COVID-19 pandemic, fundamental changes are afoot. Neoliberalism is either about to give itself a major refit or implode, leaving a murky landscape strewn with rubble real and metaphysical, in which as yet unknown forms of politics will come into being. However, the basic shapes are just about beginning to emerge. Falling profits at the turn of the millennium alerted investors to the fact that long-distance global supply chains in the real 'economy of things' are not the future. The global financial crisis revealed the derivatives economy to be unstable and unreliable as a major contributor to economic health and certainly not a long-term substitute for the real economy of tangible goods and services.

The neoliberal solution of austerity further damaged economies and ignited a populist backlash. The pandemic revealed national security issues – especially over-dependence on neoliberalism's global manufacturing hubs – and the emergence yet again of inflationary pressure as supply chains were disrupted. This provided more contemporary evidence that supply shortages and price rises are the primary factors driving rapidly rising inflation, but neoliberal ideologues still sustain the monetarist myth that wage rises, full employment and 'printing too much money' are the problems.

At the same time, the general acceptance of global warming pressed home the need for a fundamental energy transition. We should not underestimate this conjuncture. The convergence of the fall in profitability and the pressing need for infrastructural transformation to combat global warming has created a force of historically unprecedented magnitude and presented the adaptable capitalist system with opportunities. This 'great convergence' triggered a pragmatic business response that can be morally justified and might potentially save neoliberalism's global cosmopolitan project. An energy transition in the world's basic manufacturing, transport and domestic infrastructure – from fossil fuel to nuclear/renewable energy and electric/battery/ hydrogen transport – could be highly profitable and, now that the growth of China and other global production centres is slowing down, could revive the real economy as the primary investment target.

Is what economist Phil Mullan calls a world 'beyond confrontation' possible? Can we move beyond doctrinaire isolationist and globalist reactions to the global financial crisis, austerity and the pandemic to address a broken economic system and an ecological crisis with rational proposals for democratic political action in the economy? Protectionism was conflict-ridden, but the 'free trade' model of global interdependence set the context for numerous depressions, revolutionary and totalitarian reactions, the two most destructive world wars in human history and thousands of other conflicts in a general climate of national insecurity and geopolitical hostility.

The pandemic alerted nations to the dangers of global economic interdependence. Economic troubles at home are too easily blamed on the free movement of people, but when it comes down to the free movement of goods and capital, sometimes those labelled nationalists or isolationists are correct. Post-2008, more aggressive competition, trade wars and sanctions have appeared likely to escalate. On the other hand, trade protectionism can anger export-dependent nations, but of course that dependency was forged as national politicians made what they thought would be good long-term deals with global investors. Globalisation has made us susceptible to the big mistakes of supranational organisations and global finance technicians as well as the usual vagaries of market forces. Giving up sovereignty eviscerates democracy to foster powerlessness, fatalism and anxiety amongst national populations, which can, of course, breed reaction.

While globalists fear nationalism's return, globalism is understood by hard-line nationalists as the intercultural blame game writ large, the same force that is tearing apart national populations by flooding them with immigrants, either too poor and depressing wages or too rich and buying up national assets. Everything is the fault of either nativists and their xenophobia or globalists and their mass immigration policies, and the winner of that ideological war will lead us into the future. In fact, underneath this crude cultural dichotomy, the rarely discussed roots of the real economic problems we face have been slowing productivity and growth in the old industrial nations since 1945, subsequent deindustrialisation, too much concentrated power in the hands of financiers and investors, the relocation of production abroad and, more recently, the slowdown in global trade, which together form the basis for exacerbated international and intercultural tensions. To begin with, global neoliberalism's trade model is in serious difficulty. As Mullan[14] notes:

> The structural expansion in cross-border supply networks is now likely to have passed its peak rate of growth. This is why integration along global value chains appears to have slowed or even reversed in recent years... [T]he 'global trade slowdown' is the trade expression of the relative exhaustion of the internationalisation of production as a means of counteracting Western economies' domestic decay... Whatever happens to future trade levels, the key point is that changes within production relations have been and will continue to be its decisive drivers.

In other words, trade will recover and stabilise only when global production is once again internationally diversified, rationalised and modernised, when competition based on various forms of comparative advantage – some natural, such as mineral resources; some artificial, such as low currency value and cheap labour – is replaced with international collaboration structured by a configuration of national specialisms. This could have been pioneered by the EU, but its fiscal, competition and state subsidy rules kept it subservient to neoliberal doctrine.

The national energy autonomy that would be possible as technology develops – now looking more possible as breakthroughs in fusion and battery power are made – would allow nations to develop specialisms and give their populations immediate jobs, small business opportunities and a sense of renewal; in other words, a sense of security and a better future, the original promises made by the traditional and far more successful social democratic left. New national apparatuses of energy production and manufacturing could provide centres of wealth, hubs around which the ancillary small businesses and the public sector could grow, and secure communities could settle. The prospect of fostering benign national identities and international cooperation in production and raw material supply and trade with fair prices looks a long way off, but it is not impossible. Of course, in the face of today's escalating domestic and international tensions it would be more sensible to admit that it's essential.

The implication of Mullan's thesis is that the fight against global warming manifested by the current energy transition lays down material imperatives that can act as a basis for consensus and provide the opportunity for rational global decoupling and the revival of national productivity. This decoupling – the division of the world into Eastern and Western trading blocs – is, after Russia invaded Ukraine at the time of writing, being presented as inevitable by senior figures among the Western investment elite. It would encourage the Asian giants to focus more heavily on developing their domestic economies and simultaneously set the context for the development of national economies and international cooperation at the same time. The first step is to dispense with zombie production that is reliant on cheap private debt, low wages and low productivity. Today, rather than cower in the face of insurmountable difficulties, we should see a rational groundwork, a real opportunity. However, before this can be approached we encounter a fundamental problem we have stressed throughout this book and which others have explored in detail – globalism, supranational political economy and the democratic deficit.

The liberal elite's hysterical scaremongering at the sight of populist reaction – Brexiteers, the gilets jaunes, Canadian truckers or whoever – is simply one of the ways it protects the levers of economic control. To make the transition from a competitive global economy – in which the race to the bottom for nations and workers lines the pockets of financiers – we need to know precisely where these levers of control are, how they work and who pulls them. Even if agreement to move away from financialisation and create new dynamic production centres can be reached among politicians, there is no guarantee that it will attract international investment if financialisation, austerity and driving down wages remain profitable.

As we write, the price of lithium is skyrocketing in response to the surge in demand for electric vehicles, as the first stages of what the corporations are calling the 'energy transition' get under way. However, investors are slow to redirect capital, constantly waiting to be tempted by market signals, which are unreliable representations of what is needed in the real world. The future is too urgent to wait for financiers and investors to do their sums and speculate on future returns.

It is obvious that we need more proactive forms of forward planning that can readily take advantage of scientific and technological developments and cater for social and ecological needs. We know that command economies are unworkable and market signals are necessary in the realm of everyday consumption in the retail and service economy, but at the 'commanding heights' – extractive industries, energy, freight transport and essential manufacturing – democratic input, forward planning, international cooperation and a degree of governmental control are essential. This would require quite major changes to international law in such a way that supranational institutions can be challenged by democratic governments able to exercise a degree of control over central bank currency issue, capital controls and public investment as pump-priming. Nationalisation of major components of the transport and energy infrastructure, such as rail networks and power generation, would aid democratic forward planning, increase security for all nations, move some way towards energy independence and involve governments in price stabilisation at a fundamental level.

New world, new economics, new politics

We know that the fundamental levers of economic control are credit, finance and investment, but we need a more detailed understanding. Taking the first steps towards making real the vision of cooperative autonomy and democracy in a globally decoupled and reconstructed production and distribution system would require that new politics are informed by a pristine understanding of how modern economies work at their financial core. We must remember that for over four millennia all large-scale economies intent on rapid development have been dependent on the issue of money as credit.

The rapid exhaustion of the neoliberal economic model tore back the ideological veil and revealed that the supply and demand sectors on which the real economy rests – manufacturing, distribution and consumption – had together degenerated into a private debt zombie.[15] Neoclassical economics had made the move of excluding money and finance from its theoretical models, a move far bolder and more fundamental than excluding house prices from inflation indexes as financiers were about to use the rising house market as the basic asset for their derivatives game. Such convenient exclusions of reality reveal neoclassical economics as not a science but a defensive belief system in denial of reality.

Keynes had alerted us to the importance of *animal spirits*, the fact that investment depends on expectations of the future driven by emotional excitement, not by care about the population's future well-being or rational calculations of existing factors such as the money supply or interest rates. To preserve a system fundamentally based on emotive speculation, neoliberal ideologues have been selective about which factors to include in their models – banks, money and private debts have simply been omitted. They have also systematically misinformed the public about the role of banks and the source of credit as loans.

Banks are not simply intermediaries between savers and borrowers, and we have to clear the decks by admitting that the loanable funds, fractional reserve and money-multiplier models are also wrong. Here we arrive at a central fact that we must bear in mind as we assess the role of finance in creating a future that will benefit all people and their natural environments. Private banks actually *create money when they lend*, an unassailable fact now admitted by senior figures in the Bank of England. They do not simply lend out savings deposits or even risk lending above their reserves – they create those deposits themselves. Savings are reserved as a cushion for spikes in withdrawals and interbank lending.

What is this money that they create and lend out as interest-bearing loans? At the moment, and for the past 50 years or so, they have dealt with what we call fiat currency, which we discussed in detail in Chapter 2. Fiat currency is essentially state-authorised credit. Neoclassicism – the economic model on which neoliberalism was founded – presents the genuine diametric opposite to the truth on this matter. They claim that states borrow money from the public, who have created it by earning it in wealth-creating activities, in order to fund their policies, thus 'crowding out' more competent, free and good-willed private investors. The opposite is true – the state creates money by running a deficit and pumping debt-free money into the public and private sectors, into the accounts of private banks, institutions, businesses and individuals to make large-scale production, consumption and everyday economic transactions possible.[16]

The state and private banks create exactly the same thing. In fact, when private banks make loans, the state simply credits their reserve accounts at the central bank. Neoclassical mythology has been disseminated throughout the education system and pumped by mass media into popular culture for one fundamental purpose – to justify the role of private banks in the creation of money as interest-bearing loans. For over 4,000 years Western economic history has rested on a struggle between state authorities and private asset holders over the entitlement to create credit relationships with producers and consumers.[17]

When compound interest flows into the accounts of private lenders, it has created the foundation of oligarchies, in the ancient-world landholding families who issued private credit and in the modern-world private investment bankers, bank shareholders and corporate chiefs whose corporations – such as Volkswagen or PayPal, for instance – become big enough to risk lending credit. The entitlement to create new money and issue it as credit in the form of interest-bearing loans has become the ultimate asset, unreal and intangible yet the fulcrum of concentrated power over and above producers, consumers and democratic states. Oligarchs grounded in production are relatively rare. The oligarchs' dream is to have a global system with no barriers to free movement running on a ubiquitous and endless flow of private credit issued by themselves.

But in a system based on nothing but abstract power and abstract wealth, it is inevitable that animal spirits overwhelm ethics, rationality, care and democratic governance to fuel great rushes of speculation and irresponsible lending, especially when the economy of real things is saturated by over-production, profits begin to fall, and fraudulently pumping up asset prices to create flimsy artificial markets is the best way to maintain returns on investments. The Marxist insight of the falling rate of profit, shorn of its hasty corollary of likely political transformation, still rings true as a prime economic mover. The neoclassical paradigm, with its need to maintain its beliefs and its income streams in the face of reality, is pathological. It cares nothing for workers, communities or democracy, only the retention of its entitlement to place loans anywhere in the world it wants to in order to guarantee income streams and accumulate capital.

If cooperative international economic blocs with redistributed production and enhanced democratic governance are to be achieved, how do we control and target investment to that end? Banking could remain private with investors responding to market signals while simultaneously being tightly regulated by some combination of democratic national and supranational institutions. Alternatively, states could nationalise their central, commercial and investment banking systems and issue credit on behalf of their populations, at the same time trying to secure international cooperation and manage fair terms of trade. No matter which way we go, we run head on into the fundamental economic issues that need to be addressed at the political level – sovereignty, democracy, cooperation and economic management.

At the moment, as we have seen, the private banking technocrats who remain in control of the core around which the whole process revolves have infiltrated political systems across the West. However, even though identity politics still dominates the cultural landscape, the public's brief glimpses of the core financial system's operation are fuelling their interest in economic matters. Recently, a text by the American economics professor Stephanie Kelton, *The Deficit Myth*,[18] which outlines the role of the state in the issue of currency as deficit spending, has found its way onto the bestseller lists. Public interest is growing, which tells us without doubt that the people are far more than fodder for neoliberal ideologues, populist demagogues or conspiracy theorists.

Kelton is a proponent of Modern Monetary Theory (MMT), a perspective in the heterodox economics field that has attracted sometimes hysterical criticism from neoliberals and the more banking-friendly New Keynesians and post-Keynesians. Surveying even the more measured criticism, it's too often found to be coming from individuals associated with the finance industry to assume that it's impartial and rational. New Keynesians have their roots in light-touch market management, which challenges neoclassical market self-correction dogma by advocating temporary fiscal and monetary intervention to overcome 'stickiness' in prices and wages as they fail to respond to movements in markets. Post-Keynesians tend to be more interventionist because they stick to the basic Keynesian premise that there is no natural tendency in markets towards full structural employment, therefore the maintenance of effective demand is the best route to full employment and economic health. However, some post-Keynesians are significantly more critical of the role of banking and private debt which, rather than 'sticky' wages or prices, is the impediment to economic health, employment and improved social distribution of income and wealth.

MMT is a macroeconomic model based on a pristine understanding of the process of sovereign fiat currency issue. How does this work in relation to investment? To take Britain as an example, as soon as a commercial clearing bank makes a private interest-bearing loan, the central bank has permission from the Treasury to credit the bank's reserve account with interest-free money. In other words, High Street banks, which try to keep customers' savings in reserve for withdrawals and interbank lending, for which they pay their customers a token interest rate, are licensed by the state to create new money from thin air and expand the M1 money supply. Unlicensed investment banks and hedge funds leverage extra money from commercial banks over and above clients' investments by borrowing at a negligible rate, a back-door method of increasing the money supply by issuing the state's sovereign currency as interest-bearing loans. The compound interest is paid to them, of course, not the state.

A lot of sovereign currency used in the neoliberal era for industrial outsourcing, share buy-backs, asset inflation and derivatives trading has been created in this way. To put it very simply, the investment banking elite exert enough political influence on the state's political class and enough cultural influence on the population to maintain a relationship in which the state gives them sovereign currency to play with and enrich themselves while the people think it's just the normal run of things. This is the modern way that private moneylenders keep on top in the transhistorical struggle with states that we outlined earlier. This is not simply an issue of greed but also one of democracy – in the West, the supply of most of the credit for the business development on which whole nations rise and fall is in the hands of private banking technocrats.

Fiat currency, therefore, is technically speaking a public monopoly, or a potential public monopoly should more democratic control be exercised over its issue and where it is spent and invested. As we have seen, the legal demand to pay taxes solely in the state's official currency creates the currency's initial demand and value. This means that money must be spent into the economy before taxes can be paid, therefore taxes do not pay for public spending. The neoclassical economic model on which neoliberalism is based has, quite systematically and for ideological purposes, completely inverted the process. Governments with the ability to issue fiat currency cannot run out of money.

No pre-emptive financial constraint based on future 'debts and deficits' can be placed on a currency-issuing government. We have to suspect that the claim that tight constraints are necessary is simply part of an ideological strategy to minimise public spending and leave most of it to private bankers. The time for constraint is indicated at a point where the rate of inflation might approach a threshold into the realm of hyper-inflation. But the rare instances of this we have seen – Weimar Germany, Venezuela, Zimbabwe and a handful of others – have been triggered by external factors such as material supply shortages, low productivity, owing too much non-monetisable debt in a foreign currency, and elite corruption.

All expanding economies will inflate, but abnormally high inflation is, at root, a supply-side and not a monetary phenomenon, almost always kickstarted by price rises in supply chains followed by wage demands and increased currency issue and spending. However, governments have exerted a major influence on the setting of prices as the biggest buyers from the private sector – as well as being a monopoly currency issuer they are, to coin a phrase, a monopoly consumer. The problems in some of the less industrialised eurozone nations have been caused by low productivity and owing debts in what is effectively a foreign currency yet being unable to adjust their own currency value, interest rates, debt monetisation and methods of demand management. National sovereignty, it would appear, is economically vital and not just some regressive nativist fantasy.

Of course, if the MMT economic modellers' description of how a fiat currency system works is correct – and nothing we have read suggests they are far wrong – the truth they reveal is unattractive to neoliberal and libertarian globalists. More than that, if adopted and put into practice it could shatter the neoliberal belief system into fragments that, like Humpty Dumpty, could never be put back together again. However, this is not to say that conservative governments run scared of the awesome power of currency issue. In fact, especially since the appearance of central banks, they have consistently used deficit spending, but don't make a song and dance about it and always mislabel it as 'public borrowing', thereby avoiding the arousal of the public's curiosity and the bankers' ire.

Western political parties always criticise 'the deficit' or 'too much borrowing' and promise to exercise fiscal prudence when in office. However, now that Western populations have experienced the pandemic and the massive governmental currency issue that paid for furlough schemes without huge tax rises or runaway hyper-inflation, the cat is out of the bag. The current modest rise in the inflation rate we are seeing is being caused by disruption in overly long and complex supply chains, which provides evidence suggesting that the MMT explanation for inflation is probably correct. If so, it also provides justification for the shorter and more reliable supply chains that will be an integral part of the green revolution, the energy transition and the possibility this transition presents for a move to real democracy.

MMT is also a great threat to the current dominance of neoclassical dogma because it is not just a description of how a fiat money system works but a fully-fledged macroeconomic model. On its way to explaining how the money system works and suggesting positive policies that could have cross-party appeal to politicians who represent their constituents rather than financiers, it busts a lot of myths. The myth that a government should budget like a household is nonsense because a household cannot issue its own currency and cannot monetise its own 'debt'. The idea that large deficits are an indication of overspending is also incorrect because rapidly rising inflation is the true indicator. Inflation is a complex phenomenon, but employment, wages, currency issue and fiscal spending are certainly not its primary drivers.

More myth-busting tells us that the national debt is not a financial burden because, as we have seen, the system's processes are such that a currency-issuing government owes debts only to itself and can therefore monetise them. Private debts and government debts owed in foreign currencies are another matter, both issues that must be solved if an era of international cooperation and substantive human freedom is to be made real. The idea that fiscal deficits crowd out private investment is also wrong because analyses of public/private sectoral balances show that fiscal deficits increase wealth, savings and investments in the private sector.[19] A 'deficit' is simply the amount of money issued into the economy minus that which has not been reclaimed in taxes. It would be better renamed as something less pejorative and disturbing, maybe simply 'money currently in circulation'.

Around the issue of taxation, we meet the most ubiquitous of all the popular myths. We think many people swallow this myth because their belief that their hard work and generosity are paying for everything in the public realm is a great comfort to both their egos and their moral sense of civic duty. Unfortunately, the popular understanding that taxes pay for public spending is just plain wrong. A fundamental axiom of the fiat system is that governments must issue currency into existence before people can earn it and pay their taxes. Taxes cancel money from circulation, help to control inflation, expand fiscal space, redistribute wealth and prevent oligarchies forming to exert excessive cultural and political influence, but they don't pay for schools and hospitals.

In the meantime, it is quite amusing to watch government figures putting the big scare stories of deficit, debt and inflation back into public circulation just as we ease our way out of the pandemic. This is simply ideological preparation for putting neoliberal ideology and private investors back in the driving seat as we approach the energy transition, which promises to be an historically lucrative opportunity. According to Kelton, the United States' economy was stabilised during the pandemic because the government released trillions of dollars into the economy, mostly in the form of interest-free cash and grants rather than interest-bearing loans to workers and small businesses. The success of the scheme showed us once again, as we witnessed during the New Deal and post-war Keynesian eras, that unemployment is not 'naturally occurring' but has always been a policy choice made by incumbent politicians working with counsel from neoliberal economic advisers and central bankers. If employment is a political choice in a system where ordinary people are dependent on wages, then so is poverty.[20]

There are various ways in which governments can intervene in the sphere of employment. The Labour Party's call for modest public investment controlled within neoliberal parameters, a minimum wage and unionisation are simply nowhere near enough, while Biden's infrastructural investments and tax adjustments fall even further below the bar. A global economy founded on 40 years of deindustrialisation, outsourcing, free trade, mass economic migration and private sector domination has disempowered democratic states and occupationally and culturally atomised the working class. Unions now tend to be the preserve of the salaried public sector, whilst most workers in the private sector have to contend with the gig economy, in which they are compelled to operate as self-employed, mobile, entrepreneurial workers in a system of flexible labour. Political solidarity between the two factions is difficult to organise.

The intervention that MMT economists prefer is a Job Guarantee Programme[21] in which governments employ all unemployed workers on a fixed wage. Not only would this lift millions out of relative poverty and insecurity but, in the technical dimension, it would provide a buffer stock employment policy, setting a wages floor, stabilising prices, increasing the quality of goods and services, and helping to combat inflation as sellers respond to a greater volume of consumer demand. A job guarantee could also act as a form of spatial Keynesianism, boosting economically distressed regions and locales. There are potential pitfalls, such as making labour too expensive for fledgling small businesses, but it could be combined with some sort of enterprise allowance and rationalised income support. It is certainly feasible, although it currently vies with alternatives such as the expansion of the public sector, Universal Basic Income (UBI), a more flexible welfare system and others. For us, it looks like it's probably the best of the bunch.

The US economist Stephanie Kelton has had some success in popularising heterodox economic principles. One reason for that success is that she leads with comprehensible policy proposals rather than arcane theory, such as the subsidised scrapping of high-emission power stations and trade-in schemes for old, fuel-inefficient vehicles. However, she does not take aim at private capital, arguing instead that judicious fiscal spending would free up investors to fund a rapid transition to renewable energy. The federal government could also increase funding for research and development, helping and steering the private energy sector towards satisfactory public policy outcomes. Her objective seems to be a Blairite partnership between private enterprise and public investment to raise living standards for everyone in nations with abundant resources and labour. Although it's hardly radical thinking, and in the political sense quite conciliatory, it's substantially more interventionist than anything promised by the mainstream or cultural left. However, her claim that '[w]ith the knowledge of how we can pay for it, it's now in your hands to imagine and to help build the people's economy' still relies on the rather naïve hope that the neoliberal institutions of politics, academia and mass media will allow this understanding to be taught as truth.[22]

The fundamental principle is simple: the money we all use to buy the things we need and that we invest in the means of producing them hasn't been generated by businesses or generously donated by taxpayers. It is our money issued by our governments, and, if democracy is to have any meaning at all, populations, through their elected representatives and democratic institutions, must have some say in how it is issued, distributed, spent and invested. However, because very few nations are self-sufficient in the resources needed to run their energy and industrial sectors, and therefore trade in basic raw materials is still essential, we must broaden our vision beyond Kelton's domestic policy programme. If international cooperation between relatively autonomous nation-states organised in trading blocs with short supply chains is to be achieved, it is doubtful whether private global investors and shareholders operating on a global scale can be trusted to act ethically, rationally or in the interests of working populations in any nation. Animal spirits will not lead us to a future fit for the majority of humans. Whereas the MMT model and the post-Keynesians provide the practical economic basis for new politics, they do not provide the political discourse itself.

However, when one surveys the liberal left's current discourse in the institutions where it dominates, discussions about establishing a new economic model are marginal. Throughout the education, media and political systems, cultural issues dominate, and economic issues are squeezed out. Where economic issues continue to be discussed, those discussions tend to be restricted to neoclassical doctrine. The cultural antagonisms that have shredded the left into tatters and displaced the organised working class have also threatened to cleave the MMT community into two hostile camps. Recently, social media was awash with career-threatening accusations of nationalism, nativism and racism aimed at some activists who argued that specific nations such as Greece and Italy should leave the EU and the eurozone. Yet, inherent in the MMT economic model is that democratic political control of sovereign currency issue at the national level is essential. The nation-state is not an absolute evil[23] but the only feasible site of democracy,[24] and nation-states are the essential nodes required for a democratic form of internationalism.[25]

The first lesson that the new politics must learn is that patriotism is not a surface indicator of hidden horrors. The need to care for the nation and its population, and the ability of the sovereign state to act as the democratic hub of economic renewal in a mixed economy are essential building blocks for a future politics. As we have tried to make clear, if you can't love your own people, you can't love any other people or act as an inspiration for others to do the same. The more the cultural left encourages guilt, shame and self-hatred, the more these destructive sentiments will be projected outwards.

Those on the left who propose such policies as the nationalisation of central banks[26] and remind us of the unavoidable fact that leftist politics have been electorally successful only when they have shown empathy towards patriotism[27] have been ignored or condemned as 'nativists' by the cultural left. To label with symbols of absolute evil those who simply air such possibilities or state such truths is to be a true ideological servant of the undemocratic neoliberal globalism that reproduces the context in which periodic economic convulsions and genuine far-right reaction are inevitable. The cultural left has diverted three generations along a path of division to the current destination of general confusion over vital issues. The dismal fact is that many of the left's most vocal activists have no deep understanding of either nationalism or globalism, and, when pressed, they seem to want neither. In fact, they don't really know what they want.[28] When the progressive Western left's cultural or political leaders find their way onto mainstream media to present us with their beautiful visions, simple questions about the details of the economic context required to realise those visions make them look as clueless as anyone else.

The individuals behind a new political movement must become economically literate, reject neoclassical orthodoxy, establish and widely disseminate a renewed economic discourse and accept the fact that the territory we should be allowed to love again – the sovereign nation-state – evolved as the optimal unit of political organisation.[29] It is the powerful issuer of the sovereign currency essential to economies based on credit and investment.[30] It is the only potentially democratic interface that can bring together working people, their social needs and economic management. This cannot be done on a small regional or vast global scale without ceding power to the global investment class and the supranational institutions that work on their behalf. A form of sovereignty external to, and where necessary in opposition to, the forces of the global market and its supra-national institutions is essential.

Cultural leftists are damaging politics in both a positive and negative mode, with what is present in its discourse and with what is absent – on one hand stirring up divisive cultural antagonisms, while on the other distracting attention away from the efficacy of exerting democratic control over currency issue and investment. Just behind and to one side of us on the trail blazed by the bold cultural leftists is a little siding that leads to a scrapyard of important ideas and analysis that have been dismissed or marginalised. Susan Strange's detailed analysis of 'casino capitalism'[31] doesn't appear at the top of the cultural left's discursive list, and more recent notions such as Mazzucato's 'entrepreneurial state'[32] risk being side-lined too. Academia and media pay them lip-service, while established party politicians such as Clinton, Obama, Blair, Brown and latterly Corbyn have allowed themselves to be surrounded by neoliberal advisers who either dismiss or dilute such ideas. Neoliberal technocrat Larry Summers advised Obama that any deficit over $1 trillion would discredit the government in the eyes of the population and should be avoided at all costs. The current deficit of $3.1 trillion hasn't upset the majority, and hyper-inflation is nowhere to be seen.

Summers advised former Greek finance minister Yanis Varoufakis that, because he held a responsible economic office, he was one of the 'adults in the room'[33] who should obey the rule of silence. He should never reveal to the public anything the neoliberal financial technocrats were saying or doing, otherwise club membership would be cancelled and the political wilderness would await. However, some critical voices are refusing to be silenced. Whether they can be located on the 'left' or not is becoming gradually less important, except for the possibility that distancing oneself from the extremes of the currently dominant cultural left might be in the longer term a sensible strategy. These voices are not afraid of what neoliberals and the cultural left regard as 'controversial' observations and show an awareness that any genuine movement towards the healing of cultural divisions beyond the clutches of neoliberal incorporation is dependent on political and economic contexts.

Some understand that globalisation in its current form run by the 'adults in the room' is the capture of potentially democratic sovereignty to create an external sovereignty that is incorrigibly anti-democratic[34] and conducive only to the rise of a global oligarchy consisting of financiers and corporate chiefs.[35]

Other voices are moving beyond essential criticism to promote positive ideas for the return to what we have seen was a very fragile project of democracy and solidarity amongst working people. The possibility of partial, rationalised deglobalisation which would assist the agendas of green economics and democracy[36] is now presenting itself in an era that will be defined by the impact of the pandemic, lockdowns and the gathering pace of the energy transition.[37] Moving beyond neoliberal globalisation while avoiding aggressive nationalism is possible but our current political zeitgeist, limited to the concerns of the neoliberal right and the cultural left, falls far short of the ability to realise that possibility. The current energy transition could add weight to deglobalisation; for instance, safe nuclear power combined with renewables and the energy-saving effects of shorter supply chains able to accommodate battery-powered vehicles could increase the chances of devolving and democratising economic decision-making.

However, that will be impossible without understanding the difference between the spatial and functional mobility of capital, which does not move from nation to nation before it is sifted through the stratosphere of financial instruments to benefit global rentier interests. The functional mobility of capitalism can be addressed only by economically focused democratic politics, the electoral success of which – in the face of neoliberal dogma and cultural leftist division constantly stoked by the encouragement of 'moral minoritarianism'[38] in popular culture – is unlikely.

Can popular consciousness be raised and currently unfocused populist discontent be channelled to demand these politics? In the everyday economic field, can owners of smaller businesses and workers recognise their common interests and the need either to displace or to tightly regulate their common antagonist, the private financiers, investors and rentiers? New movements such as MMT try their best to distance themselves from highly mediated cultural leftist extremism, yet at the same time suggest attractive policies that accommodate intersectional non-discrimination and set the context for the economic security of all workers across societies in a rising economic tide. Evidence from three generations of sociological studies shows that economic security and the opportunity to work together in practical tasks orientated to the common good is the context most conducive to the transcendence of cultural antagonisms. However, when we see neoliberals with their hands over their ears and cultural leftists lost in a dream of extreme personal experiences, is anyone really listening?

11

Futures

It is still possible that the left will rise to the historical challenges that define the present. However, our rather dour conclusion is that it will not. All indications suggest that the mainstream left maintains a deep but often disavowed commitment to the present status quo. Across the West, it will be either the centrists or the mainstream right who will set the course for deglobalisation and the energy transition. The primacy of neoliberal thinking will continue, and everyday people will continue to suffer as a result. The influence of the liberal left may continue to be felt in some aspects of our cultural life and in a number of key institutions, but even here little is guaranteed. It seems likely that key figures in the vaguely composed field of 'identity politics' will move seamlessly into the sub-dominant elite tasked with administering the social system on behalf of the corporate and banking elites that are the true locus of entrenched privilege and power. In the absence of an informed, serious and ambitious left, animosity and conflict on the cultural field will continue to grow. The left today displays no desire to build a new economy in which all citizens are included by right, no drive to dispense with the diverse insecurities which weigh so heavily upon our present way of life, and no capacity to bond all citizens together in a project of political renewal and mutual betterment.

In the recent 2022 French presidential election, a deeply dispiriting battle took place between Macron's unabashed neoliberal centrism and Le Pen's updated right-wing nationalism. Macron's victory, of course, failed to yield any sense that a majority of the French population are behind his depressingly familiar policy programme. Instead, the core message of the election was that the majority are not yet ready to countenance Le Pen as president. In the United States, Biden's popularity has nosedived, and the prospect of another divisive election between Trump and whichever dispiritingly cautious neoliberal candidate emerges from within the Democratic Party draws nearer. In Britain, hope springs eternal as Labour has taken a slight lead in the polls. Of course, this swing to Labour reflects popular dissatisfaction with the Tories in the wake of the pandemic rather than the ability of the centrist Starmer and his colleagues to inspire voters to dream of a better tomorrow. The electoral battle is between the right and the centre, with the cultural left making up the weight.

The time has come for some fundamental truth-telling. So many on the left are so dedicated to identifying the moral defects of those on the political right that they have entirely forgotten their traditional war against unbridled free-market capitalism, which continues to immiserate millions of ordinary working people who deserve so much more. Huge expanses of our politics today – in parliamentary debating chambers, on our news broadcasts, and especially on social media – seem to have descended into simple-minded squabbling in which the fundamental issues that can change our experience of everyday life are studiously avoided. What does the left really hope to achieve today? Will it continue to make the effort to win over ordinary working people, or are those days now gone? Our investigation into the history and present form of the left has led us to the sad conclusion that the left no longer represents a serious political force.

And so, we are back where we started. The left, in any true sense, is dead. Its principal goals were abandoned along with its traditional sources of support. Its sacred vow to fight to the very last defending the interests of ordinary working people lies in tatters. The only hope to save this great and still vital tradition is for a new generation to arise and take on the task of building something beautiful where the left once stood. Our great hope is that an entirely new opposition can quickly grow, garner popular support and begin to address the towering challenges humanity currently faces.

The first step will be to renew the traditional and apparently forgotten commitment to the common good. The left must rediscover the beauty of obligation and the wonders to be found in common cause. The second will be to dismiss identitarian activists, transcend divisions and unite ordinary people of all backgrounds. It is pointless to stick implacably to the left's 'broad church' mythology. The left must split if it is to stand any chance of remaining true to itself. The third step will be to construct a range of new economic policies that people can believe in and rally around. The final step is to promise to itself that it will press on and never waver, because the enemies of this new political project will use every trick in the book to split it apart and encourage all involved to give up and walk away. Out of adversity clearly understood renewed strength can arise. And one thing is clear: as the global financiers and corporate chiefs implement bold and effective plans to capture the world's political, financial, industrial and media infrastructures, we now need a true left – a true *new* left – more than ever. If a new generation does not emerge, and if these pressing tasks continue to atrophy in the background, the left's death will be eternal.

Notes

Introduction

1 We explore the hollowing out of politics in our book with Briggs and Treadwell, *Riots and Political Protest*, published in 2015 by Routledge, and in *Rethinking Social Exclusion: The End of the Social?*, which was published in 2012 by Sage. Other useful sources on post-politics include: Fukuyama's *The End of History and the Last Man*, published in 1992 by the Free Press; Žižek's *Living in the End Times*, published in 2011 by Verso; Ali's *The Extreme Centre*, published by Verso in 2015, and Badiou's *The Meaning of Sarkozy*, published in 2009 by Verso.

Chapter 1

1 Winlow et al's *Riots and Political Protest* (n 1 in Introduction).
2 *Riots and Political Protest* (n 1 in Introduction).
3 Reinhart and Rogoff's *This Time is Different*, published by Princeton University Press in 2009.
4 A nation's 'household wealth' is a standard form of measurement in economics. A household's wealth is usually assessed by calculating its assets minus its liabilities. A nation's household wealth is simply the sum total of all wealth held by the nation's households. This crude figure is usually only the starting point for analysis. See for example: https://www.ons.gov.uk/peoplepopulationandcommunity/personalandhouseholdfinances/incomeandwealth/bulletins/totalwealthingreatbritain/april2018to march2020
5 Reinhart and Rogoff's 2009 article, 'The Aftermath of Financial Crises', published in *American Economic Review*; Swagel's 'The Cost of the Financial Crisis: The Impact of the September 2008 Economic Collapse', published by PEW Financial Reform Project: https://core.ac.uk/reader/71350480
6 These figures are taken from the BBC's investigation into the effects of the 'credit crunch' and the subsequent recession. While these figures do not adequately capture the reality of the economic consequences of the crisis in the UK, they do manage to communicate a general sense of the scale of the crisis and its effect upon the UK economy. An overview can be found here: news.bbc.co.uk/1/hi/business/8241480.stm
7 See Duhigg's 2009 article in the *New York Times*, 'Stock Traders Find Speed Pays, in Milliseconds': www.nytimes.com/2009/07/24/business/24trading.html

[8] Tooze's *Crashed*, published in 2019 by Penguin.

[9] MacDonald's 2009 book, published by Ebury Press, *A Colossal Failure of Common Sense*; Farrell's 2018 article in *The Guardian*, 'Lehman Brothers collapse: where are the key figures now?': https://www.theguardian.com/business/2018/sep/11/lehman-brothers-collapse-where-are-the-key-figures-now

[10] Martin's *Making it Happen*, which was published by Simon & Schuster in 2014.

[11] Minsky's *Stabilizing an Unstable Economy*, republished in 2008 by McGraw Hill, and his *Ending Poverty*, published by the Levy Economics Institute of Bard College.

[12] Mazzucato's *The Entrepreneurial State*, published in 2018 by Penguin.

[13] *Riots and Political Protest* (n 1 in Introduction).

[14] This phrase was actually first uttered by Lloyd George in the wake of the First World War, but it is commonly attached to discussions about the aftermath of the Second World War, the common desire to ensure the people had a better standard of living and the eventual creation of the British welfare state. Judt's *Postwar*, published in paperback by Vintage in 2010, deals well with this period of British history.

[15] For a useful account of the Marshall Plan and its impact upon post-war geopolitics, see Steil's *The Marshall Plan: Dawn of the Cold War*, which was published in 2021 by Oxford University Press.

[16] Keynes' magnum opus, *The General Theory of Employment, Interest and Money*, was published in 1936 by Palgrave Macmillan.

[17] Perhaps the most notable of Keynes' supporters was Joan Robinson. She was a great economist in her own right, producing such classics as *The Economics of Imperfect Competition*, republished in 1969 by Palgrave Macmillan, and *Freedom and Necessity*, published in 1970 by Allan & Unwin.

[18] Attempts to rid the American academy of committed Keynesians are discussed at length in Carter's *The Price of Peace*, published in 2020 by Random House.

[19] Wolff's *Capitalism Hits the Fan*, published in 2013 by Interlink Books.

[20] Lloyd's *The Harms of Work*, published in 2019 by Bristol University Press; Cederstrom and Fleming's *Dead Man Working*, published in 2012 by Zero Books.

[21] David Cameron's 'Big Society' policy agenda is particularly illustrative of this trend. See Kisby's article in *The Political Quarterly*, Vol 81, No 4, 2010, entitled 'Big Society: Power to the People?'.

[22] This phrase is commonly associated with Gordon Brown. He discusses his time as chancellor in his autobiography, *My Life, Our Times*, published by Random House in 2017. Bower's book, *Gordon Brown Prime Minister*, published by Harper Perennial in 2007, offers useful detail on Brown's time as chancellor and the power he wielded behind the scenes. Brown remains a staunch advocate of global free market, despite admitting that his desire to free the market from government regulation contributed to the global financial crisis. A *mea culpa* of sorts can be found here: 'Gordon Brown

admits "big mistake" over banking crisis', 2011: https://www.bbc.co.uk/news/business-13032013

23 Milton Friedman's work is indicative of this trend. He was considered the prophet of the new economic liberalism, and his work was hugely influential in both academic economics and in the political realm. His *Why Government is the Problem*, published in 1993 by the Hoover Institute, is a useful place to start, but his *Capitalism and Freedom*, originally published in 1962 by the University of Chicago Press, offers a more detailed account of his economic thought.

24 Milne's *The Enemy Within*, published in 2002 by Verso; Beckett and Hencke's *Marching to the Fault Line*, published in 2009 by Constable.

25 El-Gingihy in *How to Dismantle the NHS in 10 Easy Steps*, published by Zero Books in 2015; *NHS for Sale*, by Davis, Lister and Wrigley, published by Merlin Press in 2015. Whitehead's *Transforming Probation*, published by Policy Press in 2016, offers a detailed exploration of the marketisation of the probation service.

26 Darling's *Back from the Brink* was published in 2012 by Atlantic Books.

27 Bernanke's *The Courage to Act* was published in 2017 by Norton.

28 Neate's article in *The Guardian*, published on 19 March 2019, titled 'Most people want higher taxes on rich to support poor – OECD': https://www.theguardian.com/business/2019/mar/19/most-people-want-higher-taxes-on-rich-to-support-poor-oecd

29 Forms of local government do not produce a currency of their own, and so their position is quite unlike that of central government. Forms of local government tend to rely upon central government and locally imposed taxes to cover the costs of their various operations.

30 Piketty's *Capital in the Twenty-First Century*, published in 2014 by Harvard University Press.

31 O'Connor's article, published 8 February 2013, in the *Financial Times*, entitled 'Amazon unpacked'; Lloyd's *The Harms of Work* (n 20).

32 Piketty's *Capital in the Twenty-First Century* (n 30); Mitchell and Fazi's *Reclaiming the State*, published in 2017 by Pluto.

33 Piketty's *Capital in the Twenty-First Century* (n 30); Harvey's *A Brief History of Neoliberalism*, published in 2007 by Oxford University Press; Streeck's *How will Capitalism End?*, published in 2017 by Verso.

34 Shaxson's *Treasure Islands*, published by Vintage in 2011.

35 Kelton, *The Deficit Myth*, published in 2020 by John Murray; Tcherneva's *The Case for a Job Guarantee*, published in 2020 by Polity; Mitchell and Fazi's *Reclaiming the State* (n 32).

36 Piketty's *Capital in the Twenty-First Century* (n 30), contains a wealth of useful evidence on the inequalities of the neoliberal age.

37 Varoufakis's *Adults in the Room*, published by Vintage in 2018.

38 Winlow et al's *Riots and Political Protest* (n 1 in Introduction); Lapavitsas's *The Left Case Against the EU*, which was published in 2018 by Polity.

39 Winlow et al's *Rise of the Right*, published in 2016 by Policy Press; Embery's *Despised*, published in 2020 by Polity.

40 Hall and Winlow's 2020 article, 'Back to the future: On the British liberal left's return to its origins', in the *International Journal of Media & Cultural Politics*.

41 In relation to the decline of working-class support for the Labour Party in Britain, see Cutts, Goodwin, Heath and Surridge's 2020 article in *The Political Quarterly*, entitled 'Brexit, the 2019 General Election and the Realignment of British Politics': https://onlinelibrary.wiley.com/doi/full/10.1111/1467-923X.12815 With regard to working-class conservatism, see Lipset's *Political Man*, republished in 2019 by Forgotten Books. Lipset famously notes 'the more well-to-do are liberal, the poorer are more intolerant'.

42 In the UK in the 1990s, it seems that around 50% of the population were against interracial marriage. By 2011, this figure had fallen to 15%. See the report from the think tank British Future, entitled 'The Melting Pot Generation': https://www.britishfuture.org/wp-content/uploads/2020/09/The-melting-pot-generation.pdf

43 In the aftermath of Brexit, it was much easier for rattled liberals to believe that some malevolent conspiracy had destabilised democracy and secured victory for the forces of evil. It was much harder to face up to the fact that a slender majority was unpersuaded by the liberal left's campaign to remain part of the EU. A hunt for the culprits brought about the Cambridge Analytica story, which ran in the liberal broadsheet press for many months. A typical example of the liberal left's coverage of this issue can be seen in Cadwalladr and Townsend's article, 'Revealed: the ties that bound Vote Leave's data firm to controversial Cambridge Analytica', which was published in *The Guardian* in 2018: https://www.theguardian.com/uk-news/2018/mar/24/aggregateiq-data-firm-link-raises-leave-group-questions

44 Rawlinson's *How Press Propaganda Paved the Way to Brexit*, published in 2020 by Palgrave Macmillan.

Chapter 2

1 Anderson's *Imagined Communities*, republished in 2016 by Verso.

2 *The Spivak Reader*, edited by Landry and published in 1996 by Routledge.

3 Antonopoulos' article, 'The Current Economic and Financial Crisis: A Gender Perspective', published in 2009 by the Levy Economics Institute, Working Papers Series No. 562, available at SSRN: https://ssrn.com/abstract=1402687, and Emejulu and Bassel's 'Whose Crisis Counts? Minority Women, Austerity and Activism in France and Britain', in Kantola and Lombardo's edited book, *Gender and the Economic Crisis in Europe*, which was published by Springer in 2017. Our goal here is not to pour scorn upon those who have investigated the effects of the global financial crisis upon particular sections of the general population. In our judgement, such investigations are valuable.

4 Wainwright's article 'General Election 2019: The untapped influence of the non-voter': https://www.bbc.co.uk/news/election-2019-50393317

5   This is an academic concept we have written about at length. See for example Hall's *Theorizing Crime and Deviance*, published in 2012 by Sage; and Hall and Winlow's *Revitalizing Criminological Theory*, published in 2015 by Routledge.

6   Guilluy's *Twilight of the Elites*, published in 2019 by Yale University Press.

7   Mudde's article for *The Guardian*, 'The Problem of Populism', published on 17 February 2015: https://www.theguardian.com/commentisfree/2015/feb/17/problem-populism-syriza-podemos-dark-side-europe

8   See for example Rummens' 2017 article 'Populism as a Threat to Liberal Democracy', published in Rovira Kaltwasser, Taggart, Ochoa Espejo and Ostiguy's edited book, *The Oxford Handbook of Populism*, by Oxford University Press.

9   Bhambra's chapter 'Locating Brexit in the pragmatics of race, citizenship and empire', in Outhwaite's 2017 edited collection *Brexit: Sociological Responses*, published by Anthem Press.

10 See Frank's *The People*, published by Scribe in 2020, for discussion.

11 Frank's *The People* (n 10).

12 Guilluy's *Twilight of the Elites* (n 6).

13 Jacobson's *100% Clean, Renewable Energy and Storage for Everything*, published by Cambridge University Press in 2020.

14 Roussinos's 2021 article for *Vice*, 'How Hungary's Orban is winning support by out-socializing the socialists': https://www.vice.com/en/article/a3bgpg/how-hungarys-orban-is-winning-support-by-out-socializing-the-socialists

15 Žižek's *Violence*, published in 2008 by Verso, and his *Living in the End Times*, published in 2010 by Verso.

16 Schmitt's *The Concept of the Political* and his *Political Theology*. Both were republished by the University of Chicago Press, in 2007 and 2006 respectively.

17 Fukuyama's *The End of History and the Last Man*, republished by Penguin in 2020.

18 See Badiou's *The Rebirth of History*, published in 2012 by Verso.

19 See 'Margaret Thatcher: A Life in Quotes', published by *The Guardian* on 8 May 2013: https://www.theguardian.com/politics/2013/apr/08/margaret-thatcher-quotes

20 Winlow and Hall's *Rethinking Social Exclusion* (n 1 in Introduction).

21 Ehrenreich's *Blood Rites*, published in 1997 by Virago Press.

22 Pogrund and McGuire's *Left Out*, published in 2021 by Vintage.

23 Jacobson's *100% Clean, Renewable Energy and Storage for Everything* (n 13); Newell's *Power Shift*, published in 2021 by Cambridge University Press.

24 Pogrund and McGuire's *Left Out* (n 22).

25 L. Daniel Staetsky's study for the Institute for Jewish Policy Research 'Antisemitism in contemporary Great Britain', published in 2017: https://cst.org.uk/public/data/file/7/4/JPR.2017.Antisemitism%20in%20contemporary%20Great%20Britain.pdf

26 See YouGov's 'Roma people and Muslims are the least tolerated minorities in Europe', published in 2015: https://d25d2506sfb94s.cloudfront.net/cumulus_uploads/document/g96awulgzv/Eurotrack_Minorities_W.pdf

27 Boyd's 2011 report for the Institute for Jewish Policy Research, entitled 'Child poverty and deprivation in the British Jewish community': https://archive.jpr.org.uk/download?id=1510

28 Boyd's 2011 report for the Institute for Jewish Policy Research (n 27).

29 YouGov's March 2021 Voting Intention Poll: https://docs.cdn.yougov.com/u9wuynpn2e/TheTimes_VI_Track_210319_W.pdf

30 The Trilateral Commission is a shadowy non-governmental globalist organisation whose ostensible aim is to foster closer economic links between Europe, North America and Japan. Its core membership contains key powerbrokers from Europe and North America, and the organisation is broadly considered to be dedicated to the maintenance of global free trade.

31 Nagle and Tracey's 2020 article 'First as Tragedy, Then as Farce: The Collapse of the Sanders Campaign and the "Fusionist" Left', in *American Affairs*. It can be read for free here: https://americanaffairsjournal.org/2020/05/first-as-tragedy-then-as-farce/

32 Sanders' 2020 policy proposals can be read here: https://berniesanders.com/issues/

33 Nagle and Tracey's 'First as Tragedy ...' (n 31).

34 Based on exit poll data. A brief digest of the study from which these statistics were taken can be accessed here: https://www.bbc.co.uk/news/world-us-canada-54972389

35 Swales' study 'Understanding the Leave vote' for NatCen Social Research. This study suggests that 32% of Asian voters, 29% of Black voters and 37% of 'mixed' ethnicity voters supported Brexit.

36 Bhambra's 2017 paper for the *British Journal of Sociology*, titled 'Brexit, Trump, and "methodological whiteness"': On the misrecognition of race and class'; Botterill and Burrell's 2019 paper for *Environment and Planning C* entitled '(In)visibility, privilege and the performance of whiteness in Brexit Britain: Polish migrants in Britain's shifting migration regime'; and Emujulu's 'On the Hideous Whiteness of Brexit', which can be read for free here: https://www.versobooks.com/blogs/2733-on-the-hideous-whiteness-of-brexit-let-us-be-honest-about-our-past-and-our-present-if-we-truly-seek-to-dismantle-white-supremacy

37 The Pew Research Center, in its 2019 study of 'race in America', found that 64% of white Democrats believe the United States has 'not gone far enough' when it comes to giving black people equal rights, with a further 30% believing the country has 'been about right'. For white Republicans, 53% believed things were 'about right' and 31% believed 'things have 'gone too far'. A synopsis of the project's findings can be accessed for free here: https://www.pewresearch.org/social-trends/2019/04/09/race-in-america-2019/

Chapter 3

[1] Ritzer's thesis attempted to shed light of the forms of homogeneity that quickly became synonymous with globalisation. One can buy a McDonald's Big Mac in virtually any city in the world and expect it to be pretty much the same as any other Big Mac you have ever eaten. Its ingredients are pretty much the same, the cooking process is pretty much the same, and its presentation is pretty much the same. Globalisation, Ritzer claimed, was creating similar forms of banal standardisation. Individual towns and cities were losing their unique character as high streets and shopping arcades became virtually indistinguishable from those in other towns and cities. See Ritzer's *The McDonaldization of Society*, which was republished in 2000 by Sage.

[2] See Johnston's *Žižek's Ontology*, published in 2008 by Northwestern University Press.

[3] See McIntyre's *After Virtue*, which was republished by Bloomsbury in 2013.

[4] Groseclose and Milyo's 2005 article for *The Quarterly Journal of Economics*, 'A measure of media bias', identifies a strong liberal bias in many major media outlets. The obvious exceptions are Fox News and *The Washington Times*. Here, 'liberal bias' is understood in the pejorative sense of being nominally 'left wing'.

[5] While there are many examples of this trend, perhaps the most telling is the Disney Corporation's introduction of the 'Reimagine Tomorrow' programme, which pushes staff to consider 'white fragility', 'systemic racism' and 'white privilege', and other concepts and tropes associated with critical race theory and the contemporary activist left. A basic description of the programme has been published in *The Washington Post* and can be accessed for free here: https://www.washingtontimes.com/news/2021/may/10/walt-disney-catches-critical-race-craze/

Coca-Cola also seems to have been bitten by the bug. In a course designed by Robin DiAngelo, the bestselling author of *White Fragility*, members of staff are invited 'to be less white'. Being less white apparently means to: 'be less oppressive; be less arrogant; be less certain; be less defensive; be less ignorant; be more humble; listen; believe; break with apathy' and 'break with white solidarity'. This quote in taken from the article 'Coca-Cola accused of telling employees to "be less white" in training course by critical race theory peddler DiAngelo', which was published on the *Russia Today* website and can be accessed for free here: https://www.rt.com/usa/516114-coca-cola-race-training/

See also Eberhart's article for the *Daily Mail*, entitled 'Disney is slammed for "woke" anti-racism training that tells white staff to "decolonize their bookshelves", participate in reparations and complete a "privilege checklist"': https://www.dailymail.co.uk/news/article-9556947/Disney-slammed-woke-training-documents-claiming-America-fundamentally-racist-country.html

6   This figure is taken from the article 'What is Bob Iger's net worth?', which was published in *The Sun* and can be accessed for free here: https://www.thesun.co.uk/tvandshowbiz/11042627/what-is-bob-igers-net-worth/

7   This figure is taken from an article that appeared in Forbes.com titled 'How much of Lockheed Martin's revenue comes from the U.S. government?'. It can be accessed here: https://www.forbes.com/sites/greatspeculations/2020/12/31/how-much-of-lockheed-martins-revenues-comes-from-the-us-government/?sh=37656483629d

8   Rufo's article, 'The woke-industrial complex', appeared in *City Journal* on 26 May 2021: https://www.city-journal.org/lockheed-martins-woke-industrial-complex

9   For example, in June 2021, MSNBC announced with some pride that 'the military industrial complex is now run by women'. The brief segment can be accessed here: https://www.msnbc.com/velshi-ruhle/watch/the-military-industrial-complex-is-now-run-by-women-1419183171559

Chapter 4

1   Kirby's 2003 book for Palgrave Macmillan, *Child Labour in Britain, 1750–1870*, offers an overview.

2   E.P. Thompson's *The Making of the English Working Class* was republished in 2013 by Penguin.

3   Hobsbawm and Rude's *Captain Swing*, republished in 2014 by Verso Books; McLeod's *Religion and the Working Class in Nineteenth Century England*, published by Macmillan in 1984, and Gilbert's *Religion and Society in Industrial England 1740–1914*, published by Longman in 1976.

4   Marquand's *Ramsay Macdonald*, published in 1977 by Jonathan Cape.

5   Grossman's 1978 article, published in *Monthly Labor Review*, titled 'Fair Labor Standards Act of 1938: Maximum struggle for a minimum wage', offers a useful overview.

6   Mosley's *The Chimney of the World*, published by Routledge in 2008.

7   See: https://www.gov.uk/government/news/public-health-england-publishes-air-pollution-evidence-review

8   McIvor and Johnston's *Miners' Lung*, published in 2016 by Routledge.

9   McIvor and Johnston's *Miners' Lung* (n 8).

10   Gordon's *Phossy Jaw and the French Match Workers*, published by Routledge in 2016.

11   Besant's short article on the plight of the match girls can be read for free here: http://www.mernick.org.uk/thhol/thelink.html

12   The Fabian Society was established in the final years of the nineteenth century and immediately assumed a key role in drawing together various strands of the British left to form the Labour Party at the turn of the century. The Society took its name from a Roman general famous for his gradualist approach to securing victory. The Fabian Society continues to play a major role within the Labour Party.

13   Schneer's *Ben Tillett*, republished by Routledge in 2020.

14. Fishman's *East End Jewish Radicals 1875–1914*, published in 2004 by Five Leaves.
15. Crick's *History of the Social-Democratic Federation*, published in 1994 by Keele University Press.
16. Virdee's *Racism, Class and the Racialized Outsider*, published in 2014 by Red Globe Press.
17. The *Taff Vale* judgment of 1901 followed a labour dispute between the Taff Vale Railway and the Amalgamated Society of Railway Workers. To cut a long story short, in a resulting court case, it was determined that, following strike action, unions could be liable for the loss of private company profits. The judgment sent a shockwave through the British labour movement. Thorpe's *A History of the British Labour Party*, published in 2015 by Red Globe Press, offers a useful digest of the case and its affects.
18. These results are taken from YouGov's voting intention tracker. A detailed breakdown of these results for June 2021 can be found here: https://docs.cdn.yougov.com/zhh0oqc2h2/TheTimes_VI_Track_210624_W_BPC.pdf
19. Winlow's *Badfellas*, published by Berg in 2001; Winlow and Hall's *Violent Night*, published by Berg in 2006; Hall's *Theorizing Crime and Deviance* (n 5 in Ch 2); Hall et al's *Criminal Identities and Consumer Culture*, published by Willan in 2008, and so on.
20. See for example Pakulski and Waters, *The Death of Class*, published by Sage in 1995.
21. Baudrillard, *Symbolic Exchange and Death*, published by Sage in 2016.
22. Wilford's *The CIA, the British Left and the Cold War*, published in 2003 by Routledge.
23. Kersten's *Labor's Home Front*, published by NYU Press in 2006.
24. Taken from Winter's 1980 paper in the *Journal of Contemporary History*, titled 'Military Fitness and Civilian Health in Britain during the First World War'.
25. Greenwood's *The Health and Physique of School Children*, published in London in 1913.
26. Winter's 'Infant mortality, maternal mortality and public health in Britain in the 1930s', which appeared in the *Journal of European Economic History* in 1979.
27. Winter's 'Infant mortality …' (n 26).
28. Garvey's *Philosophy and Opinions of Marcus Garvey*, edited by Amy Garvey, published in 2014 by Martino Fine Books.
29. Washington's *Up From Slavery*, republished by Entreacacias in 2021.
30. Branch's *Parting the Waters*, published in 1989 by Pocket Books; *Pillar of Fire*, published in 1998 by Simon & Schuster; and *At Canaan's Edge*, published by Simon & Schuster in 2006.

Chapter 5

1. Our discussion of Stalin, Trotsky, Lenin and the Russian Revolution is informed by the following books: Service's biographies of Trotsky, Stalin and Lenin, all of which were republished by Pan in 2010; Conquest's *The*

Great Terror, published by Bodley Head in 2018; Montefiore's *Stalin* and *Young Stalin*, published by Weidenfeld & Nicolson in 2003 and 2007, respectively; Rayfield's *Stalin and his Hangmen*, published by Penguin in 2005; Rubenstein's *The Last Days of Stalin*, published by Yale University Press in 2017 and Trotsky's *History of the Russian Revolution*, which was republished by Penguin in 2017.

2   The Kronstadt Rebellion was a 1921 leftist uprising of sailors and soldiers against the Bolshevik leadership. The rebels were disillusioned with the overall direction of the revolution and issued a series of demands that focused on advancing the material interests of peasants and the working class and reducing the centralised power of the Bolsheviks. The rebellion was ruthlessly crushed by the Bolsheviks, at the cost of several thousand lives. The rebellion and its suppression prompted many supporters to lose faith in the revolution. Ida Mett's *The Kronstadt Uprising*, republished by Theory and Practice in 2017, offers a detailed account.

3   Tombs' *The English and their History*, published by Penguin in 2015.

4   Our discussion of Bevin and the post-war Labour government draws from the following books: Bullock's *Ernest Bevin: A Biography*, published in 1983 by Heinemann; Dale's *God's Politicians*, published in 2000 by HarperCollins; Thomas-Symonds' *Nye*, published by Taurus in 2016; Bew's *Citizen Clem*, published by riverrun in 2016; Pimlott's *Hugh Dalton*, published in 1985 by Jonathan Cape; Judt's *Postwar* (n 14 in Ch 1); and Hennessy's *Never Again* and *Having it So Good*, published in 2006 and 2007, respectively, by Penguin.

5   Stonor Saunders' *The Cultural Cold War*, published in 2013 by The New Press and her *Who Paid the Piper?*, published by Granta in 2000; Wilford's *The CIA, the British Left and the Cold War* (n 22 in Ch 4); and Krabbendam and Scott-Smith's edited volume, *The Cultural Cold War in Western Europe, 1945–60*, which was published in 2004 by Routledge.

6   Wilford's *The CIA, the British Left and the Cold War* (n 22 in Ch 4), for discussion.

7   Wilford's *The CIA, the British Left and the Cold War* (n 22 in Ch 4).

8   Stonor Saunders' *The Cultural Cold War* (n 5), p 1.

9   See Stonor Saunders' *The Cultural Cold War* (n 5); Wilford's *The CIA, the British Left and the Cold War* (n 22 in Ch 4).

10   Griffiths' *Engaging Enemies*, published in 2014 by Rowman & Littlefield.

Chapter 6

1   Raddatz's edited volume, *The Marx-Engels Correspondence*, published in 1981 by Weidenfeld & Nicolson.

2   The historical aspect of our analysis here is informed by Kenny's *The First New Left*, published in 1995 by Lawrence and Wishart; Dworkin's *Cultural Marxism in Postwar Britain*, published in 1997 by Duke University Press; and Hamilton's *The Crisis of Theory* published by Manchester University Press in 2012.

3   Hoggart's *The Uses of Literacy* was republished in 2009 by Penguin Classics.

4   Hall's *Cultural Studies*, published by Duke University Press in 2016.
5   Thompson's *The Making of the English Working Class* (n 2 in Ch 4), and his *Whigs and Hunters*, published in 1977 by Penguin.
6   Thompson's *The Poverty of Theory*, published in 1978 by Monthly Review Press.
7   Hall's 'Introducing NLR', in *New Left Review*, Jan. 1960.
8   Hennessy's *Having it So Good* (n 4 in Ch 5).
9   Hall and Jefferson's edited volume, *Resistance Through Rituals*, republished by Routledge in 2006 and Hebdige's *Subculture*, published by Routledge in 1979.
10 See Willis's *Learning to Labour*, republished by Ashgate in 2000.
11 See Winlow's article, 'Is it OK to Talk About Capitalism Again? Or, Why Criminology Must Take a Leap of Faith', which appeared *New Directions in Crime and Deviancy*, edited by Winlow and Atkinson and published by Routledge in 2012.
12 Our analysis of the Frankfurt School is informed by the following books: Wiggerhaus's *The Frankfurt School*, published in 2010 by Polity; Wolin's *The Frankfurt School Revisited*, published in 2006 by Routledge; Jeffries' *Grand Hotel Abyss*, published in 2017 by Verso; Jay's *The Dialectical Imagination*, published in 1996 by the University of California Press; Adorno's *The Culture Industry*, republished by Routledge in 2001, and Adorno and Horkheimer's *Dialectic of Enlightenment*, republished by Verso in 2016.
13 Reich's *The Mass Psychology of Fascism* was republished by Souvenir Press in 1997.
14 Marcuse's *Eros and Civilisation* was republished by Routledge in 1987.
15 Marcuse's *One-Dimensional Man* was republished by Routledge in 2002.
16 Our analysis of Fromm draws from his *Escape from Freedom*, republished in 2011 by Ishi Press; *The Art of Being*, republished in 1993 by Constable; *The Anatomy of Human Destructiveness*, republished in 1997 by Pimlico; and *The Fear of Freedom*, republished by Routledge in 2001.
17 Boltanski and Chiapello's *The New Spirit of Capitalism*, published in 2007 by Verso; Zizek's *Violence* (n 15 in Ch 2).
18 Marcuse, *One-Dimensional Man* (n 15).
19 Adorno and Marcuse's 'Correspondence on the German Student Movement', published in *New Left Review* in 1999.
20 Jeffries' *Grand Hotel Abyss* (n 12); Leslie's 1999 article, 'Introduction to Adorno/Marcuse Correspondence on the German Student Movement', which appeared in *New Left Review*.

Chapter 7

1   Griffiths' *Engaging Enemies* (n 10 in Ch 5).
2   Bauman's *Liquid Love*, published by Polity in 2003; Beck and Beck-Gernsheim's *The Normal Chaos of Love*, published in 1995 by Polity.
3   Beck's *Individualization*, published in 2001 by Sage, and Winlow and Hall's 2009 article, 'Living for the weekend: Youth identities in northeast England', which appeared in the journal *Ethnography*.

4 Adorno and Horkheimer's *Dialectic of Enlightenment* (n 12 in Ch 6).
5 Jameson's *Postmodernism: Or, the Cultural Logic of Late Capitalism*, published by Verso in 1992; Eagleton's *The Illusions of Postmodernism*, published in 1992 by Wiley-Blackwell; and Harvey's *The Condition of Postmodernity*, published in 1991 by Wiley-Blackwell.
6 Lyotard's *The Postmodern Condition*, published in 1984 by Manchester University Press.
7 Our analysis of Foucault is informed by the following books: Wade and Dundas's *Foucault in California*, published in 2019 by Heyday; Macey's *The Lives of Michel Foucault*, published in 2019 by Verso; Dean and Zamora's *The Last Man Takes LSD*, published in 2021 by Verso; and Zamora and Behrent's edited volume, *Foucault and Neoliberalism*, published in 2015 by Polity. We also drew upon the following books written by Foucault himself: *Power, The Foucault Reader, Discipline and Punish* and *The History of Sexuality* all republished by Penguin in 2020; *Madness and Civilisation*, published in 1988 by Vintage, and *The Birth of Biopolitics*, published by Palgrave Macmillan in 2010.
8 Plummer's 'Images of Pedophilia' appeared in Cook and Wilson's edited volume, *Love and Attraction*, published by Pergamon Press in 1979, and his 'The Paedophile's Progress: A View from Below' appeared in Taylor's edited volume, *Perspectives on Paedophilia*, published in 1981 by Batsford.
9 Mudie and Dorman's article 'Huge sums of taxpayers cash "handed to child sex group by the Home Office"', appeared in the *Daily Mirror* on 1 March 2014: https://www.mirror.co.uk/news/uk-news/paedophile-information-exchange-taxpayers-cash-3197625

Chapter 8

1 Royle's *Jacques Derrida*, published in 2003 by Routledge.
2 See for example Crenshaw's 1989 article 'Demarginalizing the Intersection of Race and Sex: A Black Feminist Critique of Antidiscrimination Doctrine, Feminist Theory and Antiracist Policies', which was published in the *University of Chicago Legal Forum*.
3 Here we are referring to the work of Carl Schmitt, whom we discussed at length in Chapter 2. A central theme in Schmitt's work is the functionality of enmity, and our descent into what seems like a world of ceaseless, multipolar enmity is really what we are getting at here.
4 Rachel Dolezal is the archetypal example. Tuvel, in her article 'In Defense of Transracialism', published in the journal *Hypatia* in 2020, defends those who choose to present themselves as a member of a historically oppressed minority.
5 Mckenzie's *Getting By*, published by Policy Press in 2015.
6 Winlow et al's *Rise of the Right* (n 39 in Ch 1).
7 Winlow et al's *Rise of the Right* (n 39 in Ch 1).
8 Winlow et al's *Rise of the Right* (n 39 in Ch 1).
9 Fraser's *Fortunes of Feminism*, which was published by Verso in 2013.

[10] Hall et al's *Criminal Identities and Consumer Culture* (n 19 in Ch 4); Frank's *The Conquest of Cool*, published in 1998 by the University of Chicago Press; Heath and Potter's *The Rebel Sell*, published in 2006 by Capstone.

[11] See n 3.

Chapter 9

[1] El-Enany's 2017 article, 'Brexit is not only an expression of nostalgia for empire, it is also the fruit of empire': https://blogs.lse.ac.uk/brexit/2017/05/11/brexit-is-not-only-an-expression-of-nostalgia-for-empire-it-is-also-the-fruit-of-empire/

[2] Vince Cable, once leader of the UK Liberal Democrats, told delegates at his 2018 party conference that Brexit voters "were driven by a nostalgia for a world where passports were blue, faces were white, and the map was coloured imperial pink".

[3] Judah's 2016 article for the *New York Times*, entitled 'England's Last Gasp of Empire'. He claimed 'the Brexit vote expressed white Britain's nostalgia for a lost sense of greatness'; Earle's 2017 article for *The Atlantic*, titled 'The Toxic Nostalgia of Brexit', which can be accessed here: https://www.theatlantic.com/international/archive/2017/10/brexit-britain-may-johnson-eu/542079/

[4] Bhambra's paper 'Brexit, Trump, and methodological whiteness' (n 36 in Ch 2).

[5] The work of Lisa Mckenzie is important here. Her long-running ethnographic work has allowed her to move beyond the cloying sensitivities of middle-class academia to offer a much more accurate account of what is happening on the ground. Her 2017 article for *The British Journal of Sociology*, 'The class politics of prejudice: Brexit and the land of no-hope and glory', is of particular relevance.

[6] Antonucci, Horvath, Kutiyski and Krouwel's 2017 article in *Competition and Change*, 'The malaise of the squeezed middle: Challenging the narrative of the "left behind" Brexiter'.

[7] See Khalili's 2017 article, entitled 'After Brexit: Reckoning with Britain's Racism and Xenophobia', which appeared in the journal *Poem*.

[8] See Campanella and Dassù's 2019 article 'Brexit and Nostalgia', which appeared in the journal *Survival*. They claim 'an infatuation with a distorted past deluded millions of British citizens ... about the future of their country outside Europe' which 'defies any rational cost-benefit analysis'. Leave voters, they claim, wanted to go 'back to the Edwardian era, thus restoring the country's lost imperial greatness'.

[9] 'Brexit Britain: British Election Study Insights from the post-EU Referendum wave of the BES internet panel'. A brief digest can be accessed for free here: https://www.britishelectionstudy.com/bes-resources/brexit-britain-british-election-study-insights-from-the-post-eu-referendum-wave-of-the-bes-internet-panel/#.WQsoptIrKUk

[10] Spilker, Schaffer and Bernauer's 'Does social capital increase public support for economic globalisation?', published in *European Journal of Political*

Research in 2012: https://ethz.ch/content/dam/ethz/special-interest/gess/cis/international-relations-dam/Publications/Documents/2011/Social_Capitel_EJPR_2012.pdf

11 Herreros and Criado's 'Social Trust, Social Capital and Perceptions of Immigration', published in the journal *Political Studies* in 2009, which can be accessed here: https://journals.sagepub.com/doi/abs/10.1111/j.1467-9248.2008.00738.x

12 Marcel Mauss is a central figure in anthropology. His most noted book is *The Gift*, which was republished in 2001 by Routledge Classics. In it, Mauss makes the point that a gift is never given freely. Gift-giving always involves a diverse series of social expectations. For example, receiving a birthday present from a distant relative is often treated as an imposition, because we then become obligated to give a gift in return. Mauss's point is that gift-giving sustains the forms of obligation and mutuality that give social life meaning. It would be easy for distant relatives to lose touch and drift apart permanently. The gift, however, sustains brittle relationships. It ties giver and receiver together, even if only in a rather perfunctory manner. The act of giving suggests that both giver and receiver remain cognisant of and committed to established social rules. Both giver and receiver know what is required of them, and in fulfilling their allotted role, they signal their continued commitment to the hidden structures and subtle rules of community life. Our point in this section is, however, a little more particular. Receiving the gift of cultural inheritance obliges each generation to nurture and sustain that cultural inheritance so that, when the time comes, they can in turn pass on the gift to the next generation. The gift is accompanied by the burden of expectation. The super-ego requires us to fulfil our obligations, and it will terrorise us if we do not.

13 Siedentop's *Inventing the Individual*, published in 2015 by Penguin.

14 Linebaugh's *The London Hanged*, republished by Verso in 2003; Bushnell's *Moscow Graffiti*, published in 1990 by Unwin Hyman.

Chapter 10

1 Hudson's *And Forgive Them Their Debts*, published in 2018 by Islet Publishing; Graeber's *Debt*, published in 2014 by Melville House.

2 Gibbon's *The History of the Decline and Fall of Rome*, republished by Penguin in 2000.

3 Hudson's *And Forgive Them Their Debts* (n 1).

4 See Carey's *The Intellectuals and the Masses*, published by Faber & Faber in 1992.

5 Le Bon's *The Crowd*, republished in 2002 by Courier.

6 Canetti's *Crowds and Power*, republished by Farrar, Straus and Giroux in 1984.

7 Welles' *The Time for Decision*, published in 1944 by Harper & Brothers; Sandburg's *The People, Yes*, republished in 2015 by Houghton Mifflin Harcourt.

8 Hudson's *And Forgive Them Their Debts* (n 1), p 16.

9   Hall's *Theorizing Crime and Deviance* (n 5 in Ch 2).
10 Slobodian's *Globalists*, published in 2020 by Harvard University Press.
11 Hayek's *The Road to Serfdom* was republished in 2003 by the University of Chicago Press.
12 Robinson (n 17 in Ch 1).
13 Keen, *The New Economics*, published by Polity in 2021; Mitchell and Fazi's *Reclaiming the State* (n 32 in Ch 1).
14 Mullan's *Beyond Confrontation*, published by Emerald in 2020, p 159.
15 Mullan's *Beyond Confrontation* (n 14).
16 Keen's *The New Economics* (n 13).
17 Hudson's *And Forgive Them Their Debts* (n 1).
18 See Kelton, *The Deficit Myth* (n 35 in Ch 1).
19 Kelton, *The Deficit Myth* (n 35 in Ch 1).
20 Lansley's *The Cost of Inequality*, published in 2012 by Gibson Square; Chang's *23 Things They Don't Tell You About Capitalism*, published in 2011 by Penguin.
21 Kelton, *The Deficit Myth* (n 35 in Ch 1); Tcherneva's *The Case for a Job Guarantee* (n 35 in Ch 1).
22 Kelton, *The Deficit Myth* (n 35 in Ch 1), p 261.
23 Tamir's *Why Nationalism?*, published in 2020 by Yale University Press.
24 Streeck's *How will Capitalism End?* (n 33 in Ch 1).
25 Mullan's *Beyond Confrontation* (n 14).
26 Embery's *Despised* (n 39 in Ch 1).
27 Edgerton's *Rise and Fall of the British Nation*, published in 2019 by Penguin.
28 Lonergan and Blyth's *Angrynomics*, published in 2020 by Agenda.
29 Streeck's *How will Capitalism End?* (n 33 in Ch 1).
30 Mitchell and Fazi's *Reclaiming the State* (n 32 in Ch 1).
31 Strange's *Casino Capitalism*, republished in 2015 by Manchester University Press.
32 Mazzucato's *The Entrepreneurial State* (n 12 in Ch 1).
33 Varoufakis's *Adults in the Room* (n 37 in Ch 1).
34 Cunliffe's *The New Twenty Years' Crisis*, published in 2020 by McGill-Queen's University Press.
35 Kotkin's *The Coming of Neo-Feudalism*, published in 2020 by Encounter.
36 Rodrik's *The Globalisation Paradox*, published in 2012 by Oxford University Press.
37 Briggs et al's *Lockdown*, published in 2021 by Palgrave Macmillan.
38 Hochuli et al's *The End of the End of History*, published in 2021 by Verso.

Index

Index

Lansbury, G. 133, 135

leadership 46, 58–9, 77–8, 83–5, 87, 90, 92, 95, 113, 135, 148, 181, 198, 232, 260, 266, 286

left-liberals 279

leftism 168

leftists 7, 26, 44–6, 48, 53, 57, 68, 78–9, 81–2, 119, 132, 136, 149–50, 157, 181, 183–4, 195, 214, 240, 255, 263–5, 267, 272–3, 311, 313

legitimacy 62–3, 113

Lehman Brothers bank 17–18

leisure 153, 220, 273

lenders 15, 285, 301

Lenin, V. 181–3

leveraging 13, 17, 303

LGBTQ+ 126

liberalisation 107, 153, 249

liberalism 3, 21, 46, 73–4, 82, 103–4, 120, 136, 140, 145, 150, 166, 180, 194, 213, 216, 228, 232, 235, 238, 256, 277–80, 289

libertarianism 170, 218, 243, 245, 248–9

libertinism 3, 180, 219–20, 231–2

Lippmann, W. 289

liquidity 16, 19, 30, 36, 42

literacy 203

livelihoods 13, 56, 98, 104, 157, 285, 289

Lloyd George, D. 173

loanable funds 300

lockdown (COVID-19) 61, 312

Lockheed Martin Corp. 125

Logos 220–1

LSD 328

luxury 35, 90

Lyotard, J-F. 238–9

M

MacDonald, R. 135

MacIntyre, A. 115–17

macroeconomic policies 146, 303, 306

Macron, F. 314

madmen 244

madness 243–4

Madonna (pop singer) 253

majoritarianism 170

mandate 42, 168, 170, 187, 193, 201, 212, 214, 224

Manifesto (British Labour Party) 34, 87

Marcuse, H. 220–2, 224, 231

marketability 68

marketisation 319

marriage 146, 194, 219, 320

Marx, K. 63, 129–30, 156, 192, 203, 205, 222, 230

Marxism 128–31, 156, 183, 192, 203, 205, 207, 217, 230–1, 233, 238

Marxists 129, 131, 161, 203, 206, 217, 222, 232

masculinity 121, 266

mass media 4–6, 11, 28–34, 44–8, 56–8, 73–7, 84–99, 104, 124, 164, 183, 256, 267, 288–94, 301, 308–11

materialism 233

materialists 131

Maussian anthropology 277

Mazzucato, M. 311

McDonaldization 109

McDonnell, J. 34, 78

Medicare 98

melancholia 193, 208–9, 211, 229

membership (union/Labour Party) 41, 57, 78, 83–4, 92–3, 108, 114, 156, 196, 198, 249, 261, 311

meritocracy 69

Methodism 128, 131–2, 155

metropolitan culture 73, 81, 84–6, 262

micronarratives 239

middle class 80, 113, 147–8, 275

migrants 82, 118–19, 273

millionaires 170

miners 26, 77, 142